Economic Development
in South Asia

Economic Development
in South Asia

Jogindar S. Uppal

St. Martin's Press   New York

Library of Congress Catalog Card Number: 76-28131
Copyright © 1977 by St. Martin's Press, Inc.
All Rights Reserved.
Manufactured in the United States of America.
0987
fedcba
For information, write: St. Martin's Press, Inc.,
175 Fifth Avenue, New York, N.Y. 10010

Cover design: Mies Hora

ISBN: cloth 0-312-23030-3
        paper 0-312-23065-6

FOREWORD

Dr. J. S. Uppal completed work on the present book during his stay with us as a Fulbright Visiting Professor in 1976. It was a pleasure having him in our midst.

His book deals with major critical problems of economic development in the South Asian countries. An important feature of the book is that while it gives an account of South Asia as a region, with certain common characteristics and similar problems of economic development, it does not ignore the essential differences in the national economies of this region and the consequent variations in their economic policies and plans for development.

The subject is treated within a coherent analytical framework useful to students of economic development in general and to those interested in South Asian countries in particular. At the same time, the presentation is lucid enough to be accessible to the nonspecialist general reader. I trust that the book will be received as a valuable addition to the growing literature on the subject.

V. M. Dandekar

Gokhale Institute of
Politics & Economics,
Poona, India

July 1, 1976

Preface

The South Asian region, comprising the countries of Bangladesh, India, Nepal, Pakistan, and Sri Lanka, is comparable to Europe in size and population. Although the region exhibits most of the characteristics of the underdeveloped world, it does possess some distinctive features. For example, South Asia has one of the highest population densities: about a quarter of the world's population lives here on only 3.3 percent of the world's land surface. Its per capita income and growth rate during the last two decades are the lowest among the world's underdeveloped regions. Most countries in the region are among the first underdeveloped nations to initiate comprehensive planning for economic development. The South Asian countries have democratic forms of government and their economic plans are based on democratic models. The low performance of these economies, when compared to the Communist countries with their command economies, is generally ascribed to the contraints which democratic political and economic institutions place on the development process. Recently, strains have been evident in the democratic processes of the South Asian governments, and states of emergency have been declared in some countries, ostensibly to remove obstacles to economic and social development.

The view that democratically instituted economic planning is ineffective is gaining ground not only in the nations of South Asia but in other developing countries as well. The final outcome of development efforts in South Asia is thus being watched with great interest, especially by other countries with similar development goals. In this sense, the development experience in South Asia is of great significance for the future of democracy, not only as a form of government but also as a framework for economic planning in all developing countries, which collectively include three quarters of the world's population.

In spite of the importance of economic planning in South Asia, no book deals systematically with the massive economic problems facing the entire region. Several books treat of specific countries, but none deals with the region as a whole. The present work attempts to fill this need. What is the nature of the problem of underdevelopment in South Asia? How do we explain its causes? What are the major achievements and failures of economic planning in the last two decades? Why are the critical problems of poverty, unemployment, and mounting frustration among the masses unsolved? These are some of the questions this book considers. While the focus is on South Asia as a region, variations in the economic problems and policies of individual nations are also explored.

I hope this book will prove useful in several courses: both theoretical and policy-oriented courses in economic development; courses in the economics of the Third World; interdisciplinary courses in Asian studies; and courses on South Asia itself.

My depts to those who have helped prepare this book are numerous. Professors A. Arumugam, Ram Chugh, Romesh Diwan, Prem Gandhi, Robert Pettengill, and Franklin Walker were kind enough to read and comment on the manuscript. The final version of the book was completed at the Gokhale Institute of Politics and Economics at Poona, India, where I served as a Fulbright visiting professor during the spring semester of 1976. I leaned heavily on the staff and excellent library facilities of the institute for research assistance. I am also grateful to the United States Educational Foundation in India (New Delhi), The University Grants Commission, Government of India (New Delhi), and the Research Foundation of the State University of New York for providing funds to enable me to visit the South Asian countries and to study in the major South Asian centers in the United States. I am indebted to the editorial staff of St. Martin's Press. My special thanks go to Martha Goldstein, who supervised the editing of this book, and to Evelyn Katrak, who so carefully checked the enormous quantity of data presented herein. Finally I must thank my wife, Pritam, who cheerfully accepted my preoccupation with the research and writing of the book.

J.S. Uppal

State University
of New York, Albany

CONTENTS

Economic Development
in South Asia

1

Economic Underdevelopment in South Asia

THE GENERAL SETTING

South Asia includes principally the countries of Bangladesh, India, Pakistan, Nepal, and Sri Lanka, (formerly Ceylon), as well as some small Himalayan states. Bangladesh, India, Pakistan, and Nepal are located on the mainland of Asia, whereas Sri Lanka is separated from the southeastern tip of India by about 20 miles of water, the Gulf of Mannar. The land area of these countries approximates 1.73 million square miles, with a population of 709 million; this constitutes only 3.3 percent of the world's land surface but 22.1 percent of its population. There are many similarities within the countries of South Asia; Bangladesh, India, and Pakistan formerly formed one country governed by Great Britain. In 1947 an eastern and a western region of India were formed into two separated wings of a new country—Pakistan. In 1971 eastern Pakistan emerged as the independent nation of Bangladesh. The 1947 partition of India cut across transportation routes, communication power lines, and waterways which had been built with one geopolitical entity in mind. The neglect of these considerations with the granting of independence resulted in the disruption of the economies of both India and the newly established Pakistan.

In physical features, Sri Lanka is like southern India. Though an island, Sri Lanka is in fact an extension of peninsular India; the very shallow waters separating it from India are dotted with many small tracts of land. Nepal is situated at the foot of the Himalayas in northeastern

India. Bangladesh was, before 1947, a part of the province of Bengal and is still in many respects similar to the present state of West Bengal in eastern India.

South Asia exists as a territorial unit; not only in its geological features, but also in some of its weather patterns, religious traditions, cultural values, and political organization. The economies of the countries in this region also have many similarities. The countries of South Asia share a tropical monsoon-type climate. Although most Asian countries rely upon monsoons, this area is particularly dependent upon the regularity of rain-bearing monsoon winds both in summer and in winter. In India and Pakistan, with 19.7 and 50.0 percent, respectively, of their total cultivated areas served by irrigation facilities, agricultural output is related directly to the adequacy and timeliness of the monsoons. Inadequate and untimely rains, which are not an uncommon phenomenon in this part of the world, may cause drought or floods bringing untold suffering. An overdependence on the unpredictable monsoons has made agriculture in Bangladesh, India, and Pakistan a gamble with rainfall. Uncertainties about the agricultural outcome in areas dependent on erratic monsoons may have contributed, somewhat, to the fatalistic attitudes held by the peoples of the area.

The peoples of South Asia share a common cultural heritage. Archaeological excavations in various parts of the subcontinent reveal the existence of a homogeneous culture—called the "Indo-Aryan." The people are proud of their past and this should be kept in mind when attempting to understand their attitudes, especially toward other countries. During the two hundred years the British occupied these countries, their subjects never considered themselves culturally or socially inferior. Despite their political subjugation, South Asians, especially the intellectuals, were never overly impressed by the material goods and technology of the West, because they could always point to the evidence of the cultural achievements of their own rich past. Although such an attitude might have placed a constraint on modernization, as commonly desired in the West, it allowed the South Asian people to keep the pride so essential for nation formation. Unlike Africa, where the foremost task in nation building is the development of a national pride—a self-esteem lost during centuries of subjugation under alien masters—the people of South Asia are more sure of themselves and their capabilities.

The peoples of South Asia are religious; the three major religions—Hinduism, Buddhism, and Islam—have greatly influenced their attitudes and styles of life. Their value systems have been formulated through their religious principles. To what extent the main tenets of Hinduism (Karma in the present life determining the condition of the next life; present life as an illusion and a preparation for the future life, etc.) hinder efforts for material advances presents a difficult but interesting problem for investigation.

Adherents of these religions have been able to explain away and bear many of the tragedies of life, including the hardships arising from poverty and natural disasters, through reliance on their religious beliefs. The soothing effect of religion is, however, diminishing—especially among the educated youth who have been affected by Western forms of education. Mounting frustrations have resulted and dissatisfaction exists now with poor economic conditions.

The social institutions of the extended (joint) family and the caste system are shared by the countries of the region. In the extended family system, members share their work and income. This system has a great impact on economic and social conditions. It may adversely affect the work effort and result in loss of income, by creating a false sense of security with an illusion of "full employment" among family members who, in fact, may not be contributing to the total family output. These family members are, thus, disguisedly unemployed—a term used synonymously with "surplus labor" or "hidden unemployment." It is believed that a substantial amount of surplus labor exists in most underdeveloped countries, especially in the rural sectors of Bangladesh, India, and Pakistan, which has been hidden by the extended family system. This family system, however, provides care for the young, the old, the sick, and the disabled. It creates a sense of belonging among family members and often minimizes some of the pressures that may result in nervous breakdowns, loneliness, and other kinds of emotional and mental disturbances. Despite the adverse economic conditions, the family does provide a type of social security system within these countries, which cannot, at this stage of development, afford care and protection for their economically and socially needy.

The caste system, though a part of the Hindu social structure, has influenced the social structure of the entire subcontinent, including those practicing the other religions—Islam, Buddhism, and Sikhism. Under the Hindu caste system, the lower castes—Shudras—have been denied full participation in society. Traditionally, various occupations in India are defined in terms of castes: teaching and religious service for Brahmans; the military for Khashatriyas; trade and commerce for Vaishyas; and the menial and manual tasks for the Shudras, or Untouchables. With industrialization, the caste system is weakening, but it remains, still, as an impediment to social and economic mobility. In chapter 6, we will further examine the impact of religion and the social institutions of family and caste on the economic development of South Asia.

Except for Nepal, the countries of South Asia are former colonies of Great Britain and they achieved independence at the same time—during the late 1940s. These countries have thus inherited a common administrative structure developed by the British government. During their two hundred years of political subjugation, colonialism affected all aspects of these societies—the economic, social, and political. Their economies were transformed to serve as suppliers of raw materials for, and importers of, the goods manufactured by British industries. The colonial relationship was a hindrance to their economic development in general, and to their industrialization in particular.

Nationalism developed in South Asia with the aim of establishing democratic forms of government. Since achieving independence, therefore, the South Asian countries have been experimenting with democracy, not only as a form of government but also as a technique for planning social and economic development. There have been many difficulties in adherence to democratic ideals in the various countries.[1] In India and Sri Lanka the democratic process has been practiced for the last two decades, while in Pakistan the experiment with the democratic form of government has not been so successful. Throughout South Asia, in the general elections of the last twenty years, the electorate has, however, shown overwhelming preference for democratic forms of government. Pakistan, even under successive military regimes, has been trying different versions of democracy. Nepal, though a constitutional monarchy, has been under parliamentary democracy most of the time during the last two decades. Bangladesh adopted a democratic form of government from its very inception in 1971. Economic plans in the South Asian countries call for public cooperation and mass participation in their formulation and execution. The planning process is characterized as "democratic," consistent with the political preference of the electorate. The fate of democratic institutions in South Asia has great significance, not only for the people of these countries but also for other developing nations. If democratic institutions do not prove successful in establishing political stability and reasonable economic development, the peoples of Asia (and those of Africa and Latin America) may eventually lose confidence in the effectiveness of democracy for solving their problems. People in these underdeveloped nations are apt to compare their development under democratic institutions with the communist and socialist techniques for economic development, such as those practiced in China.

ASPECTS OF ECONOMIC UNDERDEVELOPMENT

The countries of South Asia suffer from underdevelopment, as can be seen from various economic and social indicators. Their per capita income—the basic measure of relative economic development—is among

Table 1-1 Per Capita Income in Selected Countries
(1972 U.S. dollars)

Country	1972	Average annual growth rate 1960-1972
India	$ 110	1.1%
Sri Lanka	110	2.0
Nepal	80	0.3
Pakistan	130	3.1
Bangladesh	70	0.0
People's Republic of China	170	2.6
United States	5,590	3.0
United Kingdom	2,600	2.3
Canada	4,440	3.6
West Germany	3,390	3.7
Japan	2,320	9.4

SOURCE: United Nations, *Statistical Yearbook, 1973* (New York, 1974).
World Bank, *Trends in Developing Countries* (Washington, D.C., 1973).
_____, *Annual Report, 1975* (Washington, D.C., 1975).
_____, *Atlas, 1974* (Washington, D.C., 1974).

the lowest in the world. This is indicated by the figures in Table 1-1. It can be observed that per capita income, and also its annual rate of growth, in the South Asian countries is considerably lower than in the more advanced countries. The growth rates of the total gross national product and the per capita gross national product in South Asia are, in general, lower than comparable growth rates in other regions of the underdeveloped world, as shown in Table 1-2.

The low per capita income and slower growth rates are a reflection of the general state of economic underdevelopment in the region. Some of the causes of this economic underdevelopment seem to prevail in underdeveloped areas in general, and they are discussed in the following sections.

Excessive Dependence on Agriculture   About three quarters of the population in the South Asian countries work in agriculture. They, however, contribute less than 50 percent to the total income of these countries, indicating a comparatively lower productivity of agricultural than nonagricultural labor. For example, in India, according to the National Income Committee, average productivity per worker in agriculture for the year 1950-1951 was Rs 500 ($66.6), while it was Rs 1,700 ($226.6) in large-scale industries, and Rs 1,500 ($200) in commerce, transportation, and communications.[2]

Table 1-2 Estimated Average Annual Growth Rates of
Underdeveloped Countries, by Regions (1965 prices)

Region	Annual growth rate			Annual growth in per capita income	
	1950-1955	1955-1960	1960-1970	1955-1960	1960-1970
Latin America	5.1%	5.0%	4.5%	2.1%	1.6%
Near East	5.7	5.9	6.4	3.4	3.9
South Asia	3.4	4.2	3.8	2.1	1.4
Sri Lanka	3.3	3.2	3.0	0.6	0.4
India	3.9	4.4	3.5	2.3	1.1
Bangladesh[a]	2.3	1.7	5.8[b]	-0.08	3.4[c]
Pakistan[a]	1.8	-3.4	5.8	0.07	2.5[c]
East Asia	3.9	3.8	4.9	1.2	2.3
Africa	2.8	2.7	3.4	1.3	2.2
All underdeveloped countries	5.0	4.4	4.8	2.2	2.3

[a]Figures are in 1959-1960 prices. Until 1972 Bangladesh was eastern Pakistan.
[b]Annual growth rate for 1960-1964.
[c]Data are for 1960-1965.
SOURCE: Stephen R. Lewis, Jr., *Pakistan, Industrialization and Trade Policies*
   (London: Oxford University Press, 1970).
Joseph Stern, "Growth, Development and Regional Equity," in Walter Falcon and
   Gustav Papanek, eds. *Development Policy, II; The Pakistan Experience*
   (Cambridge, Mass.: Harvard University Press, 1971), p. 11.
U.S. Government, Agency For International Development. *Gross National Product:
   Growth Rates and Trend Data.* Washington, D.C., 1968.
World Bank, *Trends in Developing Countries* (Washington, D.C., 1973).

Historically, as countries developed, the proportion of the population working in agriculture diminished. For example, in the United States this ratio fell from about 75 percent in 1810 to 10 percent in 1970. In France and Japan, respectively, the proportion of the work force engaged in agriculture declined from 42 percent to 25 percent, and from 80 percent to 48 percent between 1870 and 1930. With industrial development, agriculture becomes more productive and fewer people are needed to produce a given quantity.

Deficiency of Capital The deficiency of capital is another basic characteristic of underdevelopment. In the South Asian countries it is reflected in two ways. First, the amount of capital available per head is very low. The figures on per capita production of two crucial capital goods, steel and electricity, are respectively, for India 31 lb and 188 kw as against the corresponding figures of 1,584 lb and 11,960 kw for the United States.[3] In some sectors of these economies, for example in the rural sector, the capital investment per head has been reduced to the point that with an increasing labor force marginal labor productivity has become extremely low. Second, the rate of capital formation in the South Asian countries, ranging between 12 and 14 percent during the period 1960–1970, is inadequate to achieve any significant growth rate. In these countries, with population growing at about 2.5 percent, about 8 percent of investment is required simply to offset the additional burden imposed by population increase. Another 4 percent of investment is required to cover depreciation. Thus, South Asian economies require about 12 percent of gross capital formation simply to cover depreciation and to maintain existing living standards. Any economic growth would emerge only from investment beyond the 12 percent level. The present rate of investment in the South Asian countries is thus grossly inadequate when viewed in terms of their development needs.

There are two components of capital formation. Domestic capital (which includes household savings, corporate savings, and government savings) and foreign capital (consisting of foreign investments, loans, and grants). The shortage of domestic capital is due to several factors, both economic and social. As regards foreign capital, there has been a steady decline in its flow into the South Asian countries. For India, foreign capital was about 2.9 percent of the national income during the decade 1955–1965, after which it declined steadily to a low of 0.8 percent in 1975. For Pakistan, foreign capital ranged between 4.0 and 6.9 percent of the gross national product (GNP) during the decade 1960–1970, but it has since declined to about 2.7 percent. There are several reasons for this decline in the inflow of foreign capital. The capital-exporting countries are themselves facing financial difficulties including adverse balance of payments. In addition, the recipient countries of South Asia have placed some restrictions on foreign investments and have, instead, started emphasizing self-reliance—which may amount to making a virtue of necessity. In the words of the Indian Planning Commission:

> The objective is not only to take the country towards freedom from dependence on external aid for its economic development but also to generate domestic capacities that will enable it to have a steady and satisfactory rate of economic growth without dependence on external aid.[4]

We will discuss these issues further in chapter 3, Capital Formation.

Low Labor Productivity Low labor productivity is both a symptom and a cause of underdevelopment. It lies at the root of much of the poverty in underdeveloped countries. The extremely low productivity of agricultural labor in the South Asian countries can be observed in

Table 1–3. Labor productivity in the nonagricultural sectors is similarly low.

The reasons for low productivity are many and varied, and they include both social and economic factors. One important cause is the growing scarcity of such cooperative inputs as land and capital, which, together with rapid population growth, places an increasing burden on land. Let us examine this phenomenon in a rural context. Taking land, labor, and capital as the main determinants of output, let us assume that the supply of capital is fixed. To increase output, both land and labor need to be increased. But if the supply of one of these inputs, say, land, does not increase or increases at a much slower rate than the other input, labor, then after a certain point, the output will stop increasing or will increase at a relatively slower rate, giving us a proportionately reduced low output per unit of labor. This is the position in the rural sector of most of the countries of South Asia. For instance, in India, because of increased population, the amount of cultivated land per capita has been gradually declining, from 1.11 acres in 1921 to 0.62 acres in 1971. In Bangladesh the cultivated area per capita dropped from 0.75 acres in 1921 to a low of 0.25 acres in 1971.

The decline in the per capita area of cultivable land can be counteracted by increased capital investment (improved technology, use

Table 1-3 Average Annual Productivity of Agricultural Labor (1970 U.S. dollars)

Country	Average Annual Productivity
Bangladesh	$ 124
India	105
Pakistan	176
West Germany	3,495
United Kingdom	2,057
United States	
Japan	2,265

SOURCE: Ruddar Datt and K. P. M., Sundharam, *Indian Economy* (New Delhi: Chand, 1973), p. 373.
World Bank, *Trends in Developing Countries* (Washington, D.C., 1973).
United Nations, *Statistical Year Book, 1974* (New York, 1975).

of fertilizers, expanded irrigation facilities, etc.), as has been the case in such land-scarce countries as Japan. But, unfortunately, because of their low rate of capital formation, the South Asian countries have not been able to resort to this remedy. The result is that overall productivity in agriculture has not risen sufficiently to meet the demands of a rapidly growing population. In India, the overall increase in agricultural productivity per acre was 40 percent during the period 1950–1970—a 2 percent annual increase against the corresponding annual population growth of 2.5 percent. In Bangladesh, agricultural production increased by 2.1 percent during the period 1960–1970, which, again, was slightly less than the increase in population. In Pakistan, however, the overall annual increase in agricultural production during the period 1960–1970 was 5.6 percent as against a population increase of 2.7 percent.

In recent years the use of improved inputs (new varieties of seeds, more and better qualities of fertilizers, expanded irrigation facilities, etc.) has resulted in impressive increases in agricultural output in certain areas. It is referred to in the literature as the Green Revolution—providing evidence that it is mostly lack of capital investment that accounts for low labor productivity, especially in agriculture.

Unemployment and Underemployment   Another important aspect of underdevelopment in the countries of South Asia is the prevalence of serious unemployment as well as underemployment. Though estimates differ for different regions of the countries, the figure of 15 percent of the labor force being unemployed can be used as a rough approximation. The problem is more acute in the rural areas, where about one quarter of the work force is "surplus." We will discuss the nature, extent, and causes of this phenomenon later, in chapter 5, but it is important to note here that unemployment is both a cause and an effect of underdevelopment. Population increase without a corresponding increase in other inputs (land, capital, etc.) inevitably results in a part of the work force being without work. This nonutilization of an important factor of production, labor, results in a loss of the goods and services that the unemployed could produce if at work. A country is thus made poorer by its unemployment. However, the poorer the country, the less its ability to save the capital that is needed to create employment. Yet, efficient utilization of manpower is an essential prerequisite for economic development.

The Unfavorable Terms of Trade   Production in some of these countries, notably Bangladesh and Sri Lanka, is very much export oriented. Jute (burlap) and tea exports constitute a significant proportion of the gross national product of Bangladesh. Tea exports are more than 35 percent of the total national income of Sri Lanka. There is a tendency for the terms of trade to turn against raw material–exporting countries because of a fall in world demand resulting, among other things, from the use of substitutes (e.g., paper and plastics for jute). This has made it difficult for such countries to rely on their export earnings for long-term economic development.[5] A United Nations Commission for Trade and Development (UNCTAD) study (1974) shows that during the period 1958–1973, the terms of trade were moving against the economies of all the countries of South Asia.[6]

Lack of Infrastructure Inadequate economic and social overheads, such as power, transportation, and communications (also called forward linkages, or infrastructure) tend to aggravate the already serious problems related to agricultural and industrial growth. This problem is particularly serious in Bangladesh and Nepal. The 1971 war in Bangladesh caused massive damage to social overhead capital, especially for communications, transportation facilities, and irrigation projects. The 1972 United Nations Relief Operation report, *A Survey of Damages and Repairs,* published in Dacca, estimated the material damage to be around $1,200 million, which is beyond the present fiscal capacity of the new nation. It will take several years for Bangladesh to repair the wartime damage and until that time the damage will continue to impede the economic growth of the country.

The difficulties inherent in Nepal's mountainous terrain make the provision of social overhead capital, especially for transportation and irrigation, a very expensive consideration.

Inequality of Income Maldistribution of national income results in extreme economic disparities among the different groups, with a very small group tending to own a very large proportion of the country's wealth and resources. It is well known that in Pakistan, twenty-two families control a substantial part of the industrial assets of the country.[7] In India, a committee appointed by the Planning Commission reported a grim picture of the distribution of national income in 1960, with the poorest 10 percent of the population earning only 1.3 percent and 0.7 percent of aggregate income in the urban and rural sectors, respectively, and economic power concentrated in the hands of a few big companies in the private sector. Analyzing the changes in income distribution, the committee observed that:

> Even after 10 years of planning and despite fairly heavy schemes of taxation on the upper incomes, there is a considerable measure of concentration in urban incomes. This would also hold for rural incomes as in their cases, even the burden of taxation is not heavy on the higher ranges of incomes.[8]

Statistics on income distribution in India, collected in an All-India Rural Household Survey, show that between the years 1962 and 1967–1968 the gap in fact widened: the share of national income of the upper 20 percent of households increased from 48 percent to 53 percent, that of the lowest 20 percent decreased from 5.9 percent to 4.9 percent.[9]

The United Nations' estimates of Lorenz-ratios,[10] indicating distribution of income over time and by broad sectors for some of the countries of South Asia, are given in Table 1–4.

Table 1-4   Income Inequalities in Selected South Asian Countries

Country	Years	Rural	Urban	Total
India	1960-1961	0.34	0.47	0.38
	1961-1962	0.30	0.35	0.32
	1967-1968	0.28	0.31	0.30
Pakistan	1963-1964	0.35	0.37	0.36
	1968-1969	0.29	0.36	0.33
Sri Lanka	1963	0.44	0.49	0.49
	1969-1970	0.36	0.42	0.41
	1973	0.37	0.40	0.41

SOURCE: H. B. Chenerey et al, *Redistribution with Growth* (London: Oxford University Press, 1974), pp. 6-16, 253-290.
United Nations, *Economic and Social Survey of Asia and the Pacific, 1974* (Bangkok, 1975), p. 58.

The generally declining Lorenz-ratios show increasing inequalities in income distribution among both the urban and the rural populations.

This disparity in income distribution, which in the past contributed to capital formation and development in some presently developed countries, for example Japan and the United States, has not helped the low-income countries of South Asia, since the wealth of the economic elite is, in absolute terms, quite small in relation to the needs of those countries. Also such wealth tends to be diverted to conspicuous consumption or dissipated in unproductive forms of expenditure (e.g., real estate or gold), rather than being invested to augment the productive capacity of the country's economy. The persistence of inequalities over a long period of time tends to foster apathy and cynicism among the majority of people—those in the lowest income brackets—who then tend to dismiss the "planning process" as a "rich man's racket."

Low Levels of Consumption   The low level of earnings and inequities in income distribution in South Asian countries are reflected in tragically low levels of consumption of even such necessities of life as food, housing, and essential clothing. Azizur Rahman Khan estimated the average daily per capita income in Bangladesh in 1970 at 17 cents.[11] The poorest 20 percent of the population receive only 7 percent of GNP and their per capita income is only about 6 cents per day. While 73 percent of the total expenditure of rural people (who constitute 93 percent of the total population of Bangladesh) is for food, 50 percent of the population are on a starvation diet and nearly 90 percent suffer from some kind of nutritional deficiency. According to Azizur Rahman, "Food intake is not only qualitatively inadequate on the average, but also quantitatively below starvation level for nearly half the population. It is extremely deficient in protective elements."[12] Tragically enough, even these extremely low levels of food intake are declining. The daily per capita available quantity of rice (the staple food in Bangladesh) and wheat decreased from 1.07 lb in 1960 to 1.06 lb in 1970.[13] With regard to clothing, Azizur Rahman found the annual per capita consumption of cloth in Bangladesh in 1966–1967 to be 7.5 yd in rural areas and 12.5 yd in urban areas, which "works out at one set of clothing per person in rural areas during a twelve month period. Perhaps for a vast proportion of the population there is no more than a couple of loin cloths per year."[14] The plight of the people with regard to housing is equally desperate. A study of dwellings in the three largest urban industrial centers of Bangladesh shows that in 1966,

> An average family of 5.6 members have on the average 1.5 rooms. Nearly 71 percent are temporary constructions without any masonry, 56 percent have only one room, 82 percent have no water connection and 97 percent have no electricity.[15]

In India, the monthly per capita consumer expenditure in 1963–1964 was Rs 22.37 ($3) in rural areas and Rs 32.96 ($4.4) in urban areas, of which 70.1 percent and 54.4 percent, respectively, was spent on food.[16] On the basis of various criteria, such as cost of "minimum essential food" and "expenditure to buy food for minimum caloric requirement," Indian economists have variously estimated the proportion of the Indian population living below the poverty line during the period 1968–1970 to be between 41 and 53 percent.[17] Comparing figures over time, most estimates indicate that the proportion of the population living below the poverty line has increased or remained substantially the same during the period 1960–1970.[18] Surveys of food consumption in India made in 1960 show that 63.2 percent of the rural population and 32.49 percent of the urban population suffered from nutritional deficiency. The comparable figures for 1967–1968 indicate that the deficiency had by then worsened considerably compared to 1960–1961, especially in the rural areas.[19]

According to Ram Manohar Lohia:

This implies that about three fourths of the people of India do not have more than one meal a day, even that food mainly consists of inferior cereals like bajra or jawar. Clothing is a luxury for many and even in bitter cold, poor people do not wear enough clothes. In rural areas, six to seven persons live in one roomed, ill-ventilated mud huts. Even these mud huts are not available to millions of workers in large towns like Delhi, Bombay and Calcutta. In sun and rain, in heat or biting cold, these poor people live in the open, on the pavement or on vacant plots. Many basic amenities such as water for drinking and bathing are not available for rural people.[20]

This tragically low standard of living causes ill health and reduction in the physical capability of people for sustained hard work. In 1921 Mahatma Gandhi sorrowfully observed that "the human bird under the Indian sky gets up weaker than when he pretends to retire. For millions it is an eternal vigil or an eternal trance."[21] That observation still holds true.

Thus, the countries of South Asia exhibit all the classic symptoms of economic underdevelopment: low per capita income; population growth preceding economic development, which acts as a retarding factor in the development process; and low productivity, which is linked to a lack of capital investment in land and in the essential economic overheads, or infrastructure. With their scarcity of capital relative to their abundant supplies of labor, these countries may be said to be suffering from severe structural imbalance in regard to factor inputs.

EDUCATION

One area in which the countries of South Asia have recorded impressive gains is in the expansion of educational facilities, especially at the secondary and college levels, as shown in Table 1-5. There has also been a rapid increase in the number of technically trained personnel, especially in India, which presently ranks third in the world in absolute numbers of skilled workers.

What is the impact of this pattern of increased education on the process of economic development in South Asia? In the literature on the role of education in economic development, it is generally held that there is a positive and high correlation between education and economic change.[22] This generalization is evidently based on the assumption that education, besides contributing to the individual enrichment of students, modernizing their outlook, and so on, develops the capacity and will for productive economic activity. Unfortunately, the educational systems of the countries of South Asia have not proved conducive to instilling these positive attitudes. In the words of the Bangladesh Planning Commission:

Table 1-5 Annual Growth Rate in Education in South Asia, 1960-1969

Country	First level[a]	Second level[b]	Third level[c]
India	5.4%	7.1%	11.0%
Nepal	13.0	11.7	15.4
Pakistan	8.0	7.9	12.0
Sri Lanka	1.5	4.9	8.9

[a]Ages 6-13, primary and middle schools, grades I-VIII.
[b]Ages 14-18, high school, grades VIII-XII.
[c]College level.

SOURCE: UNESCO, Regional Office for Education in Asia, *Progress of Education in the Asian Region* (Paris, 1972), table 19.
United Nations, *Economic Survey of Asia and the Far East, 1973* (Bangkok, 1974), p. 40.

The system of education prevalent was not geared to the needs of an independent nation or of a growing economy — Its purpose was primarily to produce a number of educated persons who could assist the British colonial administration in the country. In fact, the small section of people, who were educated under this system, acquired a set of values which, on the one hand, alienated them from their own people and on the other, developed in them a dislike for all forms of manual labour.[23]

Moreover, the educational facilities in these countries have expanded more rapidly than have their absorptive capacity. As a result:

The less wealthy countries which are undergoing an educational revolution more rapidly than their economic revolution, are often unable to employ more than a fraction of those they educate. Not only is this wasteful, but it also leads to bitterness and disappointment as painful to the individual as it may be dangerous to social and political stability. Education is often thought of as the way to prestige and affluence and an escape from the uncompromising drudgery of agriculture. The school leaver consequently tends to not remain in the village where his education might be put to the best use; instead he usually makes his way to the town where he constitutes a focus of discord.[24]

These sentiments were echoed by the 1972 Task Force on Education, appointed by the Government of India:

We have, unfortunately, at present a top heavy, lopsided, educational structure which does not seem to be commensurate with the socio-economic needs of the society. This is not, however, a recent phenomenon, it has its roots in the pre-independence period, only it has become more acute of late.[25]

Thus, the South Asian countries have many more educated persons than they can presently utilize. Being unemployed, they are unable to contribute their talents to economic development and in fact constitute a burden on the economies of those countries. Estimates by the United Nations of the incidence of unemployment among educated persons in the countries of South Asia reveal two disquieting tendencies. First, the rate of unemployment increases with level of education and second, during the period 1960–1970 the rate of increase of unemployment was greater for college graduates than for holders of high school diplomas.[26] Paradoxically, even engineers and other persons with advanced technical education are facing unemployment in India. Thus, at the present level of development the expansion of educational facilities, especially beyond secondary level, is not contributing to economic expansion. What is needed is a reconstruction of the educational systems of these countries to meet their development needs and also to strike a better balance between the number of graduates emerging from their institutions of higher education and the demand for such skills and services. Despite repeated government proclamations over the last twenty-five years, there has been no noticeable effort on the part of these countries to change their educational systems and work toward a planned growth of manpower; if anything, the situation has worsened.

PLANS FOR ECONOMIC DEVELOPMENT

Historically, at least during the current century, the countries of South Asia have remained poor, with per capita income at static low levels. Data on the changes in output in preindependent India (which comprised present-day Bangladesh, India, and Pakistan) are given in Table 1–6. There were negative rates of growth in per capita output during the three decades 1916 to 1945, largely explained by low productivity in agriculture. Over the five decades under review, agricultural output increased by only 12 percent, whereas total population increased by 34 percent. This imbalance is partly a reflection of the fact that the area under cultivation per head decreased from 1.11 acres in 1921 to 0.94 acres in 1941. The considerable increase in industry and mining output did not affect total productivity significantly because of its minor share (less than 5 percent) in the value of total output.

The position of Sri Lanka (Ceylon) was, however, different from that of the Indian subcontinent. From the late nineteenth century, there was substantial development in the plantation sector (tea, rubber, and coconut), which accounted for one-half of Sri Lanka's gross domestic product during the period 1888–1939.[27] According to rough estimates by Snodgrass, the overall annual growth rate was around 5.1 percent. Taking into account the population growth rate of 1.4 percent during this period, growth in per capita income was about 3.7 percent. While the overall trend in Sri Lanka's domestic product has been distinctly

Table 1-6 Long-term Changes in Net Output in India, 1896-1945

	1896-1906	1905-1915	1916-1925	1926-1935	1936-1945
Per capita output[a]	158	159	164	155	144
Per capita output[b]	100	101	104	98	91
Agricultural crops[b]	100	106	108	110	112
Industry and mining[b]	100	154	200	267	420
Population[b]	100	107	108	119	134
Decennial rate of percentage growth in per capita output	1	3	-6	-7	-5

[a]In rupees, 1952-1953 prices.
[b]Index: 1896-1905 = 100.

SOURCE: S. Kuznets, ed. *Economic Growth: Brazil, India, and Japan* (Durham, N.C.: Duke University Press, 1955), pp. 120-124.
Surendra J. Patel, *Essays on Economic Transition* (New York: Asia Publishing House, 1965), p. 44.

upward, growth in the plantation sector did not touch off any remarkable corresponding growth or transformation in the rest of the economy. According to Snodgrass, "Most of Ceylon's rural population relied heavily on the traditional cultivation of paddy (rice), yet per acre yields in the crop were among the lowest in the world."[28]

The static nature of the South Asian economies can be described in terms of Leibenstein's hypothesis:

(1) It is useful to characterize a backward economy as an equilibrium system whose equilibrium state (or states) posesses a degree of "quasi-stability" with respect to per capita income. . . (2) If the equilibrium of a backward economy is disturbed, the forces or influences that tend to raise per capita income set in motion, directly or indirectly, forces that have the effect of depressing per capita income. (3) In the disequilibrium state (in the backward economy), for at least the lower incomes above the equilibrium level, the effects of the income-depressing forces are greater than the effects of the income-raising forces.[29]

The static nature of these economies prior to World War II (the preindependence period) corresponds to Leibenstein's "quasi-stability" condition. Minor changes in some economic variables, such as investment and technology, did occur, creating sporadic increases in the income levels. But as Leibenstein notes, these stimulants have not led to sustained growth in per capita incomes but rather to a "pattern of change that leads to an eventual return to the low, underdeveloped equilibrium income."[30]

Sustained growth requires a transformation of the economic and social structures of the economy. Efforts toward sustained growth were not encouraged under British rule. Prior to 1947 the attitude toward economic growth can be characterized as one of indifference. Those economic changes that did take place in the countries of South Asia under alien rule, such as the growth of private consumer goods industries, the setting up of plantations, the emergence of a banking system, and the development of railways, roads, and other means of communication and transport, were either due to local enterprise or as a result of the deliberate policy of the British government to transform the region into a supplier of raw materials to Britain and an importer of manufactured goods from it. Some nationalist writers have suggested that during the period of British rule, there was an enormous drain of wealth from South Asia, resulting in the impoverishment of the countries of the region. One could debate the question of the overall impact of British rule on the countries of South Asia. There is no denying the fact, however, that by the late 1940s, on the eve of their independence, India, Pakistan, Sri Lanka, and Nepal were all in an economic backward state. Their public sectors were insignificant and there existed a serious lack of social and economic infrastructure throughout the region.

After political independence, the countries of South Asia adopted conscious and ambitious plans for economic and social development. India's five-year plans, beginning in 1950–1951, incorporated strategies to promote rapid and balanced economic development, to strengthen the economy at its base, and to initiate institutional changes that would facilitate rapid advances in the future. In Nepal,

> serious efforts to plan economic development took place after the establishment of the Planning Board in 1955. The First Five Year Plan prepared by the Board covered the period 1956–1961. The Second Plan gave priority to activities which would establish the base for more comprehensive future plans.[31]

In the words of the Pakistan Planning Commission:

> The process of economic development which commenced in Pakistan almost immediately after independence and continued through the period 1955–60 with the First Five Year Plan, had made significant advance by the end of the decade and achieved considerable results. The most significant advance was in the awareness of economic development, its need and urgency which was created in the country.[32]

The development plans of the South Asian countries[33] are comprehensive in the sense that they cover all aspects of the society. They are intended to

> accelerate the institutional changes needed to make the economy more dynamic and more progressive in terms no less of social than of economic

ends. Development is a continuous process; it touches all aspects of community life and has to be viewed comprehensively. Economic Planning thus extends itself into extraeconomic spheres, educational, social and cultural.[34]

The government of Pakistan declared its planning objectives as follows:

Man does not live by bread alone and a national plan has to take into account not only the production and distribution of goods, but also social services and civilizing activities. The standard of living of a people is a composite whole comprising material, social and cultural amenities. A proper equilibrium amongst these factors probably determines the fullness of life of a people. For the formulation of a national plan, it is necessary to state the norms for the attainment of which the nation must strive. These norms will constitute the measure of the standard of living which, within a specified time, it is desired to achieve—though the social objectives of Pakistan have not been defined, it is certain that they are higher than a mere provision of a standard of living very near the minimum requirements of human life.[35]

The first five-year plan of Nepal, started in September 1956, echoes similar purposes, "to raise production, employment, standard of living and general welfare throughout the country."[36]

Another important feature of these development plans is their declared hope and intention of benefiting the underprivileged:

The benefits of economic development must accrue more and more to the relatively less privileged classes of society, and there should be a progressive reduction of the concentration of incomes, wealth and economic power. The problem is to create a milieu in which the small man who has so far had little opportunity of perceiving and participating in the immense possibilities of growth, through organized effort, is enabled to put in his best in the interest of a higher standard of life for himself and increased prosperity for the country. In the process he rises in economic and social status.[37]

These high-sounding objectives combined with the direct promises made to the underprivileged by their political leaders, that they would share in the benefits resulting from development, created great hopes and expectations of a brighter future.

Twenty or more years have elapsed since the first of these plans was evolved—20 years of heavy investment, involving both domestic and foreign resources. In 1975 India was in the midst of its fifth five-year plan; Pakistan, completing its third five-year plan. Sri Lanka's ten-year plan was launched in 1959; Nepal began its first five-year plan in 1956.

The performance of the South Asian countries during the past two decades has been mixed. While achievements on the whole have not been impressive, some progress is evident from changes in the major economic indicators (see Table 1-7).

While growth rates are grossly inadequate to match increased demands—arising from a considerable growth in population and some rise in incomes—they do represent some progress in economies that, viewed historically, had been virtually stagnant over the last century or so. K. N. Raj observed in 1965:

> The rate of economic growth that has been achieved in India since 1950-51 is 2 to 3 times as high as the rate recorded earlier in British administration. As a result, the percentage increase in national income in the last thirteen years has been higher than the percentage increase realized in India over the entire preceding half a century.[38]

Comparing the performance of the Indian economy under the three five-year plans with preindependent India, Max Millikan observed:

> The Indian growth rate of nearly 4 percent in this period represents a notable acceleration over the annual growth rate of British India for the first half of the twentieth century, which has been estimated at no more than 1 percent, and compares very favorably with the growth rates of the presently advanced countries during their earlier development history.[39]

As the Pakistan Planning Commission noted, economic development began in Pakistan with independence and continued through 1960 with the first five-year plan. It made considerable advances and achieved significant results. The most significant was the awareness of development created in the country. "The government services as well as the potential class of entrepreneurs developed new attitudes towards problems of development. There was a new alertness and the country was poised for a big effort."[40]

By mentioning the achievements of planning in the South Asian countries, we are not trying to play down the desperate economic plight of their teeming millions. The per capita income in these countries is, perhaps, the lowest in the world. Malnutrition and disease are widespread. These countries still suffer almost all the symptoms of underdevelopment, and it will take much effort and much time before they are able to provide even a reasonably humane standard of living for their peoples. Population increases continue to outpace increases in productivity. Unless the population explosion is kept under reasonable control, these countries will continue to be threatened by social and political explosion. Nevertheless, there is no denying that planning in South Asia has, in the words of A. H. Hanson, "effected a break with economic stagnation. Dynamism has been created in the hitherto static economies and today, instead of the stagnation of the previous decades,

Table 1-7 Annual Growth Rates: Some Economic Indicators in South Asia (Constant Prices 1960-1961)

Country	Years	Gross national product	Per capita income	Agricultural production	Industrial production	Population growth
Bangladesh	1960-1970	4.5%	1.4%	1.0%	6.1%	3.1%
	1970-1973	-9.0	-12.0	-4.7	-7.5	3.0
India	1951-1966	3.5	1.5	3.0	5.6	2.0
	1960-1970	3.6	1.1	2.9	6.1	2.5
	1970-1972	3.4	0.9	-.4	4.9	2.5
Pakistan	1960-1970	5.4	3.1	4.9	11.7	2.3
	1970-1973	2.6	0.1	3.0	0.0	2.6
Nepal	1960-1970	2.1	0.3	2.6		1.8
Sri Lanka	1960-1970	3.9	1.5	2.1	5.3	2.4
	1970-1972	2.0	-.04	0.0	6.3	2.4

SOURCE: Jagdish N. Bhagwati and Padma Desai, *India: Planning for Industrialization* (New York: Oxford University Press, 1970), pp. 61-83.
Government of Nepal, National Planning Council, *The Third Plan, 1965-1970* (Khatmandu, 1965).
Government of Pakistan, Ministry of Finance, *Economic Survey, 1969-1970,* pp. 2-5, and *1972-1973.*
United Nations, *Economic Survey of Asia and the Far East, 1972, 1973, and 1974.*
World Bank, *Trends in Developing Countries* (Washington, D.C., 1973).

clearly and unmistakingly the economies have been pushed into motion and are gathering momentum, and a new vitality marks South Asian Societies."[41]

The forces that have pushed these stagnant economies into motion, moreover, have directly or indirectly created counterforces. Chief among these are population growth, a slower rate of capital formation, and unemployment, all of which tend to act as a brake on progress. In terms of the Leibenstein thesis mentioned earlier, the planning process has tended to disturb the low level income equilibrium, and the forces and influences that raised per capita income during the earlier stages, have set into motion forces that now have the effect of depressing per capita income. In other words, the planning process in South Asia initiated forces in its initial stages, 1950-1970, which raised per capita income, expanded the infrastructure, and achieved some economic development. But these productive forces evoked counterforces that have tended to retard further economic development and growth. Karl Von Vorys, describes the effect of these counterforces, as a "problem of accelerated reaction."[42] Moreover, during the later stages of economic development, these counterforces have tended to accelerate more rapidly than the forces of development, and "these counterforces unless controlled, they may very well not only slow down economic development but bring it to a standstill."[43]

What are some of the major counterforces which are inhibiting growth in South Asia? What is being done to control these forces and with what results? These and other problems will be discussed in subsequent chapters.

NOTES

1. In India and Bangladesh, the democratic form of government is under great strain, especially since 1974. A state of emergency has been declared and many of the civil rights granted to citizens under both constitutions have been suspended. The leaders of these countries, however, claim that extreme measures have been adopted temporarily under the constitutional provisions which deal with serious threats (from dissident elements) internal security and political stability. The Indian government contends that many emergency measures have been taken to ensure discipline, essential for the smooth functioning of a democratic society. The August 1975 military coup in Bangladesh against the popularly elected government does not augur well for the democratic process, though the military junta promises restoration of the democratic form of government in due course.

2. Quoted in Ruddar Datt and K. P. M. Sundharam, *Indian Economy* (New Delhi: Chand, 1976), p. 36.

3. United Nations, *Statistical Year Book, 1974* (New York, 1975), pp. 360, 546.

4. Government of India, Planning Commission, *The Fourth Five Year Plan—a Draft Outline* (New Delhi, 1966), p. 24.

5. There is considerable controversy on the question of terms of trade between developing and developed countries. Generally it is held (e.g., Raul Prebisch) that the terms of trade tend to turn against the raw material-exporting developing countries, but this view is now being contested (e.g., Harberler, Flanders). For this debate, see Luis Eugenio Di Marco, *International Economics & Development — Essays in Honor of Raul Prebisch* (New York: Academic Press, 1972); and G. M. Meier, *The International Economics of Development* (New York: Harper & Row, 1968).

6. Quoted in United Nations, *Economic and Social Survey of Asia and the Pacific, 1974* (Bangkok, 1975), pp. 97-113.

7. Lawrence J. White, *Industrial Concentration and Economic Power in Pakistan* (Princeton, N.J.: Princeton University Press, 1974).

8. Government of India, Planning Commission, *Report of the Committee on Distribution of Income and Levels of Living — Part I* (New Delhi, 1964), p. 28. According to this report, in the case of 12 out of 21 major industries in the private sector, no more than five business groups were responsible for more than 50 percent of production.

9. National Council of Applied Economic Research, *All-India Household Income, Savings and Consumer Expenditure* (New Delhi, 1972), pp. 26-29.

10. Lorenz ratios, also called concentration ratios, are the most commonly used measure of inequality. The estimates range from 0 (complete inequality) to 1.0 (perfect equality).

11. Azizur Rahman Khan, *The Economy of Bangladesh* (London: Macmillan, 1972), p. 25.

12. Ibid., p. 25.

13. Ibid., p. 20.

14. Ibid., p. 25.

15. Ibid., p. 25.

16. Government of India, *National Sample Survey (18th Round), 1963-64* (New Delhi, 1970).

17. Datt & Sundharam, *Indian Economy*, p. 236.

18. A. J. Fonseca, *Challenge of Poverty in India* (Delhi: Vikas, 1972), pp. 34-35.

19. Ibid., p. 40.

20. Quoted in Datt and Sundharam, *Indian Economy*, p. 69.

21. Quoted in Fonseca, *Poverty in India*, p. 30.

22. For the contribution of education to economic development, see T. W. Schultz, *The Economic Value of Education* (New York: Columbia University Press, 1963).

23. Government of Bangladesh, Planning Commission, *The First Five Year Plan, 1973-78*, (Dacca, 1973), p. 73.

24. Adam Curle, *Planning for Education in Pakistan* (London: Tavistock, 1966), p. 27.

25. Government of India, *Report of the Working Group on Education* (New Delhi, 1972), pp. 11-12.

26. United Nations, *Economic Survey of Asia and the Far East, 1973* (Bangkok, 1974), chs. 1-6, pp. 11-111. For the situation in India, see Government of India, *Report of the Committee on Unemployment* (New Delhi, 1973).

27. Donald R. Snodgrass, *Ceylon: An Export Economy in Transition* (Homewood, Ill.: Irwin, 1966), pp. 52-53.

28. Ibid., p. 54-55.

29. Harvey Leibenstein, *Economic Backwardness and Economic Growth* (New York: Wiley, 1963), p. 16.

30. Ibid., p. 34.

31. Government of Nepal, National Planning Council, *The Third Plan, 1965-1970* (Khatmandu, 1965), pp. 1-2.

32. Government of Pakistan, Planning Commission, *The Second Five Year Plan, 1960-65* (Karachi, 1960), p. 5.

33. Also, see Bangladesh, *First Plan*.

34. Government of India, Planning Commission, *The Second Five Year Plan, 1955-60* (New Delhi, 1956), p. 3.

35. Government of Pakistan, Ministry of Economic Affairs, *Report of the Economic Appraisal Committee, 1962* (Karachi, 1963), pp. 68-69.

36. Y.P. Pant, *Economic Development of Nepal* (Allahabad: Kitab Mahal, 1965), p. 48.

37. India, *Second Plan*, p. 2.

38. K. N. Raj, *Indian Economic Growth: Performance and Prospects* (Delhi: Allied Publishers, 1965), p. 2.

39. Max F. Millikan, "Economic Development: Performance and Prospects," *Foreign Affairs,* vol. 46, no. 3 (April 1968), p. 532.

40. Pakistan, *Second Plan*, p. 5.

41. A. H. Hanson, *The Process of Planning* (London: Oxford University Press, 1966), p. 526.

42. Karl Von Vorys, "Some Aspects of the Economic Development of India," *World Politics,* 13 (1960-1961), 585.

43. Ibid., p. 585.

2

The Population Explosion

SOME INDICATORS OF OVERPOPULATION

Rapid population growth poses a serious threat to development efforts in the underdeveloped countries in general and the South Asian countries in particular. All efforts for economic development are being thwarted by the vastly increasing numbers. For example, during the decades 1950–1960 and 1960–1970, whereas the gross national product (GNP) increased by 3.5 and 4.1 percent, respectively, the corresponding increase in per capita income—taking into account the increase in population—was only 1.4 and 1.8 percent, respectively. Increasing population is thus neutralizing much of the gains from development efforts and consuming the savings needed for capital formation. Population, growing more rapidly than new employment opportunities, is swelling the already large numbers of unemployed and underemployed thereby adding to the misery, apathy, and alienation in these societies. Thus population increases in South Asia are a great obstacle to their economic development. Yet, ironically, the factors chiefly responsible for population growth since 1941 are themselves the results of development.

Table 2–1 provides data on population growth in the countries of South Asia since the beginning of the present century.

It will be observed that in most of the countries the rapid rate of population growth started after 1941. In Sri Lanka, the rate jumped from 1.2 percent in 1900–1941 to 2.8 percent in 1950–1960; in India,

Table 2-1 Estimates of Population Growth in the South Asian Countries 1900-1972

Country	Estimates of population (millions)					Annual growth of population (percentages)			
	1900	1941	1950	1960	1972	1900-1941	1941-1950	1950-1960	1960-1972
Sri Lanka	4.0	6.1	7.8	10.2	13.72[b]	1.2%	2.7%	2.8%	2.9%
India	236.0	319.0	361.0	439.0	563.0	0.9	1.6	2.15	2.3
Bangladesh	28.9	41.9	43.0	53.9	74.0	1.28	1.94	2.53	3.0[e]
Pakistan	16.5	28.2	35.8	45.0	56.1	1.7	2.6	2.57	2.0
Nepal	5.5[a]	6.2	8.4	9.1	11.5	0.55[c]	3.0[d]	1.4	1.8

[a] Population for 1920.
[b] Population for 1974.
[c] Population for 1920-1941.
[d] Population for 1941-1954
[e] Population for 1961-1973.

SOURCE: Ruddar Datt and K. P. M. Sundharam, *Indian Economy* (New Delhi: Chand, 1975), p. 19.
Kingsley Davis, *The Population of India and Pakistan* (Princeton, N.J.: Princeton University Press, 1951), p. 28.
Gunnar Myrdal, *Asian Drama: An Inquiry into the Poverty of Nations* (New York: Pantheon, 1968), vol. 1, p. 435; vol. 2, p. 1397.
Y. P. Pant, *Economic Development of Nepal* (Allahabad: Kitab Mahal, 1965), p. 19.
Government of Bangladesh, Planning Commission, *The First Five Year Plan, 1973-78* (Dacca, 1973).
Government of Nepal, National Planning Council, *The Third Plan, 1965-70* (Khatmandu, 1965).
Government of Pakistan, Finance Division, *Pakistan Economic Survey, 1972-73* (Karachi, 1974).
United Nations, *Economic and Social Survey of Asia and the Pacific, 1974* (Bangkok, 1975).
Economic Survey of Asia and the Far East, 1973 (Bangkok, 1974).
Statistical Year Book, 1974 (New York, 1975).

from 0.9 to 2.1 percent. The next period saw a further increase in the rate of growth in these two countries from 2.8 and 2.1 percent in 1950–1960 to 2.9 and 2.3 percent in 1960–1972. A similar trend can be noted for Bangladesh, Pakistan, and Nepal.

Prior to 1941, the population problem did not receive much attention. Discussing the development of India's population control policy, T. J. Samuel characterizes the years before 1947 as "the period of indifference."[1] During the tour of a princely state in western India around 1878, the British governor of Bombay, Sir Richard Temple, was presented with an address by the ruler which contained a request, "to restrain. . .the inordinate aptitude of the people to increase the population." He replied indignantly that he would do everything in his power for the "increase, and nothing for the diminution of Her Majesty's subjects."[2] In 1907, Sir E. A. Gait, in his essay, "Population,"[3] in the *Imperial Gazetteer of India,* declared that he did not think that India was overpopulated.[4] There were, however, some warnings of the impending population problem on the Indian subcontinent. Discussing the land tax in India, Baden–Powell remarked that a lowering of the land tax in any section tends to be followed by such a fast increase in population that the potential rise in prosperity is soon neutralized.[5] Noting the effects of population increase in the Punjab (presently in northern India and Pakistan), Sir Malcolm Darling claimed in 1925 that the natural increase in population in the new irrigation colonies in the Punjab had been so rapid that the initial prosperity was giving way to overcrowding and indebtedness.[6] But these warnings were not taken seriously, especially by such nationalist Indian economists as R. C. Dutt and Dadabhai Naoroji, who took the view that overpopulation was a theory propounded by "experts with an anti-India bias with a view to justify the 'Do Nothing' policy of the imperial government."[7]

We do not intend to debate whether or not India and the other countries of South Asia were overpopulated before 1941. However, there is no denying that earlier increases in population had been rather slow and sporadic. According to Kingsley Davis:

> From 1871 to 1941 the average rate of increase of India's population was approximately 0.60 percent per year. This was slightly less than the estimated rate for the whole world (0.69) from 1850-1940. India's modern growth, therefore, is not exceptional either way, but close to average. It is, however, less than that found in Europe, in North America, and in a good many particular countries.[8]

This slow rate of growth is explained by the closeness of the birth and death rates—death rate being high because of poor sanitation, high infant mortality, and the scourges of famine and disease. There was, for example, the great Indian famine of 1876-1878; then in the 1890s yet another famine occurred; and then the great influenza epidemic of 1918 took a heavy toll of life.[9] In Sri Lanka and Nepal, however, there was a steady increase in population from 1900 onward.

After 1931, and particularly after 1941, the countries of South Asia entered into a period of rapid and accelerating population growth, while the Western nations were beginning to approach a state of demographic stability. What is important about recent population trends in South Asia is not simply the rate of growth but the huge increments that resulted, with prospects of even greater increments in the future.

It is interesting to note that this rapid and accelerating increase has come as a surprise to the experts, who had not foreseen this phenomenon. For example, India's first and second five-year plans assumed an annual rate of population growth of 1.2 percent from 1950 to 1960. But a committee of experts set up by the Indian Planning Commission reported the rate of population growth at 2.0 percent for the decade, while the 1961 census showed it to be 2.1 percent. When drawing up the third five-year plan (1961-1966), a population growth rate of 2.2 percent was assumed. Dr. S. Chandrasekhar, India's minister for Family Planning, reported that during the period 1966-1970, population had grown at the rate of 2.5 percent—one of the highest rates in India's demographic history. According to Chandrasekhar, "This is bound to increase further as our health measures prove effective in bringing down the death rate."[10]

The experience of Pakistan has been similar. Population increase during the period of the first plan (1955-1960) was estimated at 7.5 percent but the 1961 census indicated a much greater increase during this period. Pakistan's second plan estimated that total population by 1960 and 1965 would be 88.9 and 96.9 million, respectively, whereas the census count in 1961 had already reached 93.8 million.[11]

In Sri Lanka, the estimated annual rate of population growth of 2.7 percent written into the six-year program of investment (1954-1955 to 1959-1960) had later to be revised to 3.0 percent for the period 1956-1961, on the basis of actual population increase.

In most South Asian countries the revelation of actual rates of population increase being much in excess of the estimates has baffled the planners, and it is now generally recognized that these countries are in the midst of "demographic explosion." As Gunnar Myrdal remarks:

> As recently as ten or fifteen years ago, the question of whether, and in what sense, the countries of South Asia were faced with a problem of excessive population growth was still the subject of lively discussion and controversy. . . . By now, it is commonly recognized that all countries in the region have entered a critical phase of sharply accelerated population growth, and that the prospects for successful economic development are crucially related to population trends. Recent years have been witnessing a veritable demographic revolution, the pace and dimensions of which are without precedent anywhere in the world.[12]

Let us turn now to the symptoms of overpopulation in South Asia with special reference to their adverse impact on the economic development of these countries. As pointed out in the previous chapter, the gains from planning, in spite of huge investments and gigantic efforts in the different sectors of the economies, are being eroded by increasing population, leaving little capital for further investment. For instance, from 1950 to 1970, national income in India rose by 49.7 and 49.4 percent, respectively, but, on account of population increase, per capita income rose by only 18.5 and 13.0 percent, respectively, at constant prices. The annual average growth in national income for the period was 4.6 percent, but the rise in per capita income was only 1.5 percent. In Pakistan, while GNP increased by an annual rate of 4.9 percent from 1964 to 1970, per capita income increased by only 2.1 percent per year.[13] The position in Bangladesh (formerly East Pakistan) was much worse, with contrasting increases in GNP and per capita income of 4.0 percent and 1.4 percent, respectively, for the period 1964–1970. In Sri Lanka from 1960–1966, the increase of 3.0 percent in GNP was reflected as a mere 0.4 percent rise in per capita income.

Since the size and growth of population have a direct bearing on the rate of economic development, two questions arise: Will levels of productivity in the countries of South Asia, both in the short run and in the long run, increase sufficiently in relation to population growth? If so, will real per capita income (holding prices constant) increase sufficiently in these countries to eradicate poverty and also to provide the savings needed to meet the investment needs of planning for economic development? Demands on national resources from the projected 2.5 percent increase in population over the next few decades, and also from the revolution of rising expectations (a topic to be discussed in a later chapter), would appear likely to leave little capital for investment, hindering further progress and dimming prospects for an overall increase in per capita income.[14]

Apart from absolute numbers or percentage rates of increase, there are other ways of viewing the population problem. One is to examine it from the viewpoint of density per square kilometer of arable land and to relate this to increases in agricultural productivity and food production. Population density in relation to arable land increased considerably from 1960 to 1969, as shown in Table 2–2. This means that the area of cultivated land per capita has greatly decreased; in India, for example, it has dropped from 1.11 acres in 1921 to 0.62 acres in 1971.

To counter this decrease in cultivated land per capita and meet the increasing demand for agricultural goods, including food, it is necessary to raise agricultural productivity. From 1900 to 1945 the increase in

Table 2-2 Population Density per Square Kilometer of Arable Land in South Asia, 1960-1969

Country	1960	1969	Percentage increase
Sri Lanka	643	849	32.0%
India	240	290	21.0
Nepal	236	283	20.0
Pakistan	56	71	27.0
Bangladesh	356	475	33.0

SOURCE: Sultan Hashmi, "Constraints in Economic Development: The Problem of Population Growth in South Asia," in E. A. G. Robinson and Michael Kidron, eds., *Economic Development in South Asia* (London: St. Martin's, 1970), p. 9.
United Nations, *Statistical Year Book for Asia and the Pacific, 1973* (Bangkok, 1974).

overall agricultural output was overtaken by population increase. In India (then comprising present-day India, Pakistan, and Bangladesh), population increased by 37.9 percent, the area under cultivation increased by 18.4 percent, and overall agricultural output increased by only 13 percent.[15] In other words, despite the increase in total area under cultivation the agricultural sector did not show any growth. Commenting on productivity trends during the period 1891–1892 to 1939–1940, Kingsley Davis remarks: "It is well known . . . that the productivity of land in the Indian subcontinent has not been improving and that at present it is far below that of most other agricultural areas."[16] Table 2–3 gives figures on growth in agricultural productivity since 1950, the beginning of economic planning in India. It will be noted that between 1950–1951 and 1972–1973 the production of food grains increased by 42.3 percent, while the production of non–food grains increased by only 14.1 percent. The overall index of all agricultural commodities, however, went up by 32.6 percent. Table 2–3 shows that in sharp contrast to pre-1949 patterns, after 1950 there was a noticeable trend toward increase in productivity. This was accompanied, however, by a simultaneous increase in India's population, from 361 million in 1951 to 561 million in 1972 (an increase of about 55.4 percent).

India has been a net importer of food grains since 1950; yet, even taking into account total domestic production and imports, there has been no appreciable increase in the net per capita availability of food grains, as is shown in Table 2–4.

While there has been some variation in the per capita availability of food, the per capita demand for food has steadily increased. This is largely because of increases in income and greater expectations. According to a United Nations study, the demand for food in many of

Table 2-3 Index of Agricultural Productivity in India 1950-1951–1972-1973 (Base 1959-1960 to 1961-1962 = 100)

Year	Production of food grains	Production of non-food grains	Total production—all crops
1950-1951	79.1	93.5	83.2
1955-1956	91.4	93.4	91.9
1960-1961	102.8	104.2	103.3
1965-1966	89.6	96.2	92.2
1969-1970	116.3	106.5	112.7
1971-1972	120.1	112.3	117.2
1972-1973	112.6	106.7	110.4

SOURCE: Government of India, Ministry of Food and Agriculture, *Indian Agriculture in Brief* (New Delhi, 1974), p. 116.

Table 2-4 Per Capita Availability of Food Grains in India

Year	Amount of net food available per day
1968	468.8 grams
1970	458.6
1972	469.0
1973	422.7
1974	462.4

SOURCE: Reserve Bank of India, *Report on Currency and Finance, 1973-1974*
(Bombay, January 1975), p. 15.

the South Asian countries has increased at a faster rate than food production.[17]

If the adequacy of the food supply is judged by the nutritional level of a given population, South Asia is still a long way from providing the minimum daily requirement of nutritious food. Table 2-5 shows the average daily per capita intake of food in the South Asian countries. Taking 2,400 calories as the daily minimum nutritional requirement,[18] we shall see that the South Asian countries are below that level. As a result, the bulk of the population of these countries suffers general debilitation and a lowering of physical energy and productivity.

What does the future hold for these countries as regards the race between food supply and population growth? It may be pointed out that in India, from 1949 to 1962, a greater proportion of the 3.9 percent increase in total agricultural production was contributed by an increase in the area under cultivation (1.8 percent) than by an increase of other inputs (1.7 percent).[19] More recently, increased agricultural production has resulted more from other inputs—the use of fertilizers, better varieties of seeds, and some technological developments (often referred

Table 2-5 Nutritional Content of National Average Daily per Capita Food Supply

Country	1961			1970		
	Calories	Fat (gm)	Protein (gm)	Calories	Fat (gm)	Protein (gm)
India	2,100	27.0	51.9	2,060	22.6	52.6
Pakistan	2,090	31.5	54.8	2,280	32.8	59.4
Sri Lanka	2,040	44.0	45.4	2,240	45.2	49.6
Nepal	2,020		51.0	2,050		51.7

SOURCE: United Nations, Food and Agriculture Organization, *The State of Food and Agriculture, 1968, 1974* (Rome, 1969, 1975) *1968,* Tables 8B, 8C; *1974,* pp. 144-145.

to as the Green Revolution)—and, assuming continued use of these new inputs, such gains in productivity may well continue in the future. But, in view of the limited agricultural land resources of these countries and the increasing density of population, to what extent will increases in agricultural productivity be able to meet the increasing demand? It will take nothing short of a miracle to continue to nourish the exploding populations of South Asia—even at present subminimum levels.[20]

A marked feature of overpopulation is the high ratio of nonworking dependent population ("unproductive consumers") to working population (the labor force, or "productive consumers"). These ratios are shown in Table 2-6. The ratio of nonworking dependent population (aged under 14 and over 65) to total population—that is, the dependency ratio—is much higher in the less developed than in the developed countries. Moreover, for the countries of South Asia the ratio is higher than the average for the less developed countries as a whole. A high dependency ratio (especially a high and increasing population of children) has serious implications for economic development. First, it implies that a substantial proportion of national resources must be diverted to provide nutrition, medical care, and social services, including education, for the future generations. Second, it means that households have a large number of consuming units per earning member. A large

Table 2-6 Distribution and Dependency Ratios of Population in South Asian Countries

| Country | Year | Age distribution of population (years) | | | Dependency ratio (ratio of persons of 0-14 and 65 years and above to persons 15-64 years) |
		0-14	15-64	65 & above	
India	1971	41.4%	55.4%	3.2%	80.5%
Bangladesh	1961	46.1	50.5	3.4	98.0
Nepal	1961	39.9	57.0	3.1	75.4
Pakistan	1961	42.4	52.7	4.9	89.7
Sri Lanka	1963	41.7	54.6	3.6	83.0
Less developed countries	1965	39.8	56.4	3.8	77.3
Developed countries	1965	28.1	63.0	8.9	58.7
United States	1970	25.3	64.5	10.2	55.0

SOURCE: United Nations, *Demographic Year Book, 1973* (New York, 1975).
———, *World Population Prospects* (New York, 1969).
U.S. Department of Commerce, *Statistical Abstract of the United States,* 1973 (Washington, D.C., 1974).

proportion of household income is consumed, leaving very little for savings or capital formation. As we will discuss in chapter 3, the low rate of capital formation in the South Asian economies is thus attributable to the high dependency ratio.

A further manifestation of overpopulation in the countries of South Asia is the serious and deteriorating problem of unemployment and underemployment, which poses a threat to their political and social stability. In chapter 5 we will discuss in detail the problem of unemployment and underemployment. Here we will merely attempt to relate that problem to the general problem of overpopulation. Growing unemployment, especially unemployment among the educated, has created grave tensions and driven the unemployed into the fold of dissident and radical elements. The 1971 uprising of young people in Sri Lanka is an indicator of the seriousness of the problem.

Unemployment in the underdeveloped countries, including those of South Asia, can be classified into (1) unemployment: comprising unemployed persons who are conscious of their unemployment and are actively looking for jobs, and (2) disguised unemployment, including underemployment: comprising unemployed or underemployed persons who are not aware of their unemployed status. They are seemingly working by sharing the work and income from the family farm or economic enterprise; but, if their labor was withdrawn, the total output of the enterprise would remain more or less constant. In other words, the marginal productivity of the disguisedly unemployed person is zero or negligible.

In the literature of economic development, the disguised unemployed labor force—also called surplus labor—is considered a possible source of capital formation. Since these workers are already sharing the family income, with zero contribution, they can be put to productive work at zero opportunity cost. To what extent surplus labor can be utilized for capital formation is quite an involved question. There is no denying that a proper utilization of surplus labor can accelerate the process of economic development. Utilization of the surplus labor force in China, through the communes, has contributed greatly to the economic development of that country. In the countries of South Asia, the family is organized on the joint, or extended, family basis, in which family members representing two or more generations live together and share the work in the family enterprise—and the income from it—according to their needs, rather than accounting to their contribution. Thus family members who continue to share work in the family enterprise without making any significant addition to total output are disguisedly unemployed. Any discussion of unemployment in the South Asian context must of necessity take into account not only open unemployment and underemployment but also disguised unemployment.

Various estimates of unemployment show that the problem is a serious one and that the situation is deteriorating, since population is increasing at rates greater than the labor absorption capacity of these countries at present levels of development. In India, 10.4 percent of the country's manpower was listed as unemployed from 1966 to 1969. The rest—the so-called employed—however, suffered from serious underemployment. According to the *Report of the Committee on Unemployment,* 42.3 percent of the "gainfully employed" worked less than 14 hours per week; for urban areas the figure was 45.6 percent.[21] The proportion of surplus manpower in Indian agriculture is rising, as indicated by the increase in the number of workers engaged in agriculture without corresponding increases in area under cultivation or agricultural productivity. The incidence of unemployment among educated persons is also assuming serious proportions. In India in 1972, out of the total of 20.8 million persons with the educational qualification of matriculation (high school) and above, 3.3 million were unemployed. In other words, 15.8 percent of the educated manpower were without jobs. Paradoxically, the extent of unemployment in India is greater among the educated (high school and above) than among the uneducated.

According to Pakistan's third five-year plan:

> The gravest problem confronting Pakistan is unemployment. Almost one-fifth of the available manpower, the country's most valuable resource, is wasted every year for lack of opportunities for useful work. In actual numbers, about half the labour force is affected, as unemployment in Pakistan generally takes the form of an underutilzation of at least half of the available manpower.[22]

Mahbub-ul Haq estimated surplus labor in Pakistan agriculture to be 3.7 million out of a total labor force of 17.5 million.[23] For East Pakistan (now Bangladesh), the problem of unemployment was—and is—even more serious; according to an International Labour Office study in 1955, 17 percent of the labor force worked less than 25 hours a week and 48 percent were seasonally underemployed.[24]

In Sri Lanka also, the growth of population has been responsible for increasing underemployment and unemployment levels. According to an International Labour Organization study, 10.5 percent of the total labor force of this country was unemployed in 1959; in addition, 45.4 percent of the rural labor force and 29.0 percent of the urban labor force were underemployed.[25]

CAUSES OF THE POPULATION EXPLOSION

In order to understand the population explosion confronting the South Asian countries, we need to look into the three components of population growth: fertility, as indicated by the birth rate; mortality, as indicated by the death rate (but also including emigration); and the survival rate, the difference between the fertility and mortality rates. It is the last component—the survival rate—that determines population growth in a society.

An analysis of demographic patterns in different parts of the world at varying stages of economic development indicates the following five demographic stages:

Stage I: Birth rate and death rate are both high and nearly equal, resulting in a stationary or very slowly increasing population: most African countries.

Stage II: Birth rate remains high while death rate begins to decline, resulting in moderate population growth but with the potential for rapid growth: some Asian countries including India, Nepal, and Pakistan.

Stage III: Birth rate continues high without any tendency to fall, while death rate remains fairly low, resulting in "population explosion." Population growth is very rapid in this situation: Bangladesh, Sri Lanka, Malaysia, and Taiwan in Asia, and some countries in Latin America.

Stage IV: Birth rate declines and death rate remains low, resulting in a slowing down of the rate of population growth: Soviet Union, Canada, and Japan.

Stage V: Birth rate declines substantially and, with the low death rate, the rate of population growth becomes moderate: United States and some West European countries.

Table 2–7 provides us with a picture of pertinent demographic trends in the countries of South Asia.

Table 2-7 Estimated Birth Rates, Death Rates, and Rates of Natural Increase in the Population of the South Asian Countries

Country	Period	Births per thousand	Deaths per thousand	Annual rate of natural increase
Bangladesh[a]	1951-1961	50.0	29.0	2.1%
	1963-1967	53.0	22.0	3.1
	1966-1970	47.0	20.0	2.7
India[b]	1881-1900	48.9	41.3	0.8
	1891-1900	45.8	44.4	0.1
	1901-1910	49.2	42.6	0.7
	1911-1920	48.1	47.2	0.1
	1921-1930	46.4	36.3	1.0

continued

Table 2-7 Estimated Birth Rates, Death Rates, and Rates of Natural Increase in the Population of the South Asian Countries (con't.)

Country	Period	Births per thousand	Deaths per thousand	Annual rate of natural increase
	1931-1940	45.2	31.2	1.4
	1941-1950	39.9	27.4	1.2
	1951-1960	41.7	22.8	1.9
	1961-1965	41.0	17.2	2.4
	1966-1970	38.6	14.0	2.4
	1971-1975	35.1	11.3	2.4
Nepal	1951-1961	41.1	20.8	2.0
	1965-1970	40.0	10.0	3.0
Pakistan[c]	1951-1961	49.0	26.0	2.3
	1961-1971	50.9	18.4	3.2
Sri Lanka	1870-1879	27.5	22.6	0.5
	1880-1889	28.8	23.9	0.5
	1890-1899	33.7	27.1	0.7
	1900-1909	38.1	28.9	0.9
	1910-1919	37.8	30.1	0.8
	1920-1929	39.6	26.9	1.3
	1930-1939	36.7	23.5	1.3
	1940-1949	37.3	17.9	2.0
	1950-1959	37.6	10.7	2.7
	1963-1967	33.0	8.4	2.5
	1967-1972	29.9	7.6	2.3

[a]The figures are for former East Pakistan.
[b]The figures prior to 1951 are for prepartition India, which included the present Bangladesh and Pakistan.
[c]The figures are for former West Pakistan.

SOURCE: S. N. Agarwala, *India's Population Problems* (New Delhi: Tata McGraw-Hill, 1972).
Nafis Ahmad, *A New Economic Geography of Bangladesh* (New Delhi: Vikas, 1976).
Azizur Rahman Khan, *The Economy of Bangladesh* (London: Macmillan, 1972).
Kingsley Davis, *The Population of India and Pakistan* (Princeton, N.J.: Princeton University Press, 1951), pp. 68-79, 85.
Government of Ceylon, Department of Census and Statistics, *Ceylon Year Book* (Colombo, 1968).
Government of Pakistan, *Twenty Years of Pakistan, 1947-1967* (Karachi: Pakistan Publications, 1967), p. 16.
Y. P. Pant, *Economic Development in Nepal* (Allahabad: Kitab Mahal, 1965), pp. 18-20.
Donald R. Snodgrass, *Ceylon: An Export Economy in Transition* (Homewood, Ill.: Irwin, 1966). p. 307.
Rajan Kumar Som, "Population Trends and Problems in India," in S. N. Agarwala, ed., *India's Population—Some Problems in Perspective Planning* (Bombay: Asia Publishing House, 1960), pp. 59-69.
United Nations, *Statistical Year Book, 1974* (New York, 1975), pp. 80-85.

Before 1919, Sri Lanka was in Stage II—high birth and death rates, moderate population growth with potential for rapid growth. The country entered Stage III around 1930 and is now in the midst of a population explosion. Population growth has been especially rapid since 1950. The position of India and Pakistan is more or less similar to that of Sri Lanka—they entered Stage II in 1931, and, with the rapid decline in death rate since 1941, they have now entered into the stage of population explosion.

Thus the crux of the population problem in South Asia is the continuing high birth rate especially in relation to the dramatic reduction in the death rate. Emigration has been a negligible factor and, with the tightening of immigration laws in the East African and South East Asian countries and also in Great Britain (traditionally the destinations of most South Asian emigration), the prospects for reducing population pressure through emigration seem very dim. To be effective, population policies should aim at reducing birth rates so as to bring them in line with declining death rates.

We will now discuss the patterns of birth and death rates in the countries of South Asia.

Birth Rates   Table 2-8 gives birth rates in the South Asian countries as well as in some other countries—to provide a basis for comparison. It will be noted that in general birth rates for the South Asian countries are comparatively high, although they fluctuate from decade to decade.

Let us now examine some of the reasons for the high birth rates in the countries of South Asia.

Socioreligious Background as a Determinant of Birth Rate.   The socioreligious outlook of the people in a country is an important factor determining its birth rate. One such factor is marriage. According to custom and tradition, marriage is almost universal in South Asia. In Hinduism—the dominant religion of the region—marriage is vested with religious significance and sacrificial virtue. "Every Hindu must marry and beget children—sons if you please—to perform his funeral rites lest his spirit should wander uneasily in vacant places of the earth."[26] According to Wadia and Merchant, 467 males and 493 females per thousand of population on the Indian subcontinent were married in 1951. "If we take into account widowers and widows as well as ascetics and mendicants, almost every person of marriageable age was actually married."[27] The 1961 census data show that during the reproductive period, 15–40 years, only 3 percent of India's females were unmarried; whereas, for example, the comparable figure for England and Wales was

Table 2-8 Birth Rates in South Asia and in Some Other
Parts of the World (in millions)

	1931	1941	1951	1961	1971
India[a]	46.4	45.2	39.9	41.7	38.6
Pakistan[b]	46.4	45.2	46.2	49.0	50.9
Sri Lanka[c]	39.6	36.7	37.3	37.6	29.9
Nepal	38.2	37.3	37.0	41.1	40.0
Africa	48.1	47.0	48.0	48.1	48.0
Latin America	40.9	41.0	41.0	40.0	38.0
United States	21.3	19.4	24.1	23.7	17.3
United Kingdom	17.4	17.2	15.9	18.2	16.2
Japan	32.9	33.0	24.5	17.0	18.8
France	19.3	21.0	18.0	18.1	16.7

[a]Estimated birth rates.
[b]Includes present-day Pakistan and Bangladesh.
[c]Registered births; according to Snodgrass, birth rates are much higher.

SOURCE: Government of India, Publications Division, *India 1974* (New Delhi,
1974), p. 16.
Donald Snodgrass, *Ceylon: An Export Economy in Transition* (Homewood, Ill.:
Irwin, 1966), p. 305-313.
United Nations, *Demographic Year Book,* 1973 (New York, 1974).
U.S. Department of Commerce, *Statistical Abstract of the United States, 1974,*
(Washington, D.C., 1975), p. 818.
World Bank, *Trends in Developing Countries* (Washington, D.C., 1973), Table 2.3.

36 percent.[28] Paradoxically, despite the poverty of the Indian people,
economic considerations appear to be of secondary importance in regard
to marriage. Even today the majority of marriages are arranged by
parents, with the married having little if any say in the selection of their
mates, and in most cases without regard to their present or future
financial position.

Apart from the universality of marriage, the practice of early
marriage also contributes to the high birth rate. According to Kapadia,
Indian tradition asserts that marriage is a *samskara* (Indian word
meaning "primary duty") for a girl and requires that she be married at
least around the age of puberty—if not earlier.[29] According to the 1961
Indian census, 22.1 percent of girls in the rural areas and 7 percent of
those in urban areas entered matrimony between 10 and 14 years of age.
At age 19, 74 percent of rural girls and 52 percent of urban girls were
married. The mean age of marriage for females was 15.43 while for
males it was 21.76 years. In Pakistan, the age of marriage was even

lower, but in Sri Lanka and Nepal it was similar to that in India.

Early age increases the reproductive span, and surveys have shown that as age of marriage rises, overall fertility rates decline. J. R. Rele, in a survey of one of the Indian states, found the total number of children born to women married at different ages to be as follows: 7.3 children for women married before 15 years of age; 7.05 for those married at age 15-16, and 6.8 for those married at 17.[30] Based on his studies of fertility rates in Calcutta during 1954-1958, S. B. Mukerji concluded:

> The higher the age at marriage, the lesser is the number of children born — if the marriage can be postponed up to the twentieth or twenty-first year of the girl, then the number of children born will decrease by at least one child per mother for no less than 80 percent of all married women in Calcutta.[31]

A survey in 1954 and a resurvey of rural Maharashtra state in India in 1966, made by K. Dandekar, showed that the fertility of women was reduced by 6.9 percent when the age of marriage rose from 13 to 17 years.[32]

The mores and folkways of South Asia are attuned to the ideal of a large family. Maternity is supposed to be the first concern of a woman. It is the "central fact" in her life. In such a cultural pattern, sterility is inauspicious and the woman with many children is considered fortunate. In keeping with this attitude, failure to bear a child soon after marriage becomes a serious domestic concern. Ceremonies are performed to invoke the blessings of the gods so that the new bride may be saved from barrenness. Rajani Pathare, in his survey on the family planning program in India, found that

> These psychological and social forces are reflected in the fact that the interval between the age of consummation of marriage and the first pregnancy is generally low — the first parity interval is as low as 16.92 months when the age at consummation is 24+ years and 17.15 months when the age of consummation is 20-23. It rises to 21.39 months when the consummation age is 16-19 and to 31.45 months when the consummation age is as low as 12-15 years.[33]

Another factor that makes a couple continue to have more children, is the craving for a male child. In South Asia there exists a strong preference for male children; at least one son in a family is a must. He is a potential earner and therefore an asset to his parents. According to the findings of Kothari,[34] "It is he who saves them from hell. A son is also needed to perform religious ceremonies like Sraddha and by continuing the family Sraddha, [he] becomes himself indispensable."[34] It is thus not uncommon even today for a man to marry—or at least wish to marry—a second wife in order to father a child—more so a male child. Couples who produce female children one after another will not be willing to increase the interval between children until their desire for a male child is fulfilled. Tara Patel, in a study conducted in western India, found that more than 91 percent of couples were reluctant to limit births until they had borne the desired number of children, with at least one male child.[35]

It may be pointed out that the above sociocultural patterns influencing birth rate are, to a great extent, maintained and supported by the joint, or extended, family system, which still predominates in the South Asian countries. In the joint family, the members work together, pooling their income and sharing it on the basis of individual need rather than individual productivity. An individual family member does not feel responsible for supporting his or her own nuclear family. The joint family system creates a climate of irresponsibility. Since the joint family supports all members—those living as well as those still to be born—individual members within the family have no economic deterrent against having an additional child; the additional burden will be borne by the entire family. As mentioned earlier in the chapter, this tendency to keep adding children to a joint family is what creates surplus labor, resulting in the further impoverishment of all.

In the context of South Asian cultural and social traditions, what are the future prospects for the birth rate? As Gyan Chand remarks:

> The high birth rate in India is a part of our culture and it is only when the moral sentiments of the community change either by choice or by the force of circumstances that a fall in the birth rate comparable with the fall which has taken place elsewhere can be expected.[36]

The extent and manner of the change in the moral sentiments of the community, then, is what will bring about a change in birth rates. One can notice change occurring through factors like the spread of education, urbanization, and mobility—both geographical and social. But since the change is by "choice" and not by "force" (as in totalitarian societies) the results are inevitably slow. As mentioned in chapter 1, the South Asian countries have by and large, opted for democratic techniques of planning, in which social, political, and economic reforms take place by the choice and free will of the public, consistent with their cultural and social traditions. In general, the people of South Asia have great reverence for their social and cultural values and would not wish them to be abolished by command—as might occur in a totalitarian context—with speedier results.

The cultural and traditional values of South Asia are well summed up in India's third five-year plan:

Each major culture and civilization has certain distinctive features, rooted in the past, which bear the impress of that culture. India, with thousands of years of history, bears even now the powerful impress of her own distinctive features. . . . They are in fact a set of moral and ethical values which have governed Indian life for ages past, even though people may not have lived up to them. . . . These values are a part of India's thinking, even as, more and more, that thinking is directed to the impact of the scientific and technological civilization of the modern world. To some extent, the problem of India is how to bring about a synthesis between these two.[37]

The synthesis between India's cultural values and its scientific and technological advancement has to be brought about through education and persuasion. The objective of the South Asian countries is to create conditions in which their future generations are less traditional in their approach to solving life's problems while at the same time remaining true to their ancient civilizations and cultures. Against such a background, it is quite understandable that changes in the cultural values affecting birth rates will be slow.

Economic Conditions as a Determinant of Birth Rate.   It is a well-known axiom in demography that birth rate is universally related to level of income, level of education, extent of urbanization, and the like.

Table 2-9 shows the impact of economic factors on the birth rate in the United States. The data show a striking inverse relationship between level of family income and years of school completed, on the one hand, and total number of children born, on the other. Also, birth rate is higher for rural than for urban dwellers. The data for India show a similar relationship between birth rate and various socioeconomic factors (see Table 2-10).

It seems that a higher standard of living does result in some reduction in birth rate. But we do not know at what level of income the turning point is reached. Not every increase in standard of living can be expected to bring about a decline in birth rate; in order to have this effect, level of income must first rise sufficiently for the household to enjoy a reasonable minimum standard of living. It is possible that when living standards rise from the initial levels of destitution and mere subsistence there may actually be an increase in the birth rate and that only after a reasonable living standard has been attained will birth rate start to decline. On the basis of demographic patterns described by the National Sample Survey reports in India, Mahalonobis has suggested:

It is possible that the number of children born (or surviving) is very small in the case of couples who are almost destitute; that the number born (or surviving) increases quite rapidly at first with an increase in the level of living up to a peak point at some critical level of living and then gradually decreases as the level of living rises beyond the critical peak value for fertility. On this view, a comparatively small rise in the level of living, especially in the lowest group, would increase the total number of children born (or surviving) and lead to an increase in the rate of growth of population. As the level of living further rises and more and more couples pass beyond the critical level of living for fertility, the rate of growth would gradually slow down. At this stage, an increasing level of living may be expected to exercise a retarding effect on the growth of population in India as was observed in the more developed countries of the world in the past.[38]

Table 2-9 Number of Children Born per Thousand Married Women 15 to 44 Years Old, by Selected Characteristics, in the United States, 1972

Characteristic	Number of children
Residence	
Urban	2,942
Rural—nonfarm	2,986
Rural—farm	3,694
Schooling completed	
Elementary:	
less than 8 years	3,647
8 years	3,487
High school:	
1-3 years	3,410
4 years	2,920
College:	
1-3 years	2,716
4 years or more	2,378
Annual income of husband	
Under $2,000	2,736
$2,000-$2,999	2,551
$3,000-$3,999	2,374
$4,000-$4,999	2,274
$5,000-$6,999	2,252
$7,000 and over	2,270

SOURCE: U.S. Department of Commerce: *Statistical Abstract of the United States, 1964* (Washington, D.C., 1965, 1973, 1974), *1965,* p. 52; *1972,* p. 53; *1973,* p. 55.

Table 2-10 Average Number of Children Born per Couple, by
Selected Characteristics, in India, 1961-1965

Characteristics	Average number of children
Household income and expenditure (1960-1961)	
Up to Rs 10 per month	3.40
Rs 11 - 20 per month	3.02
Rs 21 - 30 per month	2.95
Rs 30 and over per month	2.70
Educational level attained by women (1961)	
Illiterate	3.5
Primary school	3.4
Secondary school	3.1
College	3.0
Postgraduate	2.5
Residence (1963-1964)	
Urban	3.19
Rural	3.76
Occupation of head of household	
Agriculture	4.4
Industry	4.2
Professional—law, medicine, teaching	3.7
Average for all occupations	4.3

SOURCE: S. N. Agarwala, *India's Population Problems* (New Delhi: Tata McGraw-Hill, 1972), pp. 126-128.
P. A. Wadia and K. T. Merchant, *Our Economic Problem* (Bombay; New Book Co., 1954), p. 118.

We do not know what exactly constitutes the critical level of living referred to in Mahalonobis's statement, but it can be inferred from the Indian experience (Table 2–10), that the South Asian countries are in the demographic stage where a gradual improvement in living standards would result in a corresponding decrease in birth rates.

What is the rationale for people with little means tending to have larger families than the well-to-do? In simple words, when life is at mere subsistence level, each additional child is seen as a source of future additional income, as the child can be put to work at an early age to supplement the meager resources of the family. To explain the paradox—the poorer the household, the larger the size of the family—we can apply the tools and concepts of microeconomic analysis.[39] Consider a household as a "firm" producing children as "economic goods" to maximize profit. To arrive at the point of maximum profit, the household would compare the marginal cost of an additional child with the marginal revenue to be desired from that child. When a household is poor, the marginal cost of rearing the additional child is insignificant—he shares starvation and sleeps on the floor of the hut, his schooling costs nothing, his clothing very little (he can even be without clothes, particularly in tropical regions). At an early age the child becomes a source of revenue to the household as a shepherd, domestic servant, or whatever. So, when the household is poor, marginal revenue exceeds marginal cost, and such a household will continue to produce more children until these two variables are equalized. However, once the income and living standards of the household "firm" improve, the marginal cost of rearing children increases. Additional space and baby furniture is needed; money must be spent on food, diapers, medicine, and clothing. Expenses are incurred to educate the child. Against all these costs, the labor laws of affluent societies and the social norms of the upper-income classes in poor countries generally prevent the remunerated employment of children of less than a certain age. In the circumstances, at this economic level, the marginal cost of an additional child is much greater than its marginal revenue; the rational household will plan for "optimum" size and will not lightly incur the loss resulting from having an additional child.[40]

Where do the economies of the South Asian countries stand in terms of the above analysis? It is difficult to give a conclusive answer. Different countries, and even different regions of the same country, may be at different levels of economic well-being. In general, we can say that the South Asian countries are in a border zone—that is, they are within range of the turning point between the two stages of the above analysis. On the basis of the demographic income structure (rural–urban, occupational, etc.) we can predict some decrease in birth rates with increased levels of economic development in these societies.

Death Rates   After birth rate, death rate (or mortality rate) is the next most important component of population growth. As already noted (Table 2-7) the underdeveloped areas of the world including the South Asian countries, are facing an explosion in population mainly because, while birth rates have registered some decrease, there has been a drastic decline in death rates, especially in the post–World War II period—a period that also marks the beginning of economic planning in the countries of South Asia.

All the countries of South Asia have experienced declining death rates in recent decades. In Sri Lanka during the period 1941-1967, while birth rate declined by 16 percent, death rate declined by 57 percent. In India, the comparable figures for the period 1941–1971 are 14 percent and 59 percent, respectively. It will also be noted that earlier—starting with the turn of the century—the population of these countries was stationary or increasing very slowly and in irregular fashion because birth and death rates were both high, moving, as it were, in unison. It is the growing imbalance between the two demographic variables, birth rate and death rate, that accounts for the rapid increase in population—or the population explosion.

Death rate in any society is an index of the well-being of its people. Wars, epidemics, famines, and natural calamities are reflected in increased death rates (e.g., the high death rate in Sri Lanka, India, and Pakistan during the decade 1910–1920—see Table 2-7) while low death rates are usually indicative of increased prosperity (measured by such variables as income and housing) and of the society's efforts to improve the wellbeing of its people through better health education and social welfare programs and the application of improved medical technology to the problems of health and sanitation. A study of historical trends in the demography of the present advanced countries indicates that, with economic advancement and the resultant improvements in the factors mentioned above, both death rates and birth rates declined, leading to a significant but gradual percentage net increase in population, as shown in Table 2-11.

A study of the demographic patterns of the present-day advanced countries shows that population growth was gradual and that it followed economic development.[41] Increasing population following economic development was an asset and an important factor contributing to that development. What has happened in the present underdeveloped countries, including those of South Asia, is that, with birth rates still high, death rates have declined sharply, resulting in a buildup of population pressures—while the economies are still in a state of underdevelopment. That is to say, unlike the case of the developed nations, population pressures have preceded economic development. Evidently, when population explosion precedes development, it becomes a retarding factor in the development process—and this is the position in the countries of South Asia.

In short, the now advanced countries had their take off before their population explosion, whereas many of the now underdeveloped countries have had their population explosion before a take off.[42]

What is the reason for the drastic decline in death rates in South Asia. To some extent, this is part of a worldwide phenomenon. With the

Table 2-11 Percentage of Annual Average Population Increase in Northern Europe and South Asia, 1735-1971[a]

Countries	1735-1799	1800-1849	1850-1899	1900-1949	1963-1971
England and Wales	0.60%	1.20%	1.27%	0.65%	0.40%
Denmark	0.30	0.85	1.22	1.09	0.70
Norway	0.70	0.93	1.40	0.90	0.80
Sweden	0.56	0.81	1.15	0.69	0.80
Average for developed countries	0.50	0.90	1.17	0.81	2.00
Bangladesh					2.90
India			0.30[b]	1.40	2.30
Nepal				1.60	3.00
Pakistan				1.00[c]	3.20
Sri Lanka				2.00	2.40

[a]To some extent, population growth of the advanced countries was affected by migration from countries like Great Britain to the countries of the New World, including the United States. The overall picture, however, remains unaffected insofar as the historical trend is concerned.
[b]Includes present-day Bangladesh and Pakistan.
[c]Figure for former West Pakistan.

SOURCE: Kingsley Davis, *The Population of India and Pakistan* (Princeton, N.J.: Princeton University Press, 1951).
Calculated from Benjamin Higgins, *Economic Development* (New York: Norton, 1959), p. 695.
U.S. Department of Commerce, *Statistical Abstract of the United States, 1973* (Washington, D.C., 1973), pp. 803-806.

introduction of new scientific discoveries, especially the "wonder drugs," (such as antibiotics), vaccines, and insecticides in to the underdeveloped countries, many diseases responsible for wiping out large numbers in the past, such as malaria, typhoid, and pneumonia, have been practically eradicated.[43] And the three great killers — cholera, smallpox, and the plague, which, according to Kingsley Davis, were the "most common and most fatal of the epidemic diseases which periodically devastate[d] India,"[44] have been brought under control. To a great extent, however, the decline in mortality rates in the South Asian countries can be attributed to the massive programs of disease eradication and health improvement undertaken in the development plans. Under India's five-year plans, medical facilities were stationed all over the country—especially in the rural areas. Nationwide programs for the control of malaria, filaria, leprosy, and smallpox, including the BCG (Bacillus Calmette-Guerin) vaccination program, were undertaken, enabling India to control many mass-killer diseases. From 1951 to 1971 the number of doctors more than doubled, the number of medical colleges increased from 30 to 100, with annual admissions up from 2,500 to 12,000, and the number of hospital beds increased from 113,000 to 250,000.[45] In Pakistan, Sri Lanka, and Nepal, similar programs were undertaken to eradicate these and other epidemic diseases and to improve the health of the common man.

The South Asian countries have not yet solved their massive health problems; they have still a long way to go when compared to more-advanced nations. But there is no denying that there have been significant gains in some important health indicators. For instance, in India, from 1950 to 1970, the expectation of life at birth increased from 32.5 years to 53.2 years for males and from 31.7 to 51.9 for females, resulting from a decline in the death rate from 27.4 per thousand in 1950 to 11.3 per thousand in 1971. Sri Lanka has witnessed the most dramatic decline in death rate in the world—from 20 per thousand in 1940–1944 to 7.6 per thousand in 1972. As a result, life expectancy at birth in Sri Lanka increased from 46 years in 1946 to 60–65 years in 1960.

Now let us correlate birth and death rates. There has been only a minor decrease in birth rates, resulting mainly from improved living standards, while death rates have been substantially reduced — hence a widening gap between the two, resulting in a virtual population explosion. The crucial question, in the words of Kingsley Davis, is, "Will fertility be brought down in time to avoid either a disastrous growth of population or a calamitous rise in the death rate?"[46] Davis arrives at a negative conclusion. The increase in income and urbanization are not likely to be significant enough to cause a substantial decline in birth rates. And if birth rates decline, death rates might also continue to drop, thus perpetuating population increases. The way out is clear, "No sharp decline in the birth rate can be expected until deliberate control by means of contraception, sterilization, abortion, etc., is inaugurated."[47] The Indian Planning Commission arrived at the same conclusion, "It is apparent that population control can be achieved only by the reduction in the birth rate to the extent necessary to stabilize the population at a level consistent with the requirements of national economy."[48] According to India's fourth five-year plan, "Without a successful effort at limiting population growth, it would be difficult to achieve the degree of acceleration in improvement of living standards implied in our projections."[49]

The Planning Commission of Pakistan is also conscious of the perils of population explosion. According to the commission, "Since population growth can threaten to wipe out the gains of development, the Plan clearly recognizes the paramount need for a conscious population policy and its implementation."[50] The commission had earlier observed:

> Pakistan with other countries in Southern Asia, confronts a serious population problem. . . . The country must appreciate that population growth is a rock on which all hopes of improved conditions of living may founder. It admits of no approach except that the rates of growth must be low.[51]

Sri Lanka's ten-year plan devoted considerable attention to the population problem, and it urged that the "whole question of population policy in all its aspects be made the subject of nationwide discussion."[52] Similarly, the Planning Commission of Bangladesh—a country that has one of the highest man-land ratios in the world—views the prospect of further increases in population as "frightful" and disturbing, and it considers no civilized measure too drastic to keep the population within control.[53]

POPULATION PLANNING IN THE SOUTH ASIAN COUNTRIES

Having become acutely aware of the consequences of increasing population, the countries of South Asia have made population planning an integral part of their economic planning.

India was the first among the underdeveloped countries to incorporate an official family planning program into its economic plans, starting in 1951.[54] With substantial allocations for various related schemes, the program envisaged using "the cafeteria approach," that is, making available all of the scientifically approved contraceptives, rather than concentrating on any single method. The various methods popularized included sterilization, the intrauterine device (IUD), the condom or sheath, and the oral pill. The Indian government and some major private business organizations provided such incentives as small cash amounts and transistor radios to people who would volunteer to undergo sterilization after the third child. It is estimated that from 1952 until March of 1973, 14 million sterilization operations had been performed, giving a rate of 24.4 per thousand of population. The intrauterine contraceptive coil (IUCC) or loop, introduced in 1965, did not prove a popular method. In about 10 percent of the cases, the loop had to be removed due to hemorrhaging and other complications. By March 1973 about 4.6 million loops, had, however, been distributed nationwide (8.1 per thousand of population). The method most favored is the use of the rubber contraceptive, the condom or sheath, which is distributed free of charge by the family planning centers set up all over the country, as well as by clinics and hospitals. "The pill" and abortion are not common methods of prevention except among educated urban middle class women.

By 1973, 40,000 family planning centers were functioning in India—3,600 in urban areas and 36,400 in rural areas. In addition, 1,592 hospitals and urban institutions and 7,401 rural institutions were providing family planning assistance by August 1969. The Indian Family Planning Program aims at reducing the annual birth rate from about 39 per thousand in 1969 to 25 per thousand by 1981. The operational goals are adoption of family planning by the people as a way of life, through group acceptance of a small-family norm, widespread knowledge of family planning methods, and the ready availability of supplies and services. By the end of 1973, 15 percent of couples of reproductive age were practicing contraception. The goal is to increase that figure to 60 percent of those couples by 1980. The Indian fifth five-year plan (1974–1979) continues to emphasize the necessity for family planning.[55] It provides for an intensification of the methods currently in use and also for integration of family planning with health and nutrition facilities.

Under the second five-year plan of Pakistan, a National Family Planning Board was constituted by the central government with provincial branches. By June 1974, 2,110 doctors, 380 health visitors, and 478 nurses and midwives had been trained in family planning techniques; 2,750 clinics (1,161 in East Pakistan, now Bangladesh, and 1,589 in West Pakistan, now Pakistan) were established and 1.07 million persons obtained help from these clinics. A National Research Institute of Family Planning was set up to conduct research on various approaches and techniques. In Pakistan's third five-year plan, provision has been made to induce 20 million couples, representing almost all women in the reproductive ages in 1970, to practice family planning in one form or another. Pakistan also provides monetary incentive to couples who practice contraception and to the personnel who popularize it. According to the Pakistan Planning Commission, a vigorous and broadly based program of family planning would reduce the fertility rate sufficiently to compensate for declining mortality by 1985.

For several years, the government of Sri Lanka has encouraged a Swedish government agency to organize birth control services throughout the country and also to give training courses to medical and paramedical personnel on a fairly wide scale. A private organization, the Family Planning Association of Ceylon, spreads propaganda and runs family planning clinics in Sri Lanka under a grant from the government.

What has been the result of these family planning programs? Progress reports indicate a growing realization of the need for using contraceptives to reduce family size. In India, as of November 1973, 20 percent of couples in the reproductive age had been converted to family planning, although only 15 percent of these couples were using contraceptives. It is estimated that, since 1966-1967, about 5 million births have been averted.[56] According to Agarwala, this means a reduction in birth rate by 2 points, from 41 per thousand in 1965-1966 to 39 per thousand in 1970-1971.[57] Nevertheless, going by the experience of the period 1973-1975, the target of reducing the birth rate to 25 per thousand by 1980—by protecting 60 percent of couples in the reproductive age group—is unlikely to be achieved.

The Indian Planning Commission calls for a "strong, purposeful government policy supported by [an] effective program and adequate resources"[58] to save the country from the crippling effect of population growth. Some state governments in India are contemplating punitive measures to compel limiting the size of families. For example, the Maharashtra government is considering legislation for the compulsory sterilization of persons with three or more living children. The Punjab government is considering draft legislation that will make having more than two children a cognizable offense. The success of such measures would ultimately depend on their administration. Related laws already in existence (e.g., the Child Marriage Restraint Act of 1930 — known as the Sarda Act — amended in 1949 and fixing the minimum marriage age for males at 18 and for females at 15) have been observed more in defiance than in practice. In Bangladesh, awareness of family planning has been created among 85 percent of married women in the age group 15-44 years.

However, family planning studies have reported serious shortcomings, such as lack of trained medical personnel in the clinics, inability on the part of poor people to afford the price of contraceptives, and lack of follow-up efforts on couples using contraceptives. For example, a study conducted in the city of Lucknow (India) on the use of the IUD revealed that 48.5 percent of women retained IUDs at the end of 12 months; the number fell to 27.0 percent at the end of 24 months and 11.7 percent at the end of 36 months.[59] The Bangladesh Planning Commission reports an "absence of intensive supervision leading to fictitious reporting of results" and "monetary corruption distorting programme perspective" as some of the weaknesses in the family planning program.[60]

Even if the planned targets of decline in birth rates are achieved, the population is expected to grow at approximately the present rate of 2.5 percent in the coming decades because of the expected decline in death rates resulting from improved living standards as well as from improvements in health and sanitation following huge planned investments under the development plans. By around 1985 birth rates are expected to fall sufficiently to counter declining death rates, bringing a fall in net rates of population increase. But by 1985 the population problem of the South Asian countries will already have assumed serious proportions. The Indian Planning Commission, contemplating projected increases in India's population, observed, "Population growth on this scale can be a crippling handicap since our population in relation to resources is already large, incomes are low and economic development is a desperate need."[61] S. Chandrasekhar, a noted demographer and former minister for Family Planning in the Indian government made these comments on India's projected population:

> The prospect of a billion Indians by 2000 A.D. is an alarming one. Theoretically this may never come to pass, for if food production (or supply) does not keep pace with this increase in numbers, famine conditions would come to prevail all over the country, with their aftermath of an increase in disease and the death rate. The resulting poverty and miserable level of living can hardly be imagined. A government that could control India's millions in a state of such misery would clearly have to be some form of totalitarianism, embracing every aspect of the citizen's life with the tentacles of an octopus. Individual freedom as we understand it would be extinct, for teeming millions with almost literally no elbow room would imply choking government and social organization and control, utterly incompatible with individual human liberty, freedom or dignity.[62]

Whether this anticipated hell visits India or not remains to be seen. But there is no denying that the alarming increase year after year in the population of South Asia as a whole tragically nullifies most of the progress achieved in the region through planning and development over the past two decades.

NOTES

1. T. J. Samuel, "The Development of India's Policy of Population Control," *The Milbank Memorial Fund Quarterly,* vol. 44, no. 1, part 1 (January 1968), 49.

2. Quoted in S. Chandrasekhar, *Population and Planned Parenthood in India* (London: Allen & Unwin, 1961), p. 93.

3. Ibid.

4. E. A. Gait, "Population," *Imperial Gazetteer of India,* vol. 1 (1907), pp. 461–462.

5. B. H. Baden-Powell, *Land Systems of British India,* vol. 1 (Oxford: Clarendon Press, 1892), p. 346.

6. M. L. Darling, *The Punjab Peasant in Prosperity and Debt* (London: Oxford University Press, 1925), pp. 252, 286–288.

7. For the views of the Indian nationalist economists, see Bipan Chandra, *The Rise and Growth of Economic Nationalism in India* (New Delhi: People's Publishing House, 1966), pp. 1–54.

8. Kingsley Davis, *The Population of India and Pakistan* (Princeton, N.J.: Princeton University Press, 1951), pp. 26–27.

9. Ibid., p. 27.

10. *India News,* February 1960, p. 2.

11. These figures include the population of present-day Pakistan and Bangladesh.

12. Gunnar Myrdal, *Asian Drama: An Inquiry into the Poverty of Nations* (New York: Pantheon, 1968), p. 1389.

13. Government of Pakistan, Planning Commission, *Preliminary Evaluation of The Third Five Year Plan* (Islamabad, August 1970), pp. 78, 200-201.

14. For a detailed discussion of the demographic aspects of savings and investments in developing countries, see United Nations, *The Determinants and Consequences of Population Trends,* vol. 1, ch. 13, (New York, 1973), pp. 434-504.

15. J. P. Bhattacharjee, ed., *Studies in Indian Agricultural Economics* (Bombay: Indian Society of Agricultural Economics, 1958) p. 10.

16. Davis, *Population of India and Pakistan,* p. 208.

17. United Nations, Food and Agricultural Organization, *The State of Food and Agriculture, 1967* (Rome, 1968).

18. The Food and Agriculture Organization of the United Nations has estimated caloric requirement on the basis of essential nutrients for the Near East, including South Asia, at 2,400 per day. United Nations, Food and Agriculture Organization, *Agricultural Commodity Projections,* vol. 1, (Rome, 1971), pp. 43-46.

19. Government of India, Ministry of Food and Agriculture, *Agricultural Situation in India* (New Delhi, 1963).

20. According to United Nations projections of food demand in the Asian countries—taking into account such factors as income levels, population size, and accelerating urbanization, and extrapolating food production to 1985—while the demand for food will rise at the rate of 3.4 percent per annum, the rate of food production will rise at a rate of only 2.6 percent. Most of the countries in Asia will thus continue to face food shortages and malnutrition during the next decade. See United Nations, Food and Agriculture Organization, *The State of Food & Agriculture, 1974* (Rome, 1975), pp. 116-122.

21. Compiled from data in Government of India, *Report of the Committee on Unemployment* (New Delhi, 1973).

22. Government of Pakistan, Planning Commission, *The Third Five Year Plan, 1965-70,* (Islamabad, 1965), p. 149.

23. Mahbub-ul Haq, *The Strategy of Economic Planning: A Case Study of Pakistan* (Karachi: Oxford University Press, 1963), p. 241.

24. Ibid., p. 242.

25. "A Survey of Employment, Unemployment and Underemployment in Ceylon," *International Labour Review,* March 1963, pp. 247-257.

26. P. K. Wattal, *Population Problem in India* (Bombay: Bennett, Coleman, 1934), p. 23.

27. P. A. Wadia and K. T. Merchant, *Our Economic Problem* (Bombay: New Book Co., 1954), p. 115.

28. Wattal, *Population Problem in India,* p. 24; Agarwala, *India's Population Problem,* pp. 74-75.

29. K. M. Kapadia, *Marriage and Family in India,* 3rd rev. ed. (Bombay: Oxford University Press, 1960), p. 30.

30. J. R. Rele, "Some Aspects of Family and Fertility in India," *Population Studies,* vol. 15, no. 3 (March 1962).

31. S. B. Munkerji, *Studies on Fertility Rates in Calcutta,* quoted in A. Nevett, *Population: Explosion or Control?* (London: 1964), pp. 148-149.

32. K. Dandekar and Vaijayanti Bhate, *Socio-Economic Change during Three Five-Year Plans* (Poona: Gokhale Institute of Politics and Economics, 1975), p. 400.

33. Rajni Kothari, "The Family Planning Programme: A Sociological Analysis," *Sociological Bulletin,* vol. 15, no. 2 (September 1966), 51.

34. Ibid., p. 54.

35. Tara Patel, "Some Reflections on the Attitudes of Married Couples towards Family Planning in Ahmedabad," *Sociological Bulletin,* vol. 12, no. 2 (September 1963), 7, mentioned in Pathare, "Family Planning Programme," p. 55.

36. Gyan Chand, *India's Teeming Millions* (London: Allen & Unwin, 1939), p. 145.

37. Government of India, Planning Commission, *The Third Five Year Plan,*

1960–65 (New Delhi, 1961), p. 1.

38. Government of India, *National Sample Survey Report,* No. 7 (New Delhi, 1955), foreword.

39. For a discussion of this point see Ram Chugh, "Population Growth in India," in J. S. Uppal, ed. *India's Economic Problems* (New Delhi: Tata McGraw-Hill, 1973), pp. 3–22.

40. for alternative explanations, see T. Paul Schultz, "An Economic Perspective in Population Growth," in National Academy of Science, ed., *Rapid Population Growth,* vol. 2 (Baltimore: Johns Hopkins Press, 1971), pp. 148–174.

41. See Benjamin Higgins, *Economic Development* (New York: Norton, 1959), pp. 190–191 for a detailed discussion of this point. According to Higgins: "Where population grows in a country with less than optimum population, that growth provides an additional stimulus to expansion, by encouraging investment in housing, transport, public utilities, and the like. . . . But where populations are already above optimum levels, further increases act only as a drag on economic development." (p. 190).

42. Ibid., pp. 190–191.

43. Philip M. Hauser, "World Population," in National Academy of Science, ed., *Rapid Population Growth* (Baltimore: Johns Hopkins Press, 1971), p. 108. According to Hauser, "In the economically advanced nations the means by which the death rate was decreased were developed gradually over the modern era; then they became available to the less developed nations all at once. Ships anchored off Bombay, Rio de Janeiro or Dakar could carry in their holds all the material means of reducing mortality which Western nations acquired after 3 centuries of experience and effort."

44. Davis, *Population of India and Pakistan,* p. 49.

45. Government of India, Ministry of Information and Broadcasting, *India: A Reference Manual* (New Delhi, 1974), pp. 79–90.

46. Davis, *Population of India and Pakistan,* p. 81.

47. Ibid., p. 82.

48. Government of India, Planning Commission, *The First Five Year Plan, 1950–55* (New Delhi, 1951), p. 21.

49. Government of India, Planning Commission, *The Fourth Five Year Plan, 1969–74,*)new Delhi, 1970), p. 31.

50. Government of Pakistan, Planning Commission, *The Second Five Year Plan, 1960–65,* (Karachi, 1960), p. 334.

51. Government of Pakistan, Planning Commission, *The First Five Year Plan, 1955–60* (Karachi, 1957), pp. 189–196.

52. Government of Ceylon, *The Ten Year Plan* (Colombo, 1959), p. 17.

53. Government of Bangladesh, Planning Commission, *The First Five Year Plan, 1973–78* (Dacca, 1973), p. 538.

54. For details of the family planning program in India, see S. N. Agarwala, *India's Population Problems* (New Delhi: Tata McGraw-Hill, 1972), pp. 157–169, and Government of India, Fifth Lok Sabha Estimate Committee, *Family Planning Programme* (New Delhi, 1972).

55. Government of India, Planning Commission, *Towards an Approach to the Fifth Plan* (New Delhi, 1972), p. 11.

56. Agarwala, *India's Population Problem,* p. 167.

57. Ibid., p. 167.

58. Bangladesh, *First Plan,* p. 537.

59. Quoted by Ruddar Datt and K. P. M. Sundharam, *Indian Economy* (New Delhi: Chand, 1975), pp. 65, 66.

60. Bangladesh, *First Plan,* pp. 537–38.

61. India, *Fourth Plan,* pp. 31–32.

62. S. Chandrasekhar, "A Billion Indians by 2000 A.D.?" *New York Times Magazine,* April 4, 1965.

3

Capital Formation

THE GENERAL SETTING

The chronic poverty prevailing in the countries of South Asia can be explained by what is sometimes referred to as the vicious circle of poverty. According to Nurske,

> On the supply side there is the small capacity to save, resulting from the low level of real income. The low real income is a reflection of low productivity, which in its turn is due largely to the lack of capital. The lack of capital is a result of the small capacity to save, and so the circle is complete.[1]

In other words, the vicious circle of poverty is composed of low income→ low savings and investment→ low productivity→ poverty. The essence of the task of economic development is somehow to break this vicious circle. The economic histories of the presently developed countries show that in their development processes the vicious cycle of poverty was broken somewhere along the way between income and savings. In other words, today's developed nations, at one time or another, adopted measures for capital formation by channeling income into savings, though the method adopted differed according to the economic and political systems of the particular country. In the capitalist countries, economic development was financed mainly by taxing agriculture at high rates (as in Japan) or through the accumulation (and investment) of profits by keeping wage increases lagging behind productivity increases (as in England and the United States). The colonial powers of Europe (e.g., England, France, Spain, Portugal, the Netherlands, and the Soviet Union) and Japan extracted huge sums from their colonies in Asia, Africa, and Latin America. The Communist countries obtained capital by expropriating private properties and the assets of foreign firms (e.g., Cuba and the Soviet Union), by appropriating capital from the landowning and wealthy, and by enlarging the social surplus through the general tactic of restraining consumption alternatives (e.g., Soviet Union) and earmarking a part of the total product for investment before distributing it for consumption (China).

The fundamental task of economic development facing the underdeveloped countries, including the South Asian countries, is to prevent their incomes from being entirely consumed somehow and, by this means, to provide capital sufficient to put their economies on a self-sustaining growth path.

It should be pointed out, however, that not all economists assign importance to capital in the development process. According to Nevin: "Capital, like Patriotism, is not sufficient."[2] Letwin regards the view that "more capital is better than less capital" as a fallacy.[3] Some econometric studies[4] assert that more economic growth occurred in some countries than can be explained solely by the input of capital. It is asserted, on the basis of the historical experience of the developed countries, that, in addition to capital, other variables—such as managerial capacity, technology, education, work attitudes, and government policy—are also important determinants of economic growth.

Our contention is that the availability of capital may not be a sufficient condition but is one very necessary condition for growth. First, many of the factors (other than capital) mentioned above are dependent on the prior investment of capital. Second, present conditions in the underdeveloped nations are quite different from those which prevailed in the developing countries during the nineteenth and early twentieth centuries. In most underdeveloped countries today, especially in South Asia, the factor endowment position can be characterized by "labor abundance" and "capital scarcity," such that with the existing stock of capital and technology, the value of the marginal product of labor may well be zero or close to zero. In such a situation, increased productivity depends mainly on an increase in the supply of capital. In these circumstances, lack of capital can be regarded as one of the major impediments to economic development in the underdeveloped countries in general and in the labor surplus countries like Bangladesh, India, and Pakistan in particular. According to the Indian Planning Commission:

"Mobilization of resources for securing an adequate rate of growth is the crux of the problem of planning in an underdeveloped economy."[5]

Capital formation of considerable magnitude will be required for accelerating economic development in the South Asian economies for the following purposes:

1. The reorganization and revitalization of agriculture so as to raise current low levels of productivity
2. The building of necessary economic and social overheads, such as transportation and communications networks, electricity and irrigation projects, educational and research institutions, and hospitals
3. The effective exploitation of natural resources and the setting up of basic industries

While overall agricultural productivity is low throughout the region, the countries of South Asia differ with regard to their supply of social and economic overheads; India is relatively better equipped than Bangladesh and Nepal in this respect. Even in the case of India, Wilfred Owen finds transportation and communication systems extremely poor, and

> Poor transport is also an obstacle to making effective use of India's natural resources. The extent of transport deficit in India is indicated by comparisons with transport resources in the rest of the world. India accounts for 16 percent of the world's people but only 4 percent of its improved roads, 2 percent of its rail freight and 1 percent of its trucks and buses.[6]

Providing adequate transportation and communication facilities alone would require amounts of capital that are presently far beyond the capacity of the Indian economy. Writing about Pakistan, S. M. Akhtar remarks, "lack of physical capital in the sense of buildings, machinery and tools, raw materials and other intermediate goods, is a serious obstacle to economic development."[7]

What do we mean by "capital formation" and what are its various components? Traditionally, economists have defined capital in terms of the physical assets used for further production.

> The meaning of "capital formation" is that society does not apply the whole of its current consumption, but directs a part of it to the making of capital goods; tools and instruments, machines, and transport facilities, plant and equipment. . . all the various forms of real capital that can so greatly increase the efficiency of productive effort. . . the essence of the process, then, is the diversion of a part of society's currently available resources to the purpose of increasing the stock of capital goods so as to make possible an expansion of consumable output in the future.[8]

This definition emphasizes real physical assets as the major factor in the productive potential of the society. Recently, however, economists have suggested enlarging the definition of capital to include the "abilities of man" as a form of capital.

> Surely one of the major reasons for the widely held popular belief that economics is materialistic is the overcommitment on the part of the economist to a partial concept of capital restricted to material objects. The failure to include the acquired abilities of man that augment his economic productivity as a form of capital, as a produced means of production, as a product of investment, has fostered the retention of the patently wrong notion that labor is capital force and it is only the number of manhours worked that matters. But . . . laborers have become capitalists in the sense that they have acquired much knowledge and many skills that have economic value. Clearly what is needed in this connection is an all-inclusive concept of capital.[9]

According to this view, capital should include both physical capital (additions to the stock of producer goods, i.e., machines, tools, equipment, transportation facilities, etc.) and human capital (acquired abilities through education, training, and experience). In our discussion, however, we will deal mainly with physical capital, since in the South Asian countries lack of physical capital is the main impediment to economic development.[10] In fact, there presently exists an excess of education, indicated by high rates of unemployment among the educated, relative to South Asian development needs.

RATES OF CAPITAL FORMATION

What level of capital formation in the South Asian countries would initiate the process of self-sustained economic growth? The answer to this important question depends on two major factors (1) the desired rate of economic development in the context of the socioeconomic conditions of the region and (2) the capital requirements of the particular country as determined by quantitative estimates of such factors as capital-output ratios in the different sectors of its economy.

The historical experience of such developed countries as the United States, Great Britain, Germany, the Soviet Union, and Japan during their development phases can provide some valuable guidelines.[11] In the United States, the rate of investment rose from about 15 percent of the national income in 1869–1878 to 19.5 percent at the end of the century. In the Soviet Union, between 1937 and 1948, excepting the war years, the rate of capital formation remained at a level of about 15 percent. In Britain, the rate of capital formation as a proportion of GNP ranged between 15 and 20 percent during the years 1870–1914. For Canada, the rate of capital formation from 1870 to 1929 is estimated to have been between 15 and 23 percent. In Japan during the decade 1920–1930, the rate of capital formation was between 16 and 17 percent. In Germany, the net capital formation fluctuated around 14 percent between 1850 and 1870 and rose to 16.5 in the period 1901–1913.

On the basis of the above figures, one can infer that a developing country needs to save and invest something like 15 to 20 percent of its national income. To what extent is this ratio a useful guide for the underdeveloped countries today? The advanced countries had to invest huge sums on research to develop the know-how and technology which the underdeveloped countries today can simply draw upon, making adjustments, of course, for local socioeconomic factors. On the other hand, the magnitude of the task of economic development in underdeveloped countries today is much greater than for any country in the past. Massive population pressures, with numbers increasing much more rapidly than they did in the past, and the growing gap between the incomes and living standards in the poor and underdeveloped countries as compared with those in the advanced and affluent countries, is resulting in mounting frustration and dissatisfaction. This makes the task of development today much more formidable than it was in the past and calls for correspondingly higher rates of capital formation.

The level of capital formation also depends on the desired rate of economic growth within the context of the social and economic conditions in the region. Let us review the estimates of some well-known scholars in the field. W. W. Rostow suggests that before an economy can enter the "take-off stage" it is necessary that "the proportion of net investment to national income . . . rises from, say, 5 percent to 10 percent . . . yielding a distinct rise in output per capita."[12] According to W. Arthur Lewis, "The central problem in the theory of economic growth is to understand the process by which a community is converted from being a 5 percent to a 12 percent saver."[13] The rate of capital formation to raise an underdeveloped economy out of the cycle of poverty is also indicated in several mathematical models explaining the process of growth. One such is the simple "Harrod-Domar model": $g = s/k$ where g is the rate of growth, s is the rate of saving and k is the capital-output ratio (also referred to as the capital coefficient which is the relationship between the increment of capital and the increment of output both in the same period of time).[14] This simple equation suggests that the growth rate of income is equal to the rate of saving in the economy divided by its capital-output ratio. Assuming that the capital-output ratio is 3 (this is a realistic assumption for the South Asian economies), and since, as their development plans suggest, the South

Asian countries plan to achieve about 5 percent annual rate of growth, the desired rate of savings and capital formation would be about 15 percent. It may be noted that there are several conceptual problems involved in the concept of the capital coefficient,[15] but it does provide a good and simple way of estimating the approximate level of capital formation required for the amount of economic growth desired.

From the above discussion, it would seem that an underdeveloped economy requires capital amounting to about 15 to 18 percent of its national income in order to initiate a process of self-sustained economic growth. Against this estimated requirement, the actual rates of capital formation in the South Asian countries are given in Table 3-1. Note that Sri Lanka is ahead of both India and Pakistan in regard to domestic savings as a proportion of national income. This may be due mainly to the importance of plantations—with their high savings-income ratio—in the Sri Lanka economy and to comparatively lower expenditures by Sri Lanka on defense. In the postindependence years, while India and Pakistan have engaged in bitter wars and have felt it necessary to devote a considerable proportion of their national income to defense, Sri Lanka has enjoyed relative peace. The 1971 internal disturbance in Sri Lanka may, however, adversely affect capital formation. Comparing India and Pakistan, India started out with a higher rate of domestic savings; but, around 1965, Pakistan drew level, and in fact its domestic savings' rate exceeded that of India during 1967-1968. Pakistan's total gross investment exceeded that of India after 1965 because of a receipt of higher rates of foreign capital (as a proportion of GNP). Of all the South Asian countries, government savings were of significance only in India. This is due to the expansion of the public sector in India—the launching of new public undertakings (e.g., steel mills and fertilizer factories) and the nationalization of many financial institutions, such as life insurance and the banks, in pursuance of the leadership's declared objective of transforming India into a socialist society. The other countries, particularly Pakistan, have remained committed to the development of private enterprise.

On the whole, in the South Asian countries, total gross investment as a proportion of national income has been around 12 percent—except in the case of Pakistan, where total gross investment has been around 15 percent since 1964-1965 because of its high rate of foreign capital entry (around 6 percent of the national income). This ratio is much lower if we consider only the component of domestic capital. Considering the levels of capital formation required by these economies to enable them to move toward self-sustained growth, the actual rate of capital formation is well below that need. We will now discuss capital formation under its various components.

Table 3-1 Capital Formation by Source, in South Asian Countries, 1950-1974
Percentage of national income at constant prices[a]

Country	Period	Government savings	Corporate savings	Household savings	Total domestic savings	Foreign capital	Total gross investment
Bangladesh[b]	1960-1961				4.5%	3.3%	7.8%
	1964-1965				6.1	3.3	9.4
	1973-1974				4.5	7.4	11.9
India	1950-1955	1.2%	0.5%	4.9%	6.6	0.4	7.0
	1955-1960	1.6	0.4	6.5	8.5	2.9	11.4
	1965-1966	3.2	0.4	7.2	10.8	2.9	13.7
	1969-1970	0.9	0.4	6.8	8.1	0.8	9.2
	1972-1973	2.2	0.3	7.0	9.5	1.0	10.5
	1973-1974	2.8	0.3	9.1	12.2	1.5	13.7
Pakistan[c]	1949-1950	-0.6	5.1		4.5		4.5
	1954-1955	0.2	6.2		6.5	1.1	7.5
	1955-1956				7.9	2.7	9.2
	1959-1960	0.2	6.3		6.5	4.0	10.5
	1964-1965	0.8	7.8		8.6	6.8	15.4
	1967-1968				10.1	5.4	15.4
	1969-1970				10.3	2.7	13.0
Sri Lanka	1959-1960	3.9			11.0		14.5
	1964-1965	0.6			12.0		12.5
	1968-1969				12.4		13.1
	1969-1970				13.1		13.5
	1970-1971				13.0		
	1972-1973	-0.3			13.4		14.0

[a]Figures for the columns left blank are not available.
[b]Separate estimates on capital formation in Bangladesh (formerly East Pakistan) are not available for the period prior to 1973-1974.
[c]The figures for Pakistan include the present areas in both Pakistan and Bangladesh.

SOURCE: S. M. Akhtar, *Economic Development of Pakistan* (Lahore: Publishers United, 1971), p. 165.
Ruddar Datt and K. P. M. Sundharam, *Indian Economy* (New Delhi: Chand, 1975), pp. 102-105.
Government of Pakistan, Planning Commission, *The Second Five Year Plan, 1960-1965* (Karachi, 1960), p. 28.
    Preliminary Evaluation of the Third Five Year Plan, Islamabad, 1970).
Stephen R. Lewis, Jr., *Pakistan, Industrialization and Trade Policies* (London: Oxford University Press, 1970), pp. 145-147.
United Nations, *Economic and Social Survey of Asia and the Pacific, 1974* (Bangkok, 1975).
Bangladesh Planning Commission, *The First Five Year Plan, 1973-1978*, (Dacca, 1973).
    Economic Bulletin for Asia and the Pacific, 1974 (Bangkok, 1975).
    Statistical Year Book for Asia and the Pacific, 1973 (Bangkok, 1974).

THE SOURCES OF CAPITAL

The major sources of capital are (a) domestic capital (or savings), comprising corporate, household, and government savings; and (b) foreign capital (or inflow of foreign funds), comprising foreign aid and foreign investments.

Domestic Capital

Corporate Savings.   The corporate sector includes corporations, cooperative societies, and all other companies registered with the government, except government companies and nonprofit companies and associations. Corporations are classified as financial or nonfinancial by the nature of their major business activities. Banks, insurance companies, and loan, investment, and other financing companies are treated as financial, while the category "non-financial" includes large companies principally engaged in manufacture, mining, trading, transport, and the operation of plantations (mainly tea and rubber).

Corporations have played an important role in the capital formation of the present-day advanced countries in several ways. First, the ploughing back of profits has been an important source of corporate investments. Abramovitz estimates that in the United States in 1925, total net profits were about 10 percent of national income and savings from profits were about 41 percent of total savings.[16] In the advanced countries, it is normal practice on the part of large corporations to claim larger depreciation allowances than are normally adequate to maintain the productive equipment of industry. This results in further savings. Modern business corporations also help to mobilize savings by issuing shares, floating bonds, borrowing directly from financial institutions, and so on. In the underdeveloped countries in general, the number of large corporations is small and most of the business enterprises are organized on a family partnership or individual proprietorship basis. The savings of such small-scale enterprises are included in the category "household savings."

Within South Asia, India has the most developed corporate sector. Even there, however, as Table 3–1 shows, the contribution of this sector to total capital formation is only 0.4 percent, and it is declining. One of the reasons for this decline is that with the nationalization of such large companies as the Imperial Bank of India (now the State Bank of India) and the life insurance companies (now grouped under the Life Insurance Corporation), the private sector is shrinking. The savings and investments of these companies, included in the corporate (private) sector until nationalization, now appear in the government (public) sector.

The South Asian countries provide a variety of tax incentives with a view of encouraging the private sector to plough back its profits in the form of investments. India, for instance, offers development rebates, partial "tax holidays," deductions in respect of intercorporate dividends, and priority industry allowances. These tax incentives, however, have not proved effective in inducing higher rates of corporate capital formation.[17]

It may be noted that the generation of high rates of profit by the corporate sector—a major source of capital formation in the advanced countries—is a device not available to corporations today. The social, economic, and political climate of the nineteenth century, which made huge profits possible, simply does not exist any more. During the last century, the labor unions were not strong and aggressive, the business community possessed enormous political power, and egalitarian ideals did not affect income distribution and labor legislation. According to Schumpeter, capitalism owes its spectacular growth during the eighteenth and nineteenth centuries to a special type of social and political climate in which the daring and unconventional enterpreneur could amass huge profits, build a "private kingdom," and create a "business dynasty" by maintaining a high profit-wage ratio.[18] In societies accustomed to unequal income and wealth distribution, the powerful enterpreneur enjoyed the support of the public as a whole and especially of the rulers. But times have changed. The democratization process that transferred power from strong rulers to the people, and the growth of egalitarian ideas that led to payroll taxes to finance social security programs and labor welfare programs, such as minimum wages and workmen's compensation—these are some of the important factors for the decline of the Schumpeterian entrepreneur. As a result, earning high rates of profit, an important source of corporate capital, is not easy any more.

Whatever the truth of Schumpeter's analysis, it is clear that the political and social climate responsible for the decline of corporate profits followed the attainment of a high level of industrial development in the West. In the underdeveloped countries, and especially in South Asia, the order of events has been reversed. The sociopolitical climate that prevents capital accumulation through a high profit-wage ratio, prevailed from the start of the economic development effort. For example, India has a strong labor union movement guarding labor interests in the industrial sector. It is the policy of the Indian government to encourage the settlement of wages and fringe benefits, including bonus payments, by joint consultation between labor, management, and government, keeping in view productivity and profit trends. India has a considerable body of labor welfare legislation in its statutes, including the Employees State Insurance Act, 1948 (providing benefits for sickness, medicines, maternity, disablement, and dependents in all perennial, or nonseasonal, factories, using mechanical power and employing 20 or more persons); the Employees Provident Fund Act, 1952 (providing for a compulsory contribution of 6-1/4 percent of workers' wages by both employee and employer); and the Minimum Wages Act, 1948 (fixing minimum fair wages for workers in major industries). Efforts are being made to extend the scope of the fair wages legislation to other sectors of the economy.

Indian labor is very conscious of its rights, and through the organized labor union movement efforts are constantly made to keep real wages in line with productivity increases in the manufacturing sector. The labor unions often resort to militancy on the question of wages. For example, during 1972 there were 2,912 industrial disputes, including work stoppages, involving 1.6 million workers and resulting in the loss of 17.9 million work days.[19]

Besides labor welfare legislation, South Asian governments are adopting equalitarian policies for the redistribution of income and wealth on a more equal basis. The introduction of land reforms, fixing ceilings on rent, and taking land from big landowners and distributing it among the peasants; the fixing of ceilings on holdings of urban land; abolition of the privileges of the princes; the introduction of taxes on wealth; and the nationalization of major industries, including banks and insurance companies—these are some of the measures that have been taken to redistribute the country's wealth.

While labor welfare legislation and income redistribution policies are to be commended on the basis of social justice, there is no denying that the corporate sector in the South Asian economies cannot, as did its historical counterpart in the presently advanced countries, amass huge profits by keeping wages lagging far behind increasing productivity. No wonder, then, that the contribution of the corporate sector to total capital formation is low and unlikely to increase in the future. Table 3-1 shows that in India, corporate savings constituted only 0.5 percent of total capital formation, and this ratio has remained more or less constant during the decades 1950-1970. It is thus clear that one important source of capital formation, namely, corporate profits, is not available within South Asia.

Household Savings. With a small corporate sector, the economies of South Asia have to rely on household savings as a major source of capital formation. In India, Bangladesh, and Pakistan household savings constitute about three quarters of total domestic savings. Thus, all hopes for raising the needed capital for development plans lie with the household sector.[20] Tables 3-2 and 3-3 give the volume and pattern of household savings in India since 1950–1951. The figures in Tables 3-2 and 3-3 show the following patterns of household savings. First, urban savings total approximately three and a half times as much as rural savings. This would suggest a particular need to intensify efforts to promote savings in rural areas. Various studies[21] on the relative prices of agricultural and nonagricultural goods in the South Asian countries show that the terms of trade have been shifting in favor of the agricultural sector during the last decade or so and it is well known that the burden of taxation is comparatively lower in rural areas. We will discuss these points further in the next section.

Table 3-2 Household Savings in India as a Proportion of National Income

Households	1950-1951	1954-1955	1960-1961	1962-1963	1973-1974
Rural	1.7%	1.7%	1.6%	1.5%	1.9%
Urban	2.6	4.8	4.9	4.9	6.1
Total	4.3	6.5	6.5	6.4	8.0

SOURCE: Reserve Bank of India, "Estimates of Savings and Investment in the Indian Economy," 1950-51 to 1962-63," *Bulletin,* March 1965, pp. 314-333.
United Nations, *Economic Survey of Asia and the Far East, 1973, 1974.* (Bangkok, 1974, 1975).

Table 3-3 Major Components of Household Savings in India as a Proportion of National Income

Components	1968-1969	1971-1972	1973-1974
Financial (net) assets excluding financial liabilities	2.7%	5.3%	4.7%
Currency	0.9	1.2	1.7
Deposits	1.8	3.2	2.8
Insurance	0.6	0.7	0.7
Provident funds	1.0	1.3	1.2
Corporate and cooperative shares and securities	0.2	0.3	0.3
Financial liabilities	-1.8	-1.4	-2.0
Physical assets	3.5	3.6	3.3
Total	6.2	8.9	8.0

SOURCE: Reserve Bank of India, *Report on Currency and Finance, 1973-74* (Bombay, 1975), pp. 5-12.

Second, the major proportion of household savings is in the form of financial assets, institutional funds (insurance and provident funds), and corporate shares and securities. This suggests the areas in which efforts to achieve a greater savings rate will have to be concentrated. It is well known that while urban areas do have the financial institutions needed to encourage and channel savings, these institutions are practically nonexistent in the rural areas.

Total household savings as shown in Table 3-2 are generally low and inadequate, judged from any angle. The rate of saving is much lower than that attained by the more developed nations during the nineteenth and early twentieth centuries, and it is grossly inadequate to initiate the process of self-sustaining economic growth.

Let us consider some of the explanations that may be offered to account for this low rate of household savings. First and foremost, of course, is the proverbial poverty and low standard of living. The crucial question is, how and to what extent can poor households be expected to save? Nevertheless, while poverty as a cause of low savings needs no emphasis, one should not over emphasize it as an explanation. As W. Arthur Lewis points out:

> No nation is so poor that it could not save 12 percent of its national income if it wanted to; poverty has never prevented nations from launching upon wars, or from wasting their substance in other ways. . . . In such countries productive investment is not small because there is no surplus; it is small because the surplus is used to maintain unproductive hordes of retainers, and to build pyramids, temples and other durable consumer goods, instead of to create productive capital.[22]

There is some truth in this statement and one should seek some additional explanations for the low rate of savings in South Asia.

Another important factor that helps to explain the low savings rate among households is the phenomenon known as the "Revolution of Rising Expectations." In the words of Willard Cochrane:

> The common man throughout the less developed world has come to believe in, indeed to expect, economic progress for himself, his family, and his nation. . . . These people want and expect to receive this year, not next, improved medical services, a richer and more healthful diet, an improved mechanical means of transportation, a transistor radio, school for their children and such frivolities as soft drinks.[23]

The economies of most countries in the developing world—including the South Asian—are not growing fast enough to meet these rising expectations. Quoting Cochrane again:

The economies of most developing countries are making good progress; but they take off from such a low product level that they cannot possibly produce the bill of goods expected of them by their populations in the next decade or even several decades.[24]

A widening gap exists between rising expectations and levels of attainment which has serious social, economic, and political implications. We will examine various aspects of the situation including its nature, sources, and implications, in the next chapter. We may, however, point out here that the existence of this gap creates an intense urge to consume using precious capital from slowly increasing, meager incomes. This type of consumer behavior is especially manifested by the increased demand for frivolous and durable goods. With its meager income, the household aspires to buy a radio and a television set, bicycles, scooters, electric fans, and so on, rather than to put aside some of its income as savings. This practice is partly the direct outcome of the development process involving mass communication facilities and partly from setting the nation's sights on high-sounding targets in the development plans. This is yet another situation that did not exist—or at least not with the same intensity—during the initial period of Western industrialization.

This situation does not prevail, equally, among the presently underdeveloped countries. Those with democratic rule are more prone to the revolution of rising expectations than are those ruled, more or less, dictatorially. In the latter the decisions to consume or save rests more with government than with individual household. As the South Asian countries have primarily opted for the democratic way, it is almost impossible to offer the right to vote while at the same time requesting a reduction in an already low level of consumption.

Certain sociological and cultural institutions also adversely affect the saving behavior of households. One such social institution is the extended family system, which, in South Asia, is the dominant form of family organization. In the extended (or joint) family system, three or four generations (grandparents, parents, and children) all live together under a common roof, eat from the same kitchen, and share the necessities of life. The earnings of all family members are put into a common pool from which each individual gets a share according to his need. Under this system, a number of people work on the family enterprise; some of them contribute almost nothing to output, and they are virtually subsidized by the productive family members.

There are various outcomes resulting from this type of family arrangement. First, it conceals a large number of persons who are in fact unemployed (from the point of view of zero contribution to total family output), although they consider themselves employed. This employment pattern is described as disguised unemployment, or surplus labor.[25] Estimates of disguised unemployment in the South Asian economies vary between 10 and 20 percent of the total labor force. The existence of such a large, disguisedly unemployed work force partly explains the poverty of the countries, and a key factor in the development of these countries is the proper absorption of this huge mass of surplus labor. This surplus labor can also be viewed as a potential source of capital formation, since it can be withdrawn from existing enterprises and used for producing additional goods and services, including capital goods, without any loss of output.[26]

We will examine this situation in chapter 5, but it is important to point out here the impact of disguised unemployment on the savings potential of households. Any savings achieved by the households are consumed by its disguisedly unemployed members. The situation can be illustrated by a simple example. Suppose there are three working members in a family fully employed in producing a total output of Rs 1,600, consuming Rs 1,200, and saving Rs 400. Their average per capita consumption and savings are Rs 400 and Rs 133.3, respectively. Now another relative comes and joins the family, which has the social obligation to share its work and income with him. Since the newcomer will be superfluous, or in other words disguisedly unemployed, he will not be contributing anything to the total output of the family, while he is sharing in the consumption of its total output. Thus, while total output remains the same, namely, Rs 1,600, the total consumption rises to Rs 1,600, leaving no savings. What has happened is that the family's savings of Rs 400, has been consumed by the addition of an unproductive member. It can be seen that with 10 to 20 percent of the labor force being disguisedly unemployed, the total impact on savings is disastrous.

Yet another factor that stands in the way of household savings is the lack of banking facilities, especially in the rural areas, through which household savings might be mobilized. In the South Asian countries, banks are concentrated in urban areas, to the neglect of the rural sector where more than three quarters of the population live. The rural areas are served by cooperative societies, which are essentially agencies for the distribution of credit; they have failed to create a deposit consciousness among their members, as is indicated by the very low level of deposits per member in the cooperatives. Citing an example from the Indian rural cooperative societies, Datt and Sundharam[27] found the average deposit per member of a primary agricultural credit society to be as low as Rs 5.8 and Rs 6.0 in the Indian states of Uttar Pradesh and Orissa, respectively. On the basis of their findings, Datt and Sundharam remark, that it is the "failure of deposit mobilization efforts that can be held responsible for the poor performance in the saving efforts of the rural areas."[28] The opening of more banks in the rural areas, the simplification of banking procedures to suit the needs and conditions of rural life, and, above all, the creation of a deposit consciousness among households are some of the measures proposed for increasing household savings.

Government Savings.   If the corporate sector is unable to save for the various reasons discussed earlier, and households are too poor to save, the government has to be the saver of last resort for capital formation in a developing economy. For the government to play the dominant role in capital formation is not uncommon. Long before the emergence of Communist governments in the Soviet Union and China, the major saver in Japan during the Meiji period (1868-1912) was the government. The technique adopted in Japan was taxing agriculture at high rates, keeping government expenditure, especially on non-developmental items, at minimum levels, and investing the budget surpluses for industrialization.

In the South Asian countries, as in most underdeveloped countries, government savings, though presently small, are assuming growing importance as a source of public investment on necessary infrastructures, particularly transportation, power, and communications. In addition, there has been a trend toward increasing investment in social capital: education, health, and social welfare. Table 3-4 shows the share of government investment in total investment in the South Asian countries.

The increasing role of the public sector in total capital formation indicates the extent of future reliance the South Asian countries will have to place on governmental efforts to obtain the much-needed capital to meet economic development targets. The proportion of government savings to incomes, however, is still quite low. It ranges from 1.2 to 2.8 percent for India and is less than 1 percent for the other countries—as shown in Table 3.1. To find out the main reasons for these low ratios, let us examine current government revenues and current government expenditures, since it is the excess of the former over the latter that is the source of government savings.

In general, revenues in South Asia are falling short of expenditures, creating huge budget deficits. The main causes for this are (1) that tax revenues are falling behind the planned outlays, and (2) that government expenditures, particularly on nondevelopment items, are increasing at a rate disproportionate to increases in revenues.

The main factors responsible for the phenomenal rise in government expenditures on current account (as distinct from expenditures on capital account) are heavy defense expenditures; the rising cost of public administration; increased expenditures on public welfare activities, including food subsidies; and expenditures on diplomatic missions and international conferences. As a proportion of gross national product, defense expenditure in Sri Lanka has increased

Table 3-4 Investments by the Public Sector in South Asian Countries

Country	Year	Government investment as % of total investment
Bangladesh	1963-1964	74.8%
	1964-1965	67.7
	1967-1968	72.5
India	1950-1951	28.3
	1955-1956	51.5
	1960-1966	61.7
	1965-1966	66.7
	1970-1971	66.8
Pakistan	1963-1964	44.6
	1964-1965	43.2
	1967-1968	38.4
Sri Lanka	1959-1960	49.5
	1964-1965	76.1
	1969-1970	41.7
	1970-1971	33.6

SOURCE: M. Akhlaqur Rahman, "The Role of the Public Sector in the Economic Development of Pakistan," in E. A. G. Robinson and Michael Kidron, eds., *Economic Development in South Asia* (London: St. Martin's, 1970), p. 72. United Nations, *Economic Survey of Asia and the Far East, 1972* (Bangkok, 1973), pp. 75-76.

from 0.2 percent in 1950–1951 to 1.7 percent in 1971–1973, and in India from 1.7 percent to 3.7 percent during the same period. Since 1947, India and Pakistan have fought three wars.

There has also been a rapid increase in government expenditures on general services (excluding national defense) ranging during 1972–1973 from 12 percent in Sri Lanka to 14 percent in India and 17 percent in Pakistan. While expansion of outlays on the civil service is inevitable in a growing economy with government playing an increasing role, there are reasons to believe that the quality and standard of efficiency of public service has not improved in proportion to its increasing cost. There is truth in the view "that the unwieldy government apparatus in underdeveloped economies covers a large measure of disguised unemployment and functions inefficiently and sluggishly."[29] The expenditures on social welfare measures including social security have also been on the increase in many South Asian countries. The figures on such expenditures in India, Pakistan, and Sri Lanka given in Table 3-5 are quite revealing.

The government of Sri Lanka has been subsidizing food by selling it

Table 3-5 Expenditure on Social Welfare 1950-1974

Country	Years	Total expenditure on social welfare[a] (Rs million)
India	First Plan 1950-1955	16.0
	Second Plan 1955-1960	134.0
	Third Plan 1961-1966	194.0
	Fourth Plan 1969-1974	413.8
Pakistan	First Plan 1955-1960	33.0
	Third Plan 1965-1970	90.0
Sri Lanka	1950	31.4
	1956	63.4
	1960	94.8
	1972	96.0

[a]Expenditure on social welfare includes social security benefits (in Sri Lanka) and expenditure for the benefit of disabled old and other weaker sections of the population.

SOURCE: Government of India, Planning Commission, *Fourth Five Year Plan, 1969-1974* (New Delhi, 1970), p. 408.
Government of Pakistan, Ministry of Finance, *Pakistan Economic Survey, 1969-1970* (Islamabad, 1971), p. 250.
Planning Commission, *Preliminary Evaluation of the Third Five Year Plan, 1965-1970* (Islamabad, 1970), p. 175.

to consumers at rates cheaper than import prices; for example, rice was sold to the consumer at less than one-third of its import price. The total expenditure on food subsidies increased from Rs 59.0 million to Rs 81.9 million during the period 1950-1960.[30] Attempts by the government to discontinue this subsidy met with serious opposition from the general public in the shape of violent demonstrations and hunger marches. During 1951-1952, one-third of government expenditures was spent on transfers and subsidies, with food subsidies bulking large in the total. We do not mean to suggest that these expenditures are uncalled for. On the contrary, it is our contention that there is need for larger expenditures on social welfare to ameliorate the desperate plight of South Asia's teeming millions. But such expenditures do divert public funds away from investment for industrial development and construction—where the yield would be much more rapid and more tangible than is investment in human capital, including social welfare. It should be emphasized that in this respect the present situation in South Asia is quite different from that which prevailed in the early stages of industrialization. The main emphasis, then, was on the increased production of goods; public responsibility for social welfare came much later, *following* development. As Irene Tauber remarks about Japan, "the state concentrated its resources on industrialization, expansion and power; it assumed no responsibility for individuals and family members."[31]

In order to meet this increasing demand for government outlays, the financial resources at the disposal of the state would have to be augmented. The normal measures adopted by governments in this connection would include taxation, internal borrowing, and deficit financing. The last two of these, internal borrowing and deficit financing, have only limited scope in an underdeveloped country because of the absence of developed money markets and financial institutions. The experience of the South Asian countries in recent years in attempting to mobilize voluntary savings through small savings schemes and the floating of loans has not been encouraging. As for deficit financing, though widely used in recent years in many developing countries, it incurs dangers and uncertainties, including inflation, that are becoming increasingly obvious. Countries like India and Pakistan, which once enthusiastically welcomed deficit financing for their development plans, have now adopted a more cautious attitude. Taxation is, thus, the most important potential source for raising the revenues needed to meet increasing government expenditures.

The experience of most underdeveloped countries in raising tax revenues has not been very happy. Normally, as economic growth takes place, tax revenues tend to become an increasing proportion of the national income. The figures in Table 3–6 show that great variations exist between the tax revenues collected by the developed countries and those of South Asia. It may be pointed out that in the case of the South Asian countries, these ratios have not seen any appreciable increase since 1970. Also, according to the Indian Taxation Enquiry Commission, the nominal value of national income increased about fourfold during World War II and in the postwar years, and per capita tax revenues went up by about the same proportion. In other words, there has been very little addition to the national tax effort for over three decades. According

Table 3-6 Tax Revenues as a Percentage of National Income, 1970

Country	Percentage
India	12.8
Pakistan	9.1
Sri Lanka	18.3
Japan	25.3
Canada	29.1
U.S.A.	30.0
U.K.	34.0

SOURCE: United Nations, *Statistical Year Book, 1972* (New York: 1973), p. 258.

to a 1960 United Nations Survey,[32] while in recent years India has made good progress, especially in industrialization, the fiscal system still remains quite underdeveloped, in that India ranks as one of the lowest in terms of the proportion of revenues collected to national income. In Pakistan, tax revenue as a percentage of national income increased from 6.4 in 1954–1955 to 9.5 in 1969–1970; the level, however, is still very low.

What are the main problems in the tax structure of the South Asian countries which prevent an increase in tax revenues commensurate with the growth in their national incomes? In other words, how do we explain the lack of flexibility in the tax structure of these countries? First, while developed nations derive a major part of their tax revenues from direct taxation, particularly taxes on personal and corporate incomes, the underdeveloped countries of South Asia rely more on indirect taxation, especially sales and excise taxes and custom duties. In the United States, direct taxation accounts for about 80 percent of federal revenues; in Great Britain, it provides 57 percent; in India and Pakistan direct taxation (on income and land) contributes only about 25 percent and 23 percent, respectively, of tax revenues.[33] Direct taxation, being more responsive to changes in income, provides more revenues as the level of national income increases. Indirect taxation—excise and sales taxes and custom duties on which the South Asian countries put their main reliance—is less responsive to changes in income (i.e., less flexible) and therefore less reliable as a source of funds for economic development.

Another serious problem in the tax structure of the South Asian countries is the narrow base, the small percentage of the population subject to direct taxation. Whereas, in developed countries the income tax base is so broad (e.g., in the United States about 95 percent of households file income tax returns) that the tax can be considered truly national, in India, Pakistan, and Nepal, less than 1 percent of the population is subject to any income tax. In Sri Lanka, only about 15 percent of total personal income is subject to taxation. The main reasons for this extremely low tax base are: the low income of the general population, high exemption limits, and laxity in tax administration (the assessment and collection of income tax), resulting in large-scale tax evasion. The South Asian countries are becoming increasingly aware of the need to introduce tax reforms, with a view toward making the tax structure (1) cover a broader population base and (2) become more flexible.

Another deficiency in the tax structure of the South Asian countries is the imbalance in the tax burden now borne by the nonagricultural sector. This imbalance causes inequity in the tax treatment of different occupational groups, and also results in a serious shortfall in revenues.[34] Since the first development plan was launched in the 1950s, there has been an income shift from the urban to the rural sector. In other words, the terms of trade have shifted in favor of the agricultural sector, as indicated by the increasing disparity between the prices received by farmers for agricultural commodities and the prices paid by them for nonagricultural commodities.[35] The nonagricultural sector seems not only to have fared worse in the matter of overall income distribution but has also borne the major brunt of the tax burden in the South Asian countries. According to E. T. Mathew, the per capita net burden of agricultural taxation (taxes paid minus the share of public expenditure by the agricultural sector) is about Rs 6.88, or 3.2 percent of per capita income in the agricultural sector, whereas the corresponding burden in the nonagricultural sector is 7.2 percent of per capita income.[36] Studies made by V. P. Gandhi on the relative burden of taxation borne by different sectors of the Indian economy confirm this view. Gandhi found that in 1951-1952, the agricultural sector contributed Rs 2 billion in direct and indirect taxes, whereas the nonagricultural sector contributed Rs 4.5 billion; thus, the ratio of tax revenues from the two sectors was 44.4. By 1968-1969, the ratio had declined to 33.61, indicating that during the period 1950-1969, the tax share of the agricultural sector, instead of rising, had actually fallen.[37]

The corresponding data for Pakistan are shown in Table 3-7. In Pakistan, as in India, the tax burden is greater on the nonagricultural sector than it is on the agricultural sector. The comparatively lower taxation imposed on agricultural income indicates that 80-85 percent of the rural population is not bearing its due burden of financing

Table 3-7 Ratio of Agricultural and Nonagricultural Taxes to Pakistan's Income and Marginal Propensity of Taxes

| Tax | Tax base | Tax revenues as proportion of national income | | Marginal propensity of tax — 1954-1955 to 1965-1966 |
		1954-1957	1963-1966	
Income tax and corporation tax	Nonagricultural income	1.10%	1.49%	3.60%
Land tax	Agricultural income	0.55	0.47	0.70

SOURCE: Government of Pakistan, *Pakistan Economic Survey 1963-64* (Karachi, 1964), pp. 175-202.
P. C. Verma, "Growth of Tax Revenue in Pakistan," *Economic and Political Weekly,* vol. 4, No. 49 (December 6, 1969), 1895.

government expenditures or providing much-needed capital for economic development. We may point out once again that there are many instances—Japan and the Soviet Union in the past, and China today—where industrial development was financed by heavy taxation of the agricultural sector. It is clear that in the South Asian economies, too, the agricultural sector will soon have to bear a greater burden of financing industrial development.

Why has the agricultural sector in the South Asian countries not been as heavily taxed as the nonagricultural sector? One reason, of course, is the comparatively lower per capita income and the general poverty among the rural masses. Heavier taxation of the nonagricultural sector, which is comparatively better off, can be defended on the grounds of ability to pay and equity. But the more important reason seems to be the reluctance of the governments in South Asia to increase taxation on the agricultural sector—which constitutes the "vote banks"—or to raise taxes at all. In fact, during the recent general elections in India and Sri Lanka, many political parties issued election manifestos calling for the lowering of taxes!

As we have shown, with increasing government expenditures and tax revenues lagging behind, the share of government savings for total capital formation in the South Asian countries is not increasing at a sufficient rate to finance development plans. The governments seem, however, to be well aware of the problem, and they are giving serious attention to savings mobilization through various fiscal measures. In India, the Direct Taxes Enquiry Committee, appointed in 1970, has recommended several measures to make the Indian tax structures more effective in reducing tax evasion, taxing agricultural incomes at a uniform rate in the various Indian states, and closing tax loopholes. India has levied additional taxes—the proportion of tax revenue to GNP rose from 6.4 percent in 1950–1951 to 12.8 percent in 1970–1971. Much of this, however, was diverted to increased defense expenditure rather than development expenditure. During the decade 1960–1961 to 1970–1971, while development expenditure increased by 171 percent, the comparable increase of nondevelopment expenditure was 288 percent. Despite efforts to levy additional direct taxes, such as those on personal and corporate incomes, indirect taxes still registered a greater increase than direct taxes. During the period 1950–1951 to 1968–1969, direct taxes increased by about 300 percent, indirect taxes by nearly 700 percent. The Indian Planning Commission justified the increase in commodity taxes to "restrain conspicuous consumption by affluent sections of the society."[38] The Indian Planning Commission has stated that during the fifth five-year plan (1975–1980) the main thrust will be on "conprehensive direct tax reform to check evasion and avoidance of all kinds and to make the tax system elastic to income growth." Efforts will also be made "to bring agricultural incomes within the tax net."[39]

In Pakistan, the rates of central excise tax and sales tax were increased substantially to raise additional revenues for development plans. As a result, tax receipts as a percentage of GNP increased from 6.1 percent in 1959–1960 to 9.1 percent in 1969–1970.[40] Efforts were also made to cut down unnecessary nondevelopment expenditure. The result was that the deficit on current revenue account (total revenues minus government expenditure, other than capital expenditure) of Rs 193 million in 1965–1966, was turned into a surplus of Rs 2,516 million in 1969–1970.

In spite of these modest attempts to gear fiscal structure to capital accumulation in the form of government savings, the South Asian countries have a long way to go to fill the growing gap between the capital needed to execute development plans and the savings contribution of households and the private business sector. In the last analysis, all hopes for economic development in South Asia may well depend on the effectiveness of government as the "saver of last resort."

Foreign Capital The importance of foreign capital in an underdeveloped country, especially during initial stages of economic development, needs no emphasis. It can augment the meager domestic savings for investment. It can facilitate the undertaking of crucial large-scale projects such as irrigation and power projects and the building up of heavy and basic industries with a high import content and long gestation periods. Foreign capital also brings with it scarce technical knowledge, entrepreneurship, and business management practices.

> External assistance becomes inevitable not merely to fill up the gap of domestic savings but also to create necessary conditions in which fuller and proper utilization of human and material resources become possible.[41]

Historically, foreign capital played an important part in the economic development of many nations. The United States and Canada owe much of their early economic development to imported capital. And, during the post–World War II period, the economic reconstruction of Western Europe and Japan owed much to foreign assistance.

In the developing economies of Asia, Africa, and Latin America about 20 percent of total investment during 1970–1974 was made possible by an inflow of foreign funds. In the case of the South Asian countries, the crucial role of foreign capital was recognized from the very beginning of economic planning. According to India's first five-year plan (1951–1956), external assistance "would make available adequate supplies of foreign exchange and also supplement the investable resources of the community."[42] India, in fact, was the recipient of a greater amount and variety of external assistance during the decade 1951–1961 than was provided for any other underdeveloped country during this period.[43] The number of countries and institutions from which India received assistance was also without precedent. Pakistan also received substantial foreign assistance, which during 1954–1955 reached a peak of 46.1 percent of total investment capital.[44]

We will now examine the problems of foreign capital—its impact and future prospects—under its component parts: foreign assistance and private foreign investments.

Foreign Assistance. Foreign assistance includes (1) financial assistance in the form of loans and credits repayable in foreign or local currencies, (2) grants, and (3) commodity assistance—surplus food such as that given by the United States under PL 480 and PL 665.

Foreign assistance authorized by India from August 15, 1947, to March 31, 1975, totaled Rs 184 billion. The assistance utilized during this period amounted to Rs 151 billion (a utilization rate of 88 percent). The breakdown of this assistance is as follows: loans, 79 percent; commodity assistance, 14 percent; grants, 7 percent.[45] The donor sources were: the United States (45.0 percent), the International Bank for Reconstruction and Development (15.8 percent), Great Britain (9.1 percent), West Germany (8.1 percent), the Soviet Union (5.4 percent), and Japan (3.3 percent). Of this total external assistance, about 20 percent was in "untied" credits while 80 percent of credits were for specific projects. During the period 1947–1974, Rs 41 billion (27 percent of the total assistance utilized) was paid for debt servicing, amortization, and interest, payments.

The overall importance of external assistance in India's total investment and GNP can be seen in Table 3–8.

External assistance is declining relative to both the net national product and aggregate investment. The main reasons for this decline are that the aid-giving nations are themselves facing financial difficulties, also the food surpluses of the 1960s are no longer available.

The pattern of foreign aid utilization by India is given in Table 3–9. It may be noted that the largest utilization of external assistance was in the area of overall industrial development and steel industry projects, followed by investments in transportation and communication systems. These investments in infrastructure have long gestation periods, and it may take several years before their full impact on the economy is known.

The pattern of external assistance received by Pakistan (including Bangladesh) is similar to that of India. Figures in Table 3–10 show its relative importance in the national economy.

Table 3-8 External Assistance as a Proportion of Investment
and Net National Product in India, 1960-1974

Years	Aggregate investment	Net national product
1960-1961	25.8%	3.1%
1968-1969	13.4	1.3
1969-1970	8.5	0.8
1970-1971	10.6	1.2
1971-1972	11.6	1.5
1972-1973	6.7	0.8
1973-1974	7.4	0.8

SOURCE: Reserve Bank of India, *Report on Currency and Finance, 1973-1974*
(Bombay, 1975), p. 11.

What has been the impact of external aid on the economic
development of the South Asian countries? Foreign aid has been a mixed
blessing. On the plus side, through commodity aid the countries have
obtained food grains, which during some lean years in India were helpful
in preventing near-famine conditions. To some extent, food aid also
counteracted the inflationary effects of heavy deficit financing
undertaken for the development plans of both India and Pakistan.
Dandekar has summed up the contribution of commodity aid:

> This aid provided substantial additional resources for investment in plans
> of economic development. In the absence of the funds obtained through

Table 3-9 Distribution of External Assistance in India
through March 1974

Purpose for which utilized	Percentage of total assistance
Industrial development and iron and steel projects	67
Transport and communications	12
Agricultural development	6
Irrigation and power projects	5
Food aid	1
Miscellaneous	9
	100

SOURCE: A. N. Agarwal, *Indian Economy* (Delhi: Vikas, 1975), p. 634.
Reserve Bank of India, *Report on Currency and Finance,* 1973-1974
(Bombay, 1975), pp. 154-185.

Table 3-10 External Assistance as Proportion of National Product and Aggregate Investment in Pakistan (Including Bangladesh)

Year	Aggregate investment	Net national product
1954-1955	46.1%	5.0%
1964-1965	40.0	6.3
1969-1970	32.1	6.0
1973-1974	21.0	5.0
1980 (projected)	9.0	1.9
1985 (projected)	5.0	1.1

SOURCE: Government of Pakistan, Planning Commission, *Third Five Year Plan, 1965-1970* (Karachi, 1965).
Mahbub-ul Haq, *The Strategy of Economic Planning: A Case Study of Pakistan* (Karachi: Oxford University Press, 1963), p. 179.

the sale of PL 480 imports in this country, India would have possibly taken to either a smaller plan, or larger deficit financing or more stringent measures for raising local resources. Apart from those, the imports under PL 480 helped raise the cereal consumption of the Indian people, which would not have been possible with the help of internal production and commercial imports.[46]

The foreign exchange component of loans and credits enabled these countries to create crucial social and economic infrastructures by importing capital goods from the hard currency areas. To that extent the external assistance also helped their balance of payments position. As a part of the technical assistance programs, improved technology was introduced in health, agriculture, and small-scale industries.

There are, however, several negative aspects of external assistance. It is held that the "productivity effect" of external assistance was rather meager. Stanley Katz, using the data on income, savings, and investment in India for the period 1951–1961, calculated that only "one-eighth of the increase in total Indian savings and over one-fifth of the increase in Indian investment during the decade were a product of external assistance."[47]

As regards the contribution of foreign assistance to the Indian economy, Katz found that, "The aid contribution to Indian economic activity in terms of the volumes of income and saving was of minor proportions."[48] External aid also did not contribute significantly to alleviating the unemployment problem, since much of the aid was used for capital intensive projects (see Table 3–10). In Nurske's view the export of capital goods, specifically machinery for producing steel, as a part of foreign assistance to India, were more in the interests of the aid-giving countries.[49]

The element of uncertainty entailed in foreign aid also created a number of problems and complications for economic planning for the recipient countries. For example, Indian economists feel that the sudden suspension of U.S. aid to India after the Indo-Pakistan conflict in 1971 threw the fourth five-year plan out of gear. Moreover, because a major proportion of foreign assistance was in the form of tied aid, or project aid, the recipient countries were expected to buy from the donor countries or to use such aid for the purchase of specified goods on specified projects. This prevented optimal use of freely available resources.

> Assistance for economic development added up eventually to large amounts, but it came in innumerable small packets, commonly tied to a particular source of supply, and often there was much uncertainty and delay before each separate packet of aid could be converted into supplies of machinery, components and materials. The disadvantages of tied aid and the behaviour costs it entails for recipient countries are now better appreciated. On the whole, the process through which assistance was received tended to increase the costs and diminish the efficiency of development.[50]

It has also been argued that commodity trade under PL 480 has had an indirect, detrimental effect on the economy, especially in agriculture. Commodity aid created a deterrent effect on Indian farmers who decreased farm output. Through the importation of huge quantities of food, the prices of farm products were held down while at the same time the prices paid by farmers for water, fertilizer, machinery, and other inputs as well as for consumer goods continued to rise. According to Katz, "the officially preserved structure of domestic prices—strongly abetted by commodity aid—did not act as an incentive to agricultural output but rather [discouraged] it."[51] Christopher Beringer and Irshad Ahmad[52] found similar effects of commodity aid for Pakistan agriculture. Moreover, the South Asian countries came to depend on the supply of foreign food "to the point of national humiliation."[53] Dependence on foreign assistance also created a state of complacency on the part of the governments, which did not pursue vigorously the promotion of local initiatives for raising agricultural productivity. The easy availability of food grains from abroad and under soft loan conditions made these countries neglectful of the urgent need for agricultural development.

However, the most serious problem in the context of external assistance facing South Asia is the problem of a mounting debt-servicing burden, including amortization payments, which is akin to "reverse flow" of resources. This reverse flow has greatly reduced net external assistance as a percentage of gross assistance.[54] In India, the percentage dropped from 86.6 percent in the second five-year plan to 50 percent during the fourth plan.[55] The problem of reverse flow has since assumed serious proportions and its implications for the future are rather grave. This is brought out in Table 3-11 giving data for India for the year 1973-1974. The figures show that India was left with only 30 percent of gross external assistance to use for development. The staggering burden of debt servicing, amounting to as much as 11.9 percent of domestic savings and 24 percent of export earnings continues to be a serious obstacle in India's economic development. It is ironic that India should have to shoulder such a heavy repayment cost for external assistance, which did not contribute greatly to increased productivity.

Pakistan's experience has been rather similar. According to Naqvi,

> In the process the economy has also been saddled with large foreign debt servicing liabilities which up to 1965-66 amounted to Rs 1413 million and formed 8.4 percent of Pakistan's total foreign exchange earnings . . . . This strain on the economy and the country's balance of payment will become gradually more severe as interest and amortization charges grow at a compound rate.[56]

In any event, South Asia appears to have reached the end of the road of foreign assistance—unless outright grants are available in the future. This seems unlikely in the light of the international situation since 1970.

Foreign   Investments   (Private).   Investments   by   foreign corporations and businesses have a multifaceted role in the development process of the developing economics. Foreign investments can bring much-needed foreign exchange and technical skills to the less developed countries. Also, they can fill gaps in the local availability of crucial inputs, particularly capital and entrepreneurship. These were precisely the reasons advanced for the flow of large amounts of Western private capital to the developing nations of Asia, Africa, and Latin America.

Table 3-11 Debt Servicing as a Percentage of Selected Variables, India, 1973-1974

External assistance	= 70.00%
National income	= 1.23
Export earnings	= 24.00
Tax revenue of central government	= 6.68
Domestic savings	= 11.90

SOURCE: Government of India, *Economic Survey,* 1975-1976 (New Delhi, 1976). Reserve Bank of India, *Report on Currency and Finance, 1974-1975* (Bombay, 1975).

Large amounts of Western capital came into South Asia during the second half of the nineteenth century, after the British government established political domination over the Indian subcontinent. The Indian nationalist writers claim that there was no real dearth of Indian capital during that period but that it was the deliberate policy of the British government to encourage British companies "to participate in the great exploits of India."[57] British companies were given various preferential terms, including a guaranteed rate of return on investments, facilities for remitting profit and capital, and virtual monopoly rights in their respective areas of investment. British capital was chiefly invested in plantations, banking and trade, and consumer goods industries, to the complete neglect of investment in capital goods.[58] Companies were staffed with British personnel, except for the local people employed as clerks and menials. These companies enjoyed the political patronage of the British government, and their investment policies were guided almost entirely by the profit motive and the interests of Britain.

For these reasons, foreign investments in South Asia did not have much "trickle down effect." While the countries remained underdeveloped and poor, the presence of foreign firms was like "small oases in the vast desert." All these circumstances were greatly resented by nationalist leaders and the need for "regulation and control of foreign investments" became a part of their program for the political and economic liberation of the Indian subcontinent. It was felt that though foreign capital was required to augment domestic investments, it was necessary to prevent some of its abuses.

Since the attainment of independence, and particularly lately, the governments of the region have shown understandable wariness toward private foreign investment. They have attempted to lay down guidelines and prohibitions on the conduct of foreign enterprises that would encourage investors and, at the same time, safeguard the interests of the host countries. In general, they have the following features in common:

1. There will be no discrimination between foreign and local undertakings; reasonable facilities will be given for the remittance of profits and the repatriation of capital and, in the event of nationalization, fair and equitable compensation will be paid.
2. Foreign firms should gradually employ more local capital and manpower. (In India, foreign firms with more than 50 percent equity held by foreigners are allowed to participate in the economy on the same terms and conditions as the domestic firms. In the event of their expansion, however, an increasing proportion of the equity capital must be owned by Indians.
3. Collaboration with foreign firms is permitted specifically in fields of high industrial priority and in areas where the import of foreign technology is necessary. In the case of foreign equity participation, a

selective policy is adopted on the basis of the priority of the industry, the nature of the technology and the export potential of the firm. India has a ceiling of 40 percent on foreign equity, to be relaxed only for exceptional cases. Foreign technical collaboration is permitted for a limited period (5 years in India) with regulated amounts of royalties payable to foreign technical personnel.

The essence of government policies toward foreign capital in the South Asian countries is summed up by the government of Sri Lanka:

It is government's policy to welcome private foreign investments in fields (i) where local private capital is not established or likely to do so in the near future, (ii) which will strengthen the country's economy, (iii) where there will be progressive domestic manufacture eliminating ultimately all imports to the most practical extent. Subject to these conditions, Sri Lanka would provide incentives and concessions (such as tax holidays, tariff protection).[59]

Foreign investments may be divided into: (1) direct investment capital, which covers the net assets of the branches of foreign companies and equity in foreign-controlled companies held by controlling foreign investors, such as the subsidiaries of foreign companies, and (2) other capital, such as creditor capital and portfolio equity holdings, which comprise foreign holdings of portfolio equity in domestic companies and foreign holdings of shares and debentures, foreign currency loans, and suppliers' credits obtained by domestic companies. Foreign direct investment differs from creditor capital, or portfolio capital, in that it confers on the investing entity an ability to exercise control over the decision-making process of the entity in which it invests.

The growth of private foreign investments in India is shown in Table 3–12.

It will be observed that although foreign investments, in absolute terms, have risen, the rate of increase has been declining from the annual 9.3 percent during 1955–1967 to only 3.4 percent during 1967–1972. Considering the fact that India provides a heavily protected and very profitable domestic market one would expect it to attract a sizable amount of private foreign capital. Compared to other developing countries, however, such as Mexico, Taiwan, and Malaysia, whose markets are far less protected than those of India, the inflows of private foreign capital into India have been meager. According to Balasubramanyam, from 1961 to 1966 the net flow of private capital into India accounted for only 7.5 percent of total investment in the private sector.[60] In the case of Malaysia, from 1960 to 1963, private foreign capital accounted, on average, for nearly 30 percent of total capital formation in the private sector.

Table 3-12 Foreign Investments in India, 1948-1972
(in millions of dollars)

	End 1948	End 1955	End 1967	End 1972
a. Direct investments		811.6	934.0	1,086.5
1. Branches		510.5	387.5	308.0
2. Subsidiaries & other controlled		301.1	546.5	778.5
b. Portfolio investment		117.4	1,042.5	1,248.0
1. Equity		82.3	84.3	129.0
2. Creditor capital		35.1	958.2	1,119.0
Grand Total (a plus b)	799.8	929.0	1,976.5	2,334.5

SOURCE: Reserve Bank of India, *Bulletin, July* 1975, pp. 414-456.
United Nations, *Economic Survey of Asia and the Far East, 1970*
(Bangkok, 1971), pp. 55-63.

The reasons for the declining importance of private foreign investments in the Indian economy are summed up by Balasubramanyam:

> The Indian policy statements, though not lacking in incentives for private foreign capital, display an ambivalent attitude towards it. Assurances regarding repatriation of profits and compensation in case of nationalization and tax incentives are proffered. But the protracted negotiations which a policy of judging each case on its merits involves, the insistence that majority ownership of capital should rest in Indian hands, and the stipulations regarding employment of local nationals may have discouraged foreign investors.[61]

The Planning Commission of Pakistan explained a similar declining trend[62] in the importance of private foreign investment in the national economy.

> Current permission about the inflow of private foreign investment can be ascribed to a number of reasons, the most important of which is the comparative return on investment in the developed countries themselves notably Canada, Australia and certain parts of Europe. Pakistan's interest in private foreign investment is primarily on account of technical knowhow and the managerial skill that accompany such investments. . . . Pakistan interest in foreign investment is primarily on account of capital goods industries, in which rate of return is lower than consumer goods industries.[63]

As regards the pattern of foreign investments, there is a continued preference for direct investments, specifically subsidiaries, rather than minority participation through equity capital or simple technical collaboration. The figures in Table 3–13 show that from 1967 to 1972 the ratio of direct investments to total foreign investments was around 47.5 percent. This continued investor preference for control is inconsistent with the Indian government policy of diverting private investments to a minority participation pattern as part of the Indianization of foreign firms and is resented by nationalist elements.

It is also contended not only that the foreign investment inflow has been declining but that a substantial part of foreign direct investment in recent years has been in the form of reinvested earnings, rather than cash inflows.[64] According to MacBean and Balasubramanyam, the ratio of reinvested earnings to direct investment inflows in India increased from 35 percent in 1963–1964 to 60 percent in 1966–1967.[65] This decreasing net inflow of fresh foreign capital shows that foreign investments are becoming less useful in improving India's balance of payments position. Another cause for concern about private foreign investments and the importation of technology are their effects on the balance of payments of the country. Indian data for the period 1964–1967 show that the outflow of capital in the form of dividends, profits, royalties, and technical fee payments exceeded the inflow of private foreign capital. In 1966–1967 the inflow of private foreign investment was Rs 1,046 million as against an outflow of Rs 2,039 million as investment income.[66] Thus private foreign investments are, in fact, adversely affecting India's balance of payments.

The composition and sources of private foreign investments have undergone certain changes in the South Asian countries. In India, changes in the distribution of foreign investments by sector are given in Table 3–13. This changing pattern shows a shift toward the

Table 3-13 Sector Distribution of Foreign Direct Investments in India, as a Percentage of Total Foreign Investments, 1948-1972

Sector	End 1948	End 1955	End 1967	End 1972
Manufacturing	27.8%	29.2%	49.0%	57.0%
Services	38.6	25.5	24.2	24.7
Petroleum	8.7	23.5	11.0	10.2
Plantations	20.4	19.7	15.1	7.2
Mining	4.5	2.1	00.7	0.9
Total	100.0	100.0	100.0	100.0

SOURCE: Reserve Bank of India, *Bulletin*—various issues.

manufacturing sector, especially of chemicals, metals and metal products, machinery and tools, and transport equipment, and a shift away from mining and plantations. This shift is consistent with the official policy of the government of India discouraging foreign investments in the service, plantation, and mining sectors. It is ironic that the role of private foreign investments has started to decline just when these investments were stepping up their relative contribution to the manufacture of much-needed capital goods.

Significant changes have also occurred in the sources of supply of private foreign capital. Traditionally, Great Britain has been the major source of direct investments for the South Asian countries. Although it still leads the field, its share declined from 80 percent of total foreign investment in India at the end of 1948 to only 36.2 percent by 1972. Investments by the United States, on the other hand, have increased from 4.2 percent of the total in 1948 to 27.2 percent by 1972. West Germany, Italy, and Japan, which did not invest at all in 1948, invested 7.7 percent, 4.8 percent, and 3.1 percent, respectively, by the end of 1972.[67] This change in sources of fiscal supply is likely to be beneficial to the Indian economy. Now, new investor nations are more likely to be willing to explore the area and make the best of available opportunities. The interest of several new investor nations provides a broader range of capital sources and technology for the South Asian countries to draw upon.

SUMMARY

The foregoing review shows that during the early stages of development, foreign investments played a crucial role in South Asia, especially in major industries such as petroleum refining, chemicals and pharmaceuticals, light and heavy engineering, and artificial fibre manufacture. These industries owe much of their development in India to the technology and skills obtained from abroad. Through the several joint ventures between South Asian business firms and foreign companies, local business has gained in technical skills and the skills of modern management, including production planning and material control. On the other hand, the inflow of new private foreign investments into South Asia, especially India, has been relatively meager. Much of the increase in direct investments that has occurred is due to reinvestment of profits rather than the inflow of new capital. At present the outflow of royalties, dividends, and the like exceeds the inflow of new foreign private capital. In these circumstances, private foreign investments do not make a positive contribution to the balance of payments position.

The South Asian nations are caught in a dilemma. Foreign funds are desperately needed and these countries have shown their willingness to provide various fiscal benefits, such as tax holidays, accelerated depreciation allowances, and assurances of facilities for remission of dividends and capital. They tend to insist, however, on (1) localization of foreign firms by employing more local capital and labor, and (2) the demarcation of specific fields for foreign capital by discouraging investments in nonpriority fields such AS consumer goods industries and plantations. Such restrictions frighten away foreign investors, who then tend to move on to other countries with more favorable terms. From various policy statements issued by the South Asian countries it seems that they have chosen to accept the declining inflow of foreign capital, including private foreign investments, rather than change their basic policies in this respect. They are tending to put greater emphasis on self-reliance and on financing their development plans through domestic sources. The Indian Planning Commission has stated:

> What we seek is a dynamic self-reliance where the rate of growth is accelerated while, at the same time, developing the capability to sustain it essentially from our own resources. It is, thus, envisaged that by 1985–86 economic growth would be basically self-sustaining.[68]

The Indian Planning Commission expects that India will not need any "significant inflow of foreign capital on normal commercial terms."[69] Self-reliance in capital formation is not easy to achieve in view of the existing deficiencies in capital formation and the difficulties in raising additional domestic capital. But the future economic development of the South Asian countries may well depend on the success of their experiment in self-reliance.

NOTES

1. Ragnar Nurske, *Problems of Capital Formation in Underdeveloped Countries* (Oxford: Blackwell, 1953), p. 5.

2. R. Nevin, *Capital Funds in Underdeveloped Countries* (New York: St. Martin's, 1961), p. xi.

3. William Letwin, "Four Fallacies about Economic Development," *Daedalus*, Summer 1963, p. 403.

4. See for example, M. Abramovitz, "Resources and Output Trends in the United States since 1870," *American Economic Review*, 46 (May 1956), 5–23; Robert Solow, "Technical Change and the Aggregate Production Function," *Review of Economics and Statistics*, 39 (August 1957), 312–320; and E. O. Domar, "On the Measurement of Technical Change," *Economic Journal*, 71 (December 1961), 709–729.

5. Government of India, Planning Commission, *Third Five Year Plan, 1960–65*, (New Delhi, 1961), p. 92.

6. Wilfred Owen, *Distance and Development* (Washington, D.C.: The Brookings Institution, 1968), pp. 3–4.

7. S. M. Akhtar, *Economic Development of Pakistan* (Lahore: Publishers United

1969), pp. 122-123.

8. Nurske, *Capital Formation,* p. 2.

9. T. W. Schultz, *The Economic Value of Education* (New York: Colombia University Press, 1963), p. x.

10. Economic development encompasses a host of variables, such as physical and human capital, social and religious structures (including the work ethic), incentive systems, and overall organization. As pointed out in chapter 1, the South Asian countries do not presently face a shortage of educated manpower in relation to their existing level of development. Work ethic tends to develop when the worker is assured of the accrual of an adequate return for his hard work and is equipped with the requisite tools of production. In the South Asian countries, the seeming disinclination for hard work could be the product of acute poverty, resulting from chronic unemployment, and the lack of scope for any economic betterment. (The precepts relating to work that are contained in the Hindu religious system, including some elements of "dualism," are discussed in chapter 6.) Thus, the lack of physical capital remains the major impediment in the way of economic development in South Asia.

11. For the historical experience of the advanced countries, see D. Bright Singh, *Economics of Development* (Bombay: Asia Publishing House, 1963), pp. 149-150; and Benjamin Higgins, *Economic Development* (New York: Norton, 1968), pp. 181-192.

12. W. W. Rostow, *The Stages of Economic Growth* (Cambridge: The University Press, 1961), p. 37.

13. W. Arthur Lewis, *Theory of Economic Growth* (London: Allen & Unwin, 1963), p. 226.

14. Denoting all changes by Δ, national income by y, savings by S, the rate of saving by s, net investment by I, capital-output ratio by k, and the growth rate of income by g, we have the following equations:

$$k = \frac{I}{\Delta Y} \tag{1}$$

$$g = \frac{\Delta Y}{Y} \tag{2}$$

Multiplying both the numerator and the denominator of (2) by I, we get

$$\frac{I}{I} \cdot \frac{\Delta Y}{Y} = \frac{I/Y}{I/\Delta Y} \tag{3}$$

Since, by the equilibrium assumption, savings equal investment, we have

$$\begin{aligned} S &= I, \text{ and since by definition} \\ s &= S/Y \end{aligned} \tag{4}$$

we can write

$$s = I/Y \tag{5}$$

By substituting (5) and (1) into (3), we obtain

$$g = \frac{s}{k}$$

15. For a detailed discussion, see D. Bright Singh, *Economics of Development,* pp. 155-164.

16. M. Abramovitz, "Savings and Investment: Profits vs. Prosperity?" *American Economic Review,* vol. 32, no. 2 (June 1942), 53-88.

17. For further detail, see V. P. Gandhi, *Some Aspects of India's Tax Structure: An Economic Analysis* (Bombay: Vora, 1970); and National Council of Applied Economic

Research, *Taxation and Private Investment* (New Delhi, 1961).

18. For a discussion of the social and political climate which helped the growth of capitalism, see Joseph Schumpeter, *The Theory of Economic Development* (New York: Oxford University Press, 1961), pp. 128–156.

19. Ruddar Datt and K. P. M. Sundharam, *Indian Economy* (New Delhi: Chand, 1975), p. 523.

20. For details on the pattern and determinants of household savings in India, see D. T. Lakadawala and R. J. Mody, *Financial Assets and Instruments for Mobilization of Savings* (Ahmedabad: Sardar Patel Institute of Economic and Social Research, 1975), pp. 10–28.

21. Government of Bangladesh, Planning Commission, *The First Five Year Plan, 1973–78* (Dacca, 1973), p. 42; P. W. Haskall, *Taxation of Agricultural Lands in Underdeveloped Countries* (Cambridge, Mass.: Harvard University Press, 1959); and Gandhi, *India's Tax Structure*, part III, pp. 129–171.

22. Lewis, *Theory of Economic Growth*, p. 236.

23. Willard W. Cochrane, *The World Food Problem: A Guardedly Optimistic View* (New York: Crowell, 1969), p. 310.

24. Ibid., pp. 310–311.

25. For a detailed discussion on the nature and measurement of disguised unemployment, see J. S. Uppal, *Disguised Unemployment in an Underdeveloped Economy* (New York: Asia Publishing House, 1973).

26. Nurske, *Capital Formation*.

27. Datt and Sundharam, *Indian Economy*, p. 139.

28. Ibid., p. 139.

29. Van Phillips and A. M. Paul, *Public Finance and Less Developed Economy with Special Reference to Latin America* (The Hague: Martinus Nijhoff, 1957), p. 95.

30. Donald R. Snodgrass, *Ceylon: An Export Economy in Transition* (Homewood, Ill.: Irwin, 1966), Statistical Appendix A–5.

31. Irene B. Tauber, "Japan's Population—Miracle Model or Case Study?" *Foreign Affairs*, July 1962, p. 597.

32. United Nations, *Economic Survey of Asia and the Far East, 1960* (New York, 1961), p. 85.

33. P. C. Verma, "Growth of Tax Revenue in Pakistan," *Economic and Political Weekly*, vol. 4, no. 49 (December 6, 1969), 1895.

34. Shetty has estimated the loss of potential revenues from untapped agricultural incomes due to inequity taxation (both direct and indirect) between the farm and nonfarm sectors in India. Removal of this inequity would yield additional tax revenues estimated at Rs 1,600 million per year (average for the years 1966–1967 and 1968–1969), or 12 to 14 percent of the total tax burden of the farm sector. In other words, taxation of the agricultural sector should be increased by about 14 percent to equity of taxation between the farm and nonfarm sectors. The additional tax revenues would raise significantly the amount of government savings—badly needed for economic development. S. L. Shetty, "Inter-Sectorial Equity in Tax Burden," *Economic and Political Weekly*, vol. 7, nos. 31–33 (1972), 1602–1612).

35. For a detailed discussion of these ratios, see M. L. Dantwala, *Agriculture in a Developing Economy* (Poona: Gokhale Institute of Politics and Economics, 1966).

36. E. T. Mathew, *Agricultural Taxation and Economic Development in India* (Bombay: Asia Publishing House, 1965), p. 26.

37. Ved P. Gandhi, *Tax Burden on Indian Agriculture* (Cambridge, Mass.: Harvard Law School, 1966), p. 35.

38. Government of India, Planning Commission, *Fourth Five Year Plan, 1969–74,* (New Delhi, 1970), p. 85.

39. Government of India, Planning Commission, *Towards an Approach to the Fifth Plan* (New Delhi, 1972), p. 17.

40. Government of Pakistan, Planning Commission, *Preliminary Evaluation of the Third Five Year Plan, 1965–70.* (Islamabad, 1970), p. 17.

41. H. B. Chenery and A. M. Strout, "External Assistance and Economic Development," *American Economic Review*, vol. 56, no. 4, part 1, (September 1966), 680–681.

42. Government of India, Planning Commission, *the First Five Year Plan, 1950–55* (New Delhi, 1951), p. 63.

43. Stanley Katz, *External Assistance and Indian Economic Growth* (New York: Asia Publishing House, 1968), p. 61.

44. Mahbub-ul Haq, *The Strategy of Economic Planning: A Case Study of Pakistan* (Karachi: Oxford University Press, 1963), pp. 179–180.

45. Reserve Bank of India, *Report on Currency and Finance, 1973–74* (Bombay, 1975), p. 11; and Commerce Research Bureau, *Basic Statistics Relating to the Indian Economy* (Bombay, October 1975), Table 9.

46. V. M. Dandekar, "Foreword," in N. Rath and V. S. Patwardhan, *Impact of Assistance under PL 480 on Indian Economy* (Poona: Gokhale Institute of Politics and Economics, 1967), p. ix.

47. Katz, *External Assistance,* pp. 46–47.

48. Ibid., p. 46.

49. Ragnar Nurske, "Reflections on India's Development Plan," *Quarterly Journal of Economics,* vol. 71, no. 1, (May 1957), 197.

50. Tarlok Singh, *India's Development Experience* (Delhi: Macmillan 1974), p. 332.

51. Katz, *External Assistance,* p. 50. Also, see Organization For Economic Cooperation and Development, *Food Aid: Its Role in Economic Development* (Paris, 1963).

52. Christopher Beringer and Irshad Ahmad, *The Use of Agricultural Surplus Commodities for the Economic Development of Pakistan* (Karachi: Institute of Development Economics, 1964).

53. Dandekar, "Foreword," p. ix.

54. See M. Arumugam, "Aid Flows and Indian Economic Crisis," *Mankind,* vol. 18, no. 4 (1974), 37–45.

55. Government of India, *Economic Survey 1974–75* (New Delhi, 1976), pp. 45–46.

56. S. N. H. Naqvi, "The Foreign Capital Requirements and External Indebtedness of Developing Country: A Case Study of Pakistan," in E. A. G. Robinson and Michael Kidron, eds., *Economic Development in South Asia* (London: St. Martin's, 1970), p. 505.

57. R. C. Dutt, *Economic History of India* (New Delhi: Manager of Publications, 1960).

58. For an illustration of this view, see V. N. Balasubramanyam "Foreign Private Investments in India," in J. S. Uppal, ed. *India's Economic Problems* (New Delhi: Tata McGraw-Hill, 1975), pp. 382–400.

59. Government of Ceylon, *The Ten Year Plan* (Colombo, 1959), p. 121.

60. Balasubramanyam, "Foreign Investments in India," p. 391.

61. Ibid., p. 392.

62. Government of Pakistan, Planning Commission, *Third Five Year Plan, 1965–70* (Karachi 1965), pp. 50–51.

63. Ibid., p. 94.

64. Ibid., p. 391.

65. A. I. MacBean and V. N. Balasubramanyam, *Benefit Cost Analysis of Foreign Direct Investment with Special Reference to Asia,* quoted in Subramanyam, *Foreign Private Investments,* pp. 390–391.

66. Ibid., p. 399.

67. Reserve Bank of India, *Bulletin,* various issues.

68. Government of India, Planning Commission, *Draft Fifth Five Year Plan 1974–79* (New Delhi, 1975), p. 4.

69. Ibid.

4

The Revolution of Rising Expectations

Today we live in the most revolutionary age that humans have ever experienced. A revolution is usually thought of as a single event or as one interconnected series of events. But, we are living through many simultaneous revolutions—all of them changing our thinking, ways of life, and ideals for the future. What are these revolutions? The first and most pervasive is the revolution for equality—equality as an all-embracing concept—the passionate desire to see oneself as equal to any other human being without distinction by class, sex, race, or nationality. Second, the revolution of freedom—the right of self-determination for all nations. Third is the biological revolution—the sudden and amazing decline in death rates in areas of the world where human beings died in large numbers, resulting in an unprecedented increase in the rate at which humans are multiplying. The fourth is the scientific and technological revolution—the application of science and technology to production processes, especially mass production which has increased the speed at which goods can be produced. A fifth revolution, of particular importance in its impact on the economic development of the underdeveloped countries, is the revolution of rising expectations—widening the gap between the expectations and "attainments" of hundreds of millions of people. According to Willard W. Cochrane:

> The common man throughout the less developed world has come to believe in, indeed to expect, economic progress for himself, his family, his community and his nation. . . . these people want and expect to receive this year, not next, improved medical services, a richer and more healthful diet, an improved mechanical means of transportation, a transistor radio, schooling for their children and such frivolities as soft drinks. . . . This is the revolution of rising expectations that has swept across the developing world.[1]

These revolutions, occurring simultaneously, have had a profound effect on the underdeveloped countries, especially since the end of World

War II. The revolutions for freedom and independence have culminated in their emancipation from the yoke of foreign domination to emerge as new sovereign nations. More than 1 billion people won independence over the last 25 years; 25 sovereign nations came into being in Africa in one year during 1960. In the few countries where alien rule still exists, there is bitter protest against foreign domination. Along with independence, the common man in the developing countries is asserting the revolution of equality in its various forms. A black African or a brown Asian is no longer prepared to tolerate any suggestion that because of color or race he is inferior in any way. The idea that Asians or Africans are not capable of self-rule, once widespread, is now spurned. Today, "black is beautiful" and "Asian civilizations are old and superior."

Inside these countries, citadels of feudalism are crumbling and the titles of princes, emperors, sheikhs, and maharajas are being cast aside. True, there are still some lingering distinctions based on economic or social factors, but the writing on the wall is clear—we are living in an era when there is a strong urge, in fact a passion, for equality. The revolution of rising expectations which is sweeping the backward areas of the world[2] has created desires and aspirations among the world's masses that have serious economic and social implications. In the words of William and Paul Paddock, "The Age of Rising Expectations—the expectations sprout upward like hothouse plants unaffected by the cold facts of life whether in Laos, India, Chad, or wherever."[3]

In this chapter, we will examine the nature and impact of the phenomenon of rising expectations on the countries of South Asia.

As already indicated, this phenomenon is explained by the widening gap between levels of expectation and attainment, as depicted in the accompanying figure. Line OA indicates rising expectations, line OB indicates needs satisfied or attained (i.e., needs which the economies are capable of satisfying). Note that while OB is rising, it is doing so at a decreasing rate, causing AB—the gap between expectations and attainments—to widen over time.

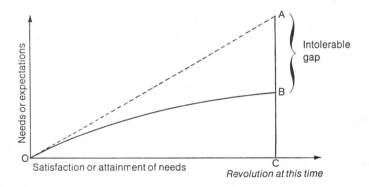

These expectations manifest themselves in different ways. In the economic sphere, there is a great increase in the demand for goods and services. In the case of food, the rural peoples of South Asia, who have for centuries been accustomed to consuming coarse food grains—and that at too low a level of consumption, are developing a taste for milk, eggs, fruit, and a variety of other foods. In urban areas, it is a common sight to see long lines of people at the government milk distributing centers. Will India be able to meet the growing food demands of mounting population? In the view of Sukhatme:

> It is doubtful whether the food supplied in animal products, especially milk, needed to attain higher levels of nutrition could be raised internally without far reaching measures, especially if the attainment of the minimum target be delayed beyond 1980.[4]

Transportation is in growing demand—people crowd the trains; sitting on roofs or clinging precariously to the sides of railway cars. Education is in growing demand—it is becoming difficult to get a child admitted to a public school, especially in the cities, and there is intense competition for admission to any of the institutions of higher education. Consumer goods are in growing demand—especially luxury goods like radios and TVs, motor scooters and cars. Since 1950, the supply of these luxury goods has increased dramatically, as shown in Table 4-1. In spite of the increased availability of luxury consumer items, it is becoming increasingly difficult to purchase a motor scooter or a car because of the tremendous demand. In India and Pakistan there are long waiting lists of families wanting to own a car or scooter, and they may have to wait as long as five years to get these highly sought-after goods. There is thus a black market for many of these items for those willing to pay prices several times higher than the retail prices fixed by the government.

There has been a massive increase in the demand for social services,

Table 4-1 Availability of Some Consumer Goods in India, 1950-1960

Item	Availability in 1950	1960	Percentage increase (1950-1960)
Radios	241[a]	732	204%
Electric fans	556	2,230	301
Refrigerators	10	30	300
Room air conditioners		29	
Cars	46	72	57
Motor scooters	6.1	89.4	1,366
Bicycles	750	3,000	400

[a]Numbers represent millions of units.

SOURCE: Government of India, Planning Commission, *Report of the Committee on Distribution of Income and Levels of Living* (New Delhi, 1969), p. 56.

including education and public health, since independence because the masses formerly denied these services now expect to be able to live decent and healthy lives. In the field of education, enrollments in educational institutions at all levels have soared over the past two decades (see Table 4-2).

Rising expectations show up in a variety of other forms. Landless laborers expect to own the pieces of land they cultivate. They are becoming increasingly frustrated by a situation in which the absentee landlord owns several hundred acres of land, while they, "tillers of the soil," do not possess any. At the very least, cultivators feel entitled to keep the major portion of their crops rather than having to pay it away as rent. The downtrodden lower castes expect to be treated with consideration and dignity by members of the higher castes and by society at large. In short, the revolution of rising expectations involves all aspects—economic, social, and political—of human behavior. The magnitude of these expectations and the amazing speed at which they are spreading among the people earns them the title of revolution. The phenomenon is real and self-evident, in spite of Gunnar Myrdal's remark that it is "rather loose and borders on meaningless unless it is quantified."[5] One can observe and feel its great intensity; and its quantitative aspect is easily observed in the serious shortages of all kinds of goods and services, despite enormous increases in supplies.

Table 4-2   Enrollment in Educational Facilities in South Asia, 1950-1972

Country	Period	Percent of primary school age (6-11) enrolled	Percent of secondary schools age (11-14) enrolled	Students attending colleges and universities—arts & sciences (in thousands)
India	1950	43.1%	12.9%	310.0
	1965	74.9	33.9	1,230.0
	1969	78.0	33.9	1,690.0
	1974	85.3	41.3	2,770.0
Pakistan	1961	40.0	30.7	205.0
	1970	70.0	42.0	270.0
Sri Lanka	1966	84.0	55.0	10.3
	1970	88.0	65.0	12.0
Bangladesh	1960	44.0	9.0	51.0
	1972	58.0	17.0	328.0

SOURCES: Government of India, Publications Division, *India: A Reference Manual* (New Delhi, 1974) pp. 62-65.
United Nations, *Statistical Year Book, 1973* (New York, 1974).

Let us now examine some of the factors that have brought about this revolution. First, there is the international demonstration effect and the countervailing forces of the economic development process. The international demonstration effect, according to Ragnar Nurske, is:

> The intensity of the attraction exercised by the consumption standards of the advanced countries—it leads to imitation of the consumption habits of the advanced countries by the people in low income countries.[6]

It is true that the strength of the demonstration effect varies a great deal among countries, but it is quite apparent that in India, Pakistan, and Sri Lanka there is a craze for such items as transistor radios, tape recorders, watches, cameras, and cosmetics—especially among the urban middle class. Contributing to this situation is the "information explosion." Foreign movies, television programs, and tourists—not to mention foreign newspapers and magazines have all contributed to knowledge of the "dream goods." *Time* and *Newsweek* magazines—from the United States, the *London Post* and other pictorial magazines from Europe, with their tantalizing full-page advertisements, are within easy reach of every college student, and they create an intense longing for all the goods and appurtenances of an affluent society.

Another major factor that has nurtured expectations in these countries is the planning and development process itself. As Myron Weiner has remarked:

> Clearly a high level of aspiration and a growing level of political organization present special problems in an underdeveloped economy where resources are scarce—economic progress is thus likely to be accompanied by a rise in organized demand.[7]

The ambitions and high-sounding objectives spelled out in the plans for development raise the hopes and expectations of the people. For example, the terms of reference of India's Planning Commission include:

A. That citizens, men and women equally, have the right to adequate means of livelihood
B. That the ownership and control of the material resources of the community are so distributed as best to subserve the common good and
C. That the operation of the economic system does not result in the concentration of wealth and means of production to the common detriment.[8]

Pakistan's first five-year plan describes its major objectives in the following words:

The economic and social objectives of Government's policy are well known. They are to develop the resources of the country as rapidly as possible so as to promote living standards and social services, secure social justice and equality of opportunity, and aim at the widest and most equitable distribution of income and property.[9]

The third five-year plan of Nepal includes among its aims that:

A.   All citizens may have equal opportunity and facility to develop their personality and to make economic progress.
B.   Citizens may have reasonable and adequate means of livelihood.[10]

Indian planning promised to "create a milieu in which the small man who has so far had little opportunity of perceiving and participating in possibilities of growth, is enabled to put in his best in the interests of a higher standard of life for himself and his family."[11] Such promises as "social justice," "adequate level of livelihood," and "equal opportunity" readily spark the imagination and expectations of the masses who, hitherto, have lived in a poverty without much hope for improvement. The "information explosion" mentioned earlier has also been fueled by development—increased educational facilities, increased circulation of domestic newspapers, a wider audience for radio broadcasts, and better transportation facilities—lifting formerly remote villagers out of their timeless isolation.

But, as noted earlier, economic advances in the countries of South Asia have not kept pace with rising expectations. Though these countries have achieved about 4 percent annual growth in GNP, taking into account the rate of population growth and increases in the general price level, the per capita increase in real income has been very low. For example, in India, measured in 1960–1961 prices, real per capita income increased by only 10.8 percent from 1960 to 1970, that is, an annual increase of only about 1 percent. Such a small increase amounts to practically nothing, even though it may look impressive statistically. For example, with a per capita income of $60, a 1 percent increase amounts to the trifling sum of 60 cents per year. For a person dreaming of a higher and better standard of living, an annual increase in income of only 60 cents is little more than a joke.

What are the consequences of this widening gap between rising expectations and attainments. To a great extent, its impact depends on the political structure of the society and the extent of the gap itself. In a dictatorship the government can, to a large extent, keep the expectations of the people at a low level simply through lack of exposure to many of the contributory factors mentioned above. On the other hand, in free, open, and democratic societies such as those in South Asia, it is difficult to prevent the exposure to mass communication. As long as the difference between the level of expectations and attainment remains small and the population is confident that its expectations are realizable, this discrepancy can provide motivation for savings and investment in the hope of economic improvement. In fact, such a gap could be conducive to economic development. But the situation becomes fraught with danger when the gap becomes excessive and people become convinced that it is not going to be reduced imminently. In such a situation, people may lose any incentive to save and invest. There is then an intense resistance to any policy that would divert any part of family income from consumption. This may be one important explanation for the low rate of household savings in the South Asian economies, discussed in the previous chapter. The serious resistance of the population to any attempt to reduce consumption results in a hostile attitude toward any increase in taxation—hostility they will vent freely as long as they have freedom of expression, freedom of assembly, and the right to vote in free elections. In the democratic societies of South Asia, where the political leadership is dependent for their continuance in power on the approval of the voters for their political and economic actions, it is not surprising that governments are reluctant to levy the additional taxes needed for capital formation.

In India, there has been strong opposition to efforts to increase taxes, especially on agricultural incomes. The opposition has held demonstrations, including hunger marches and sit-ins before the legislative assemblies. Commenting on the resistance to increasing taxes in India, Barbara Ward remarks, "In democratic India, where people are being asked for the first time in history to vote themselves through the tough period of primitive accumulation, savings are lower."[12] And, she goes on to say:

> Saving for them entails lopping off a margin from current consumption when consumption is already so low that it is barely enough to sustain life. Even though the hope is that five to ten years from now, conditions will be better, can the people be persuaded—least of all by free vote—to submit themselves to an even worse plight now?[13]

To give people with unfulfilled expectations the right to vote and then expect them to forgo consumption through additional taxes is, in our contention, difficult, if not impossible.

In addition to the resistance to taxation, there is an insistent and impatient demand from the masses for governments to satisfy some of their demands—for housing, water, sanitation, food subsidies, and other measures of social welfare. This partly explains the large government outlays by the South Asian countries on general or operating items, as opposed to development programs. In this connection, the experience of Sri Lanka is interesting. Food was subsidized—provided by the government to households at cheaper rates. According to Snodgrass:

> By 1952 these efforts had resulted in rice being sold to the consumers at less than one-third its imported prices. In 1951–52, a third of government expenditures went into transfers and subsidies with food subsidies bulking large within the total.[14]

Once such expenditures are undertaken by a government under political pressure there is a resistance to their termination, since these expenditures become a part of rising expectations. In the case of Sri Lanka

> The government tried to back out of its onerous commitment. In July 1953, it announced that all net subsidization of food would cease. Violent demonstrations and Sri Lanka's first forced change of government followed.[15]

Similarly in India and Pakistan a substantial part of government budgets are devoted to welfare expenditures to meet these rising expectations. No doubt these welfare expenditures are desirable to improve the lot of the poor, but the point being stressed here is that these expenditures divert government revenues away from investment for economic development. In other words, they impede the process of capital formation in the public sector, which in turn retards further economic growth—as discussed in the previous chapter.

A more crucial aspect of the gap between expectations and their realization is its impact on the public morale. In the words of Karl Von Vorys:

> A further consequence of a widening gap between the level of attainment and the level of expectation is the undermining of public morale or even the alienation of increased number—of population from the nation's social and political institutions. People remain loyal to institutions if these appear either inevitable or useful for achievement of their aspirations. The weakening of institutions in turn serves as a disincentive effect for such collective efforts as economic development.[16]

The position may not yet have become desperate in South Asia, but there are definite signs of a lowering of public morale, a frustration with and alienation from the existing social and political institutions of the South Asian countries. Discussing conditions in India, Dandekar and

Rath write:

> All the latent dissatisfaction about slow progress of the economy and the silent frustration about its failure to give the poor a fair deal, let alone special attention, appear to be gathering in this form. Its shape today is probably no more hideous; allowed to grow unheeded and unrelieved, it will turn ugly.[17]

The position of the poor, their economic well-being, may have even deteriorated over the last decade. Commenting on changes in the per capita consumption by different income classes in India, Dandekar and Rath came to the conclusion that whatever little gain was achieved through economic development seems to have been appropriated by the richer classes, whereas the living standards of the lower income groups have either remained stationary or actually deteriorated. In the face of the professed objective of India's plans to, "create a milieu in which the small man . . . is enabled to put in his best in the interest of a higher standard of life for himself and his family," when the low-income groups find no (or negligible) increase in real per capita in consumption, they are likely to dismiss the development plans and all reference to the planning process as a "rich man's racket." This attitude is destructive of most feelings of public cooperation and mass participation, which are supposed to constitute the cornerstone of democratic planning in South Asia.

What of the future? Is the gap between expectations and attainments likely to increase or are these countries going to accept the fact of their relative poverty and the inability to meet increasing demands on their resources? Will peoples of these countries scale down their demands? No conclusive answer can be given to these difficult questions, but William and Paul Paddock see such expectations as

> hopelessly beyond the [nations'] potential. . . . These nations are not going to achieve their exalted aspirations, no matter how hard the people may work and how much they sacrifice, no matter how wisely the foreign aid money is spent. . . . At some particular point each nation, both the leaders and the people, must realize this. The realities of life as ordained by a harsh and stern God, will eventually catch up with them.[18]

In the same spirit, Myron Weiner remarks that, "As the economic supply grows, 'consumer' political demands may increase even faster. Thus economic growth is not likely to diminish the political repercussions of scarcity."[19]

If the revolution of rising expectations grows in intensity, the countries of South Asia will find their development problems becoming increasingly difficult, because of the adverse effects on capital formation and investment and the unsympathetic public attitude toward planning. The people of these countries will have to realize and face up to the fact that their expectations will inevitably outstrip the capacity of the available resources. We can only hope, as do William and Paul Paddock, that "this realization comes within the framework of peaceful adjustment and not via internal bloody revolution or external grabbing at the possessions of neighbors."[20]

NOTES

1. Willard W. Cochrane, *The World Food Problem: A Guardedly Optimistic View* (New York: Crowell, 1969), p. 3.

2. Forrest D. Murden, quoted in DeVere E. Pentomy, *The Underdeveloped Lands: A Dilemma of the International Economy* (San Francisco: Chandler, 1960), p. 4.

3. William Paddock and Paul Paddock, *Hungry Nations* (Boston: Little, Brown, 1964), p. 12.

4. P. V. Sukhatme, *Feeding India's Growing Millions* (Bombay: Asia Publishing House, 1965), p. 154.

5. Gunnar Myrdal, *Asian Drama: An Inquiry into the Poverty of Nations* (New York: Pantheon, 1968), vol. 1, p. 115.

6. Ragnar Nurske, *Problems of Capital Formation in Underdeveloped Countries,* (New York: Oxford University Press, 1967), p. 63.

7. Myron Weiner, *The Politics of Scarcity* (Chicago: University of Chicago Press, 1962), p. 238.

8. Government of India, Planning Commission, *The First Five Year Plan, 1950-55* (New Delhi, 1951).

9. Government of Pakistan, Planning Commission, *The First Five Year Plan, 1955-60,* (Karachi, 1957), p. 1.

10. Government of Nepal, National Planning Council *The Third Plan, 1965-70* (Khatmandu, 1965), p. 13.

11. Government of India, Planning Commission, *Third Five Year Plan, 1960-65* (New Delhi, 1961), p. 5.

12. Barbara Ward, *The Rich Nations and the Poor Nations* (New York: Norton 1962), p. 92.

13. Ibid., p. 125.

14. Donald R. Snodgrass, *Ceylon: An Export Economy in Transition* (Homewood, Ill.: Irwin, 1968), p. 194.

15. Ibid., p. 194.

16. Karl Von Vorys, "Some Aspects of the Economic Development of India," *World Politics,* vol. 13 (1960-1961), 588.

17. V. M. Dandekar and N. Rath, "Poverty in India—Dimensions and Trends," *Economic and Political Weekly,* January 2, 1971, p. 40.

18. Paddock and Paddock, *Hungry Nations,* p. 12.

19. Weiner, *Politics of Scarcity,* p. 238.

20. Paddock and Paddock, *Hungry Nations,* p. 12.

5

The Unemployment Problem

PROBLEMS OF DEFINITION

Unemployment constitutes a serious economic, social, and political problem in the countries of South Asia. In its economic aspect, the existence of large numbers of unemployed means the waste of human resources and a resultant deprivation to society of the goods and services the unemployed could produce. Socially, the unemployed become alienated from the social order because of frustration and anger with the system that cannot provide them with work. If unemployment persists, these disillusioned persons can become a potential danger to political stability, being highly susceptible to subversive elements in the society. The Naxaulite movement in India and the unrest of Sri Lanka's youth are examples of political instability resulting from serious unemployment problems in those countries.

Unemployment, however, is a worldwide problem, occurring in the developed as well as in the underdeveloped countries. During the post–World War II period, unemployment in the United States has ranged from 3 to 9 percent of the total labor force and, during 1953–1954 and again in the mid-1970s, annual average unemployment reached a high of 10 percent.

Unemployment, however, is not as simple as it might appear. A given rate of unemployment depends on the way the term is defined and measured and on its nature and incidence.[1] In the United States, persons are classified by the U.S. Department of Labor as unemployed if, during the survey week, they were not employed but were available for work and had made a specific effort to find a job at some time within the preceding four weeks—or if they were waiting either to report to a new job within 30 days or to be recalled to a job from which they were laid off. The measured magnitude of unemployment changes with differing definition of the terms applied. According to the *Economic Report of the President* (1975) the definition of unemployment introduced in 1967, stipulating that unemployment should include those who had sought work at any time during the preceding four-week period, rather than, as previously, during the preceding one-week period, increased the measured unemployment rate, especially among women.

Unemployment may be classified into various categories, according to the major causes and duration of the phenomenon. Some unemployment is cyclical; that is, it is associated with fluctuations in the business cycle. During a downturn in economic activity, unemployment rises due to a general decline in business activity. Some unemployment is frictional; that is, a by-product of normal economic changes such as the closing of some firms or changing production techniques within firms. Frictional unemployment may also arise from personal factors such as completion of school or of service in the armed forces or preference for a different job environment or a certain geographical location. The unemployment arising out of imperfect market adjustments as a result of barriers to mobility, for example, unemployment among blacks in urban ghettos in the United States, is referred to as structural unemployment. Seasonal unemployment arises from seasonal fluctuations in the demand for labor and is inherent to some production processes, such as agriculture and construction, and to some consumption processes, such as vacation resorts. In terms of the duration of unemployment, the situation can be classified into short-term seasonal and frictional, short-term structural and cyclical, and long-term chronic. The causes of all these categories of unemployment, except the last, are obvious. In developed economies, long-term chronic unemployment is generally due to the lack of effective aggregate demand relative to aggregate supply, in the Keynesian sense. Aggregate demand may fall short of aggregate supply from inadequate consumption expenditure, which increases at a decreasing rate with increase in income, or private investment, or both. Unemployment resulting from the deficiency of aggregate demand can usually be reduced by appropriate fiscal and monetary policies.

The following important points of difference between unemployment patterns in a developed country and those in the developing countries of South Asia need to be borne in mind. In almost all categories of unemployment, unemployed persons in a developed economy are conscious of their state of unemployment. They are either looking for work or have a job from which they are temporarily absent. Their state of unemployment can be described as "open" or "visible" unemployment. Furthermore, most of the workers in a developed country are hired workers, as against the self-employed and unpaid workers in family enterprises. Assuming the employers to be profit maximizers, it can be safely inferred that the wages of the hired worker approximate his marginal productivity. In the United States, the ratio of self-employed or unpaid family workers to the total labor force is about 10 percent.[2] The extent of self-employment in an economy is important when assessing unemployment because self-employed persons and unpaid workers in family enterprises (mainly agricultural farms) are seldom reported as "unemployed." Also, in most developed countries the workers classified as unemployed are supported by some form of government benefits during the duration of their unemployment, and to that extent the state of unemployment is less difficult for them.

The South Asian nations have essentially rural economies, with about 85 percent of their labor force employed in agriculture. In agriculture, and also in nonagricultural small-scale and cottage industries, the unit of operation is the traditional joint, or extended family, and members of the family are associated in varying degrees with production activities. Farm work is benefited, especially by an abundance of workers, but in all family enterprises the members share the work and all share in the earnings.

Some important implications of this employment pattern may be noted. Each family member has a definite role in the enterprise that is recognized by all members of the society as justification for a share of the family product. The individual member's role may not involve "full-time work" or any "product" in the conventional sense. Yet the individual member—and for that matter the other members of the family—feels that he is employed, though he may be contributing very little, or less than what he receives from the total family output. Should such a family member be considered employed or unemployed? Applying the conventional definition of unemployed, he should be characterized as employed, since he is not seeking work; but from an economic point of view, he is unemployed, since he is not contributing anything—or is contributing less than his marginal product (i.e., his contribution to the family's total output). This pattern of unemployment is referred to as disguised, or hidden, unemployment in the literature on economic development.[3] Since disguisedly unemployed labor, with zero marginal productivity, can be removed from agriculture (and other types of family enterprise) for productive employment elsewhere without loss of total output, it is also viewed as a potential source of capital formation. The proper utilization of this disguisedly unemployed, or surplus, labor would contribute to economic growth. In most South Asian countries, the magnitude of disguised unemployment is enormous—and growing. But the phenomenon cannot be analyzed by the theoretical concepts and terminology developed in the Western world. For example, we will not be able to identify the unemployed on the family farms by applying the conventional criteria of "seeking work," "making specific efforts to find a job," or "waiting to report for a new job." Thus, applying the concept unemployment to South Asian agricultural societies, will have the ridiculous result of indicating near full employment conditions; using this definition, the 1961 Indian census estimated unemployment at 1 percent of the rural labor force. This is an absurd estimate and as Sen remarks, "These figures are low enough to put many advanced countries to shame."[4] Such estimates point up the limitation of applying theoretical concepts developed in the economically advanced countries to the conditions existing in South Asia. After examining several studies of employment, unemployment, and underemployment done in South Asia based on these theoretical concepts, Gunnar Myrdal remarked:

> In general, these studies have led to asking the kind of questions Western economists would wish to investigate in their own countries. At the same time, however, it is often acknowledged that Western categories cannot be transferred intact to a South Asian environment. . . . The orientation of these studies—fully as much as the errors in their execution—lies at the root of the problem.[5]

A committee on unemployment estimates appointed by the government of India reported:

> It is now realized that the concept as adopted in developed economies is unsuitable for an economy like ours with its preponderance of self-employment and production within household enterprises.[6]

The committee proposed that the conventional methods of estimating and presenting estimates should be discontinued. "In our complex economy, the character of the labor force, employment and unemployment is too heterogeneous to justify aggregation into single-dimensional magnitudes."[7] Similar views have been expressed by S. Selvaratram and L. S. Fernando in relation to Sri Lanka: "In developing countries like Ceylon . . . the measurement of unemployment on the criteria of 'seeking or looking for work' will not be realistic."[8] In relation to Pakistan, Sultan Hashmi and Syed Mushtaq Hussain made the following observations:

> In general, due to cultural reasons some males in the rural areas who are casual or seasonal workers might not admit that they are unemployed.

Many males will not admit that their female folks are working or looking for work even if they are, as living on the earnings of females is considered humiliating in the society.[9]

Our main purpose in pointing out the problem of applying inappropriate concepts of employment and unemployment in the South Asian context is to suggest caution in interpreting the estimates made in various studies. However, some estimate of the extent of unemployment and underdevelopment in the South Asian countries is required in order to formulate policies that will promote fuller employment. It is our contention that the concept of unemployment as developed in the advanced countries is appropriate for the urban nonagricultural sector of the South Asian economies. The need is for appropriate criteria to estimate unemployment in the rural sector, in view of the peculiarities of the socioeconomic setting.

THE NATURE OF UNEMPLOYMENT

Unemployment in the Urban Areas   Urban unemployment in the South Asian countries resembles, for the most part, the open unemployment occurring in economically developed countries—the workers are conscious of their state of unemployment and are looking for work. It may be further classified into (1) educated unemployment, that is, unemployment among educated persons and (2) other urban unemployment, that is, unemployment among laborers and industrial workers. This division is essential in order to demonstrate the serious rise in the unemployment of the educated in South Asia. For an educated person not to find a job after all the hopes and dreams acquired during the period of education, brings untold disillusionment and frustration. The educated unemployed, being highly articulate, are well able to spread their feelings of dissatisfaction with cynicism toward the existing political and economic structure. They are also very likely to sympathize with and support revolutionary movements aimed at destruction of a system that has so patently failed to use their talents and reward their skills.

Unemployment in the Rural Areas   Rural unemployment mostly takes the form of disguised or hidden unemployment and underemployment. The rural unemployed are visibly active but underutilized. A large proportion of labor in the rural sector falls into this category. As explained, rural workers, as members of an extended family, work on the family farm sharing labor and income. Since they consider themselves employed, they do not look for work. The extent of this kind of unemployment can be analyzed through the production approach or the time approach. Using the production approach, a worker is disguisedly unemployed if his marginal product (the worker's contribution to the total family farm income) is less than the average product or income of the family. In the event of zero marginal product, disguised unemployment exists. In this case, the withdrawal of workers from the family enterprise will not reduce its total output. In a situation where the marginal product is positive but less than the average product, disguised underemployment exists. In this case, the withdrawal of workers will reduce the total family output to the extent of their marginal product.

With the time approach, a certain number of hours per week (say 40 hours) is arbitrarily said to constitute full employment. Disguised unemployment or underemployment exists to the extent that workers are actually working less than that number of hours per week.

It should be pointed out that equating open unemployment with urban unemployment and disguised unemployment with rural unemployment is somewhat arbitrary. We should be cognizant of the fact that disguised unemployment may also exist in urban sectors in cases where a business firm is organized and operated on a family basis; also in private as well as in government offices, where many people are employed on a full-time basis even though the services they render may actually require less than full time. Illustrations of disguised urban unemployment are provided by Ronald Ridker:

> The street corner vendor of shoe strings may sit at his stall for fourteen hours and sell only a few pairs. The semiredundant messenger in an office may spend most of his day waiting for a message to deliver or an order to get his superior's tea.[10]

What is the relationship between the open unemployed in the cities and the disguised unemployed in the rural areas? As Edgar Edwards has pointed out,

> The most visible dimension of the underutilization of labor in developing countries namely, open unemployment in the modern sector, is but the tip of an iceberg resting on a stratum of underemployed outside the modern sector, both obscuring larger numbers of others who are visibly active, as in education or civil service, but really underutilized.[11]

On the basis of this relationship, Edwards contends that

> Efforts to clear away the visible portion of the iceberg may simply motivate other layers to emerge: for example, efforts to provide jobs for

the unemployed in urban areas may simply entice others from the countryside to take their places.[12]

This is exactly what has been happening. In the South Asian countries, as in other developing areas of the world, emphasis has been on improving employment opportunities in urban areas by creating jobs in industry and in the civil service, but this has not eased the urban unemployment situation simply because there has been a corresponding shift of unemployed and underemployed from the rural to the urban areas.

THE MAGNITUDE OF UNEMPLOYMENT

Urban Unemployment Rates Urban unemployment remains largely unmeasured in quantitative terms. Besides the conceptual difficulties already referred to, the statistical data in this area are grossly inadequate—which helps to explain why the results of different studies are so varied. Estimates on overall urban unemployment in India have been prepared at various times. Table 5–1 provides a summary of the estimates prepared by these various government agencies and by some individual studies, in chronological order.

Table 5-1 Estimates of Urban Unemployment in India, 1951-1961

Source	Reference period	Number of unemployed (in millions)	Urban unemployed as a proportion of the total labor force
B. N. Datar	March 1951	2.5-3.0	12.0%
National Sample Survey & Employment Exchange data	Sept. 1953	2.4	11.0
Second Five-Year Plan	March 1956	2.5	10.0
Wilfred Malenbaum	March 1956	2.5	10.0
National Sample Survey & Employment Exchange data	May 1956	3.4	13.6
R. C. Bhardwaj	March 1951	2.5	11.4
	March 1956	3.4	13.5
	March 1961	4.5	15.5

SOURCE: Based on R. C. Bhardwaj, *Employment and Unemployment in India* (New York: Humanities Press, 1969), pp. 109-126.

As regards educated unemployment, Bhardwaj estimates that at the end of the second five-year plan (1960–1961), out of a total of approximately 6.45 million educated people, around 1 million (or 15.5 percent) were unemployed.[13] According to the Committee on Unemployment, educated unemployment increased from 244,400 in 1951 to over 3 million in 1972—about a sixteenfold increase—as shown in Table 5–2.

Table 5-2 Educated Unemployed in India, 1951-1972 (in thousands)

Qualifications	1951	1972
Matriculation	187.0	1,744
Undergraduates	30.6	932
Graduates & postgraduates	26.8	602
	244.4	3,278

SOURCE: Government of India, *Report of the Committee on Unemployment* (New Delhi, 1973).

Paradoxically, unemployment is assuming serious proportions even among educated persons with technical qualifications. In 1968, 17 percent of engineering graduates and diploma holders were unemployed. In the decade preceding 1965, unemployment in this category was estimated at no more than 7 to 8 percent and even this appears to have been largely due to the waiting period (usually no more than one year) that the majority of new graduates had to go through before securing employment.[14]

Another disquieting aspect of educated unemployment in India during the decade 1961–1972 was the tendency for the unemployment rate to be positively correlated with more education: unemployment among matriculates (completed high school) decreased from 78.5 percent in 1961 to 53.2 percent in 1972; unemployment among undergraduates increased from 12.0 to 28.4 percent, and that of graduates and postgraduates from 9.5 percent to 18.4 percent. Clearly, the Indian economy has not developed sufficiently to absorb its increasing educated manpower; and those remaining unemployed, tend to invest in still further education in the hope of securing a job.

So far, we have considered urban unemployment in India. The situation for Pakistan and Bangladesh is depicted in Table 5–3. The problem is, however, much more serious in the major cities. From the census data, Iftikhar Ahmad has computed unemployment in the major cities in Bangladesh to range between 20 and 38 percent of the urban labor force.[15]

Estimates of urban unemployment in Sri Lanka are given in Table 5–4. Since 1965, unemployment in the urban areas has increased

Table 5-3 Urban Unemployment in Bangladesh and Pakistan as a Percentage of the Urban Labor Force, 1960-1975

	1960	1970	1975[a]
Bangladesh	6.5%	7.6%	5.6%
Pakistan	5.0	3.1	2.7

[a]Projected

SOURCE: Iftikhar Ahmad, "Employment in Bangladesh; Problems and Prospects" in E. A. G. Robinson and Keith Griffin, eds., *The Economic Development of Bangladesh within a Socialist Framework* (New York: Wiley, 1974). p. 246.
Sultan S. Hashmi and Syed Mushtaq Hussain, "A Review of Projected Manpower, Labor Force and Employment for Pakistan," in Ronald G. Ridker and Harold Lubell, eds., *Employment and Unemployment Problems of the Near East and South Asia* (Bombay: Vikas, 1971), pp. 373-375.

noticeably, especially among the educated. In 1970, when overall unemployment in Sri Lanka was 12 percent of the labor force, urban unemployment was estimated at 16 percent. About 25 percent of the unemployed in urban areas had completed the General Certificate of Education (ten years of schooling) and 24 percent had completed eight years of schooling.[16]

Rural Unemployment Rates   As discussed earlier in this chapter, disguised unemployment plagues the rural areas. The Indian Planning Commission asserts that rural unemployment is the principal cause of poverty and that the goal of "garibi hatao" (Hindi phrase meaning

Table 5-4 Estimates of Urban Unemployment in Sri Lanka, 1959-1960 to 1969-1970

	Reference period	Urban unemployment (as proportion of labor force)
International Labor office	1959-60	10.5
	1969-70	17.3
Department of Labor	1959-60	18.3
Central Bank of Sri Lanka	1963	13.8

SOURCE: H. N. S. Karunatilake, *Economic Development in Ceylon* (New York: Praeger, 1971), pp. 168-169.
Donald R. Snodgrass, *Ceylon; An Export Economy in Transition* (Homewood, Ill.: Irwin, 1966), p. 103.
United Nations, *Economic Survey of Asia and the Far East, 1972* (Bangkok, 1973), p. 21.

removal of poverty) cannot be achieved without providing work for the rural unemployed.

As pointed out, in the socioeconomic context of rural India (and other countries of the region) underemployment, rather than actual unemployment, is the problem. This explains why the estimates of unemployment made by the National Sample Survey in India in 1960–1961—that 1.62 percent of the rural population was unemployed—are considered grossly short of the mark. Underemployment includes (a) underemployment from sharing work on farms owned and operated by joint families and (b) seasonal unemployment. The National Sample Survey's estimates of severe underemployment in Indian agriculture are given in Table 5-5. (Persons working less than twenty-eight hours per week were considered severely underemployed, those working between twenty-nine and forty-two hours, as moderately underemployed.) It is interesting to note that there has been a decline in the percentage of severely underemployed, from 14.72 percent in 1958–1959 to 9.85 percent in 1961–1962. This may have resulted from additional work opportunities created in the rural areas under the five-year plan or it may be largely due to changes in survey coverage and the statistical methods applied. In its midterm appraisal of the fourth plan, the Indian Planning Commission remarked:

> The incidence of seasonal and underemployment remains as heavy as before. It is, perhaps, heavier than before except in some parts of the country where the Green Revolution has achieved significant success.[18]

The Indian peasantry continues to depend for work on the vagaries of nature. According to C.B. Mamoria,

> The period of complete inactivity in each agricultural region varies with the nature and variety of crops and cropping pattern. Broadly speaking,

Table 5-5 Percentage of Employed Males and Females Working Twenty-Eight Hours or Less in Indian Agriculture

Year	Males	Females
1958-1959	5.78%	8.94%
1959-1960	5.46	9.08
1960-1961	3.34	6.55
1961-1962	3.96	5.89

SOURCE: Government of India, Planning Commission, *Report of the Committee on Unemployment Estimates* (New Delhi, 1970), p. 10.

[the] Indian cultivator is unoccupied anywhere from 4 to 6 months in a year excepting in places where he has undertaken the cultivation of wet crops or where he grows more than one crop from the same soil in a year, while the cultivators' womenfolk are unoccupied for an even longer part of the year.[19]

Since the amount of land under double cropping is only 14 percent of the total cultivated area, enforced idleness due to seasonal factors afflicts the vast majority of the Indian rural work force.

The extent of underemployment among agricultural laborers in India was estimated by the first and second Agricultural Labour Enquiry committees, in 1950–1951 and 1955–1956, respectively. The seriousness of the problem is indicated by the following figures:

1. Casual adult male workers were on an average, employed for wages 200 days in 1950–1951 and 197 days in 1956–1957. They were self-employed 75 days in 1950–1951 and 40 days in 1956–1957. Thus, they were without work 90 days in 1950–1951 and 128 days in 1956–1957.
2. Casual adult female workers were employed for wages 134 days in 1950–1951 and 141 days in 1956–1957.[20]

As regards the problem of disguised unemployment, or surplus labor, various estimates have been prepared. Tarlok Singh estimated in 1945 that between 21 and 22 million persons out of a working population of 99 to 103 million, that is, 33 to 55 percent of the total population were surplus in British India.[21] Shakuntala Mehra, estimated surplus labor in 1956–1957 at 17.1 percent of the agricultural work force, on an all-India basis.[22] Uppal estimated disguised unemployment in Punjab agriculture at 8.41 percent of the rural work force for the year 1956–1957; on smaller holdings (e.g., on farms of less than 10 acres), more than 20 percent of the labor force was surplus.[23]

Rural unemployment and underemployment, according to the Bangladesh Planning Commission, "are widespread in Bangladesh today . . . it is frequently suggested that on the average up to 30 percent of the available labor is not used, although much of this is concealed by work sharing and in underemployment."[24] Estimates of rural unemployment in Bangladesh, based on data developed by the International Labor Office and on the census of population, are given in Table 5-6. According to the Pakistan Planning Commission, unemployment

is the gravest problem confronting Pakistan. Almost one-fifth of the available manpower . . . is wasted every year for the lack of opportunities for useful work. In actual numbers about half of the labor force is

Table 5-6 Estimates of Rural Unemployment in Bangladesh,
1950-1951 to 1969-1970

	1950-1951	1954-1955	1960-1961	1964-1965	1969-1970
Unemployed percent of rural labor force	31.29%	33.60%	34.02%	30.80%	32.42%

SOURCE: Based on Iftikhar Ahmad, "Employment in Bangladesh, Problems and Prospects," in E. A. G. Robinson and Keith Griffin, *The Economic Development of Bangladesh with a Socialist Framework* (New York: Wiley, 1974). p. 246.

affected, as unemployment in Pakistan generally takes the form of an underutilization of at least half of the available manpower.[25]

In Sri Lanka, the Department of Labour estimated rural unemployment at 11.8 percent of the rural labor force for the year 1959–1960.[26] This ratio increased to 13.5 percent during 1965, according to a survey conducted by the Central Bank of Sri Lanka. Since 1965, the situation seems to have deteriorated further. The Finance Minister, in his 1970 budget speech, characterized unemployment as the most urgent problem facing Sri Lanka; asserting that "unemployment demanded very urgent solutions to fulfill the aspiration of young men and women for whom life will lose all meaning unless they can find a useful place in our society."[27]

SOME MAJOR CAUSES OF UNEMPLOYMENT

Employment problems in South Asia can be traced to the following factors:

1. Rapid population growth and increase in the labor force
2. Use of inappropriate technology—distortion of factor prices
3. Inappropriate educational systems and attitudes towards work

Table 5-7 Estimated Growth of South Asian Labor Force, 1950-1980

Period	Growth of labor force (annual percentage increase)
1950-1965 (Actual)	1.4%
1965-1980 (Projected)	1.9
1970-1980 (Projected)	2.0

SOURCE: Adapted from Edgar O. Edwards, Editor, *Employment in Developing Nations* (New York: Columbia University Press, 1974), p. 12.

The most important cause of unemployment is, of course, the population explosion with its resultant rapid growth in the labor force. During the decade 1960–1970, population increased in South Asia by 2.45 percent per year; the ensuing increase in the labor force of the South Asian countries is shown in Table 5–7. It may be noted that the labor force is growing at an increasing rate. This is largely explained by the increase in population. But several sociological changes are contributing to the trend, in particular, the higher participation rate, particularly of women, in the labor force, and the weakening of the joint family system, especially in the urban areas, encouraging more family members to seek employment. These sociological changes have occurred mainly through the spread of educational facilities and the development of mass communications.

Increasing population is worsening the unemployment problem, both rural and urban. In the rural areas, agriculture is becoming more crowded without a corresponding increase in productivity. In India, between 1961–1973, agricultural yield per acre increased annually by the compound growth rate of 1.24 percent as against the 2.0 percent annual increase in rural population.[28] Agriculture in the South Asian countries is, thus, becoming an ever-increasing reservoir of surplus labor.

Urban unemployment is exacerbated by a persistent trend toward urbanization. In the past, overcrowding, unsanitary conditions, and unemployment in the urban centers discouraged rural folk from leaving their traditional settings and migrating to the cities. But recent developments, including worsening unemployment in the rural areas, increase in rural debt, lack of rural industries to provide alternative sources of employment, and low incomes and wages, have had a "push" effect causing a large increase in rural-urban migration. In Bangladesh, whereas total and rural population increased by 21.0 and 19.8 percent, respectively, from 1951 to 1961, urban population increased by 43.2 percent.[29] During the same period, the population of the principal cities of Bangladesh—Chittagong, Dacca, Khulna, and Narayanganj—increased by 25.6, 65.7, 209.0, and 137.0 percent, respectively. Similar conditions prevail in India, Sri Lanka, and Pakistan in regard to exploding population and the trend toward urbanization.

Increasing population and inadequate supplies of capital inputs make the South Asian countries labor abunaant and capital scarce economies, as explained in chapter 3. If the forces of supply and demand were operating freely, the relative prices of these two factors of production, labor and capital, would induce a profit-maximizing enterpreneur to use labor intensive (capital extensive) techniques, that is, techniques of production that use relatively more labor and less capital. Interestingly enough, the production techniques used in some of the

South Asian countries do not correspond to the prevailing factor endowment situation. Iftikhar Ahmad has calculated capital-labor ratios in manufacturing industries in Bangladesh and compared them with those in Japan and the United States—whose economies, when compared with that of Bangladesh, are characterized as labor scarce and capital abundant. Table 5-8 presents estimates on capital intensities in selected major industries in the three countries mentioned above. For each industry the capital intensity or capital-labor ratio for Bangladesh is set at unity and the ratios for Japan and the United States are calculated on that basis.

Figures on the value of fixed assets per worker employed in Bangladesh, Pakistan, and Japan computed by Azizur Rahman Khan, are given in Table 5-9.

It is clear that industries in Bangladesh (with the exception of basic metals) are more capital intensive than those in Japan. Many of Bangladesh's industries are as capital intensive as those in the United States. Pakistan's manufacturing industries are more capital intensive than Japanese industries. The high capital intensity of the Bangladesh and Pakistan industries seems paradoxical in view of the high level of unemployment existing in these countries. The main explanation seems to be that the techniques used have been imported from the advanced Western economies and are geared to their factor endowment situation. But an important additional cause for using capital intensive techniques is the distortion of factor prices, that is, the fact that the market prices of such factors as capital, foreign exchange, and labor do not reflect their

Table 5-8 Capital Intensities in Manufacturing Industries: Bangladesh, Japan, and the United States, 1962-1963

Industries	Bangladesh	Japan	U.S.
Cotton textiles	1.0	0.38	2.18
Paper	1.0	0.07	0.85
Leather goods	1.0	0.59	1.40
Rubber goods	1.0	0.32	4.43
All chemicals	1.0	0.33	2.49
Basic metals	1.0	4.04	13.60
Machinery	1.0	0.20	1.96
Wood products	1.0	0.40	

SOURCE: Iftikhar Ahmad, "Employment in Bahgladesh: Problems and Prospects," in E. A. G. Robinson and Keith Griffin, eds. *The Economic Development of Bangladesh within a Socialist Framework* (New York: Wiley, 1974), p. 250.
A. R. Kahn, "Capital Intensity and the Efficiency of Factor Use: a Comparative Study of the Observed Capital Labour Ratios of Pakistan Industries," *Pakistan Development Review*, vol. 10 (Summer 1970), 232-263.

Table 5-9 Value of Fixed Assets per Worker in U. S. dollars

Industries	Japan (1955)	Bangladesh (1962-1963)	Pakistan (1962-1963)
Cotton textiles	475	1,713	2,418
Paper	508	11,424	
Leather goods	422	960	1,164
Rubber goods	269	1,122	2,764
Machinery	478	3,306	1,023
Wood products	367	1,236	652

SOURCE: Azizur Rahman Khan, "Some Problems of Choice of Techniques in a Mixed Economy: The Case of Pakistan," in E. A. G. Robinson and Michael Kidron, eds., *Economic Development in South Asia* (London: St. Martin's, 1970), p. 206.

true equilibrium prices based on the factor endowment situation. A number of factors, including minimum wage rates, the provision of housing and other fringe benefits to workers, and union-negotiated wages have tended to raise the price of labor. For instance, wage rates in the urban industrial areas are, on the average, three to four times the wage rates prevailing in the rural areas. On the other hand, several factors tend to reduce the price of capital, for example, the granting of import licenses to industrialists to import capital goods at official foreign exchange rates, which, from 1948 to 1965, were overvalued to the extent of 80 to 210 percent. This is tantamount to subsidizing imported capital goods for the industrialists. Various tax advantages, such as liberal accelerated depreciation allowances, also serve as incentive to use capital rather than labor. These steps raise the market price of labor and lower the market price of capital from their equilibrium levels (also called shadow prices), thus adversely affecting the employment situation in the countries concerned. In the absence of such distortions, more labor would be hired, easing the unemployment situation somewhat.

The worsening unemployment among the educated is partly explained by the massive increase in educational facilities provided in the South Asian countries as a part of economic planning (discussed in chapter 4), beyond the absorptive capacities of their economies. The nature, or philosophical basis, of education in the South Asian countries tends to accentuate the problem. In the words of the Bangladesh Planning Commission:

> The system of education prevalent in the subcontinent before 1947 was not geared to the needs of an independent nation or of a growing economy. Its purpose was primarily to produce a number of educated people who could assist the British Colonial administration in the country. In fact, the small section of people who were educated under this system acquired a set of

values, which, on the one hand, alienated them from their own people, and on the other, developed in them a distaste for all forms of manual labour.[30]

There has been no appreciable change in the philosophy of education as it existed prior to 1947.

> The philosophy of education or its contents was not significantly changed to suit the requirements of a developing nation. . . . Our educational system thus conspicuously failed to inculcate consciousness in the minds of the educated people of their obligations towards the less fortunate masses.[31]

The ranks of the educated vainly seeking white-collar jobs continue to swell, while many jobs requiring technical skill and manual work go unfilled. However, more recently, even technically qualified personnel are having difficulty in finding employment.

> The technically qualified personnel presented no serious employment problem until about the end of the Third Plan. However, as a result of serious set-backs in the mid-sixties, to investment and growth, particularly in industry and mining, there was a sharp decline in the demand for technical personnel. This happened just as the large expansion of training facilities during the Second and Third Plan periods was beginning to yield a much larger out-turn of technical personnel. As a result, large scale unemployment appeared even among the technical and scientific personnel including degree holders, diploma holders and science graduates and post-graduates . . . serious and growing unemployment among the non-technical educated is a chronic problem. In recent years, the position has been deteriorating even faster than usual.[32]

STRATEGIES FOR IMPROVING EMPLOYMENT

Provision of employment opportunities to millions of unemployed and underemployed in South Asia is in itself a stupendous task and will require substantial changes in the economic policies pursued in the past. In this section, we shall discuss some crucial policies that would help to alleviate, if not eliminate, the unemployment problem in South Asia.

Population Control   Curbing the population explosion facing the South Asian countries is fundamental in any attempt to provide work opportunities for the swelling labor force. Most countries in the region are aware of the grave implications of their fast increasing numbers and have included population planning programs as an integral part of their development plans. But, unfortunately, the success of these programs, until now, has been mainly in creating an awareness of the problem, rather than in the adoption of family planning measures. We have already discussed the population problem in chapter 2. Obviously, failure to check population growth will further aggravate the unemployment problem.

Removal of Factor Price Distortions   Careful analysis of the market versus shadow prices of factors of production is essential in planning the production techniques that would promote a more efficient use of existing resources. As discussed earlier, most of the South Asian economies are characterized by a labor abundant, capital scarce factor endowment situation, but factor price distortions have led to the adoption of inappropriate capital-intensive techniques. Amelioration of this distortion will expand employment opportunities. Current policies which discriminate in favor of capital—such as those providing for massive depreciation allowance and other tax advantages and the granting of import licenses at lower foreign exchange rates—should be revised or discontinued. And appropriate wage policies will have to be adopted to bring wages more into line with labor productivity.

From the point of view of economic efficiency, while an underdeveloped economy with labor abundance and capital shortage should choose production techniques characterized by a lower capital-labor ratio; this adjustment should not be such as to entail loss of output. Otherwise employment creation objectives will conflict with income generation and economic growth objectives. For achieving the criterion of economic efficiency, the crucial variables are factor and product prices in competitive markets. There is, however, a school of thought in determining the appropriate techniques of production which places more emphasis on the employment creation objective—stressing the social cost of unemployment and the social benefits to be derived from providing work opportunities.

> Special care has to be taken in those countries which have a large surplus of unskilled labour for in such circumstances, money wages will not reflect the real cost of using labour. In these circumstances, capital is not productive if it is used to do what labour could do equally well, given the level of wages. Such investments may be highly profitable to capitalists but they are unprofitable to the community as a whole since they add to unemployment but not to output.[33]

Mahatma Gandhi built a strong case for using highly labor-intensive techniques of production (cottage industries and handicrafts) on the basis of the high social costs of modern capital intensive methods which he foresaw would deprive workers of the social benefits and meaningful work opportunities of the more traditional production techniques. The People's Republic of China, during its early stages of development, sacrificed economic efficiency for labor absorption by using labor-intensive techniques for the production processes normally highly capital intensive (e.g., iron and steel). The question of choice of technology is, however, quite complex and needs careful consideration. The chief aim of employment policy is to strike a balance between the objectives of greater employment and greater output.

Reform of the Educational System   The educational system as presently constituted in the countries of South Asia is not geared to the development of human resources but, in the words of Gunnar Myrdal, "to train clerks, minor officials, and low-level administrative personnel for government and business."[34] Such an educational system results in a serious waste of scarce educational (as well as human) resources because people "are not merely being insufficiently educated, they are miseducated on a huge scale."[35]

The reform of the educational system should start with achieving a proper balance in the skill structure and labor needs of the countries in this region. In other words, education should be made responsive to the specific requirements of those countries. It must have relevance to future work and life and should provide adequate preparation for productive employment. The system should produce a cadre of skilled laborers required for the development needs of the country. It should cease to turn out countless numbers of "educated" persons who remain mostly unemployed and unemployable. A reformed educational system should inculcate certain basic values, including a respect for work—whatever its nature, social prestige should be based on contribution to the needs of the society rather than on the acquisition of wealth and political power. Ideally, education should instill initiative, self-reliance, and an urge for creativity, so that an educated person is able to find or create employment for himself, rather than depending on the government to hire him. These suggested reforms may read like a list of dreams and pious hopes but, taken seriously, they are essential to the economic development of South Asia. Any other attempt to provide jobs to the fast-increasing number of educated persons on a permanent basis will fail until the educational system is linked more effectively to the demands of social and economic development.

Reform of the educational system will require long-term attention. The Indian Planning Commission has offered the following proposals for speedy generation of employment opportunities for the educated unemployed:

1. Intensification of research and development in identified priority areas
2. Formulation of a shelf of projects from which choices could be made for inclusion in the fifth plan
3. Acceleration of construction activities
4. Assistance to technically qualified persons for setting up small-scale industries[36]

The Planning Commission recognizes the fact that, "the lasting solution . . . must, eventually, be found in a greatly intensified tempo of growth. In this context, a sharp step-up in the rate of investment and industrial expansion, particularly in areas that have a high employment potential, is essential,"[37]

Rural Work Programs   The absorption of surplus rural manpower has, in the past, followed a classic historical pattern: Starting out with a predominantly agricultural economy, technological advances resulted in productivity increases, with fewer people required to produce the nation's agricultural needs, a process of industrialization emerged; the surplus rural population was absorbed into the expanding urban industrial centers; and, finally, urban and rural areas became complementary to one another in economic expansion. This was the pattern of development in all of the presently advanced countries. However, the economies of the South Asian countries cannot follow this path of development. The urban industrial sector has not developed sufficiently to absorb the surplus rural population. In fact the cities have not even been able to provide employment to new entrants to the labor force resulting from natural increases in the urban population. Serious overcrowding and urban unemployment characterize most cities of South Asia. The solution to rural unemployment thus lies in the overall development of the economies in the long run and in launching rural work programs to absorb the existing unemployed in the short run. Almost all of the South Asian countries have emphasized work programs. According to the Pakistan Planning Commission, "The Works Program is a multi-purpose experiment in socioeconomic development. Its objectives are: to provide additional and seasonal work for the unemployed and underemployed." These programs would create

necessary infra-structure such as roads, bridges, irrigation canals, flood protection embankments, drinking water supply facilities, etc. and provide larger employment opportunities in the rural areas.[38]

Such programs are also an integral part of India's five-year plans.

The rural works program has a vital contribution to make, both towards relief of unemployment and underemployment and assuring of minimum earnings and towards acceleration of the pace of agricultural and rural development.[39]

To face the deteriorating unemployment position, the Government of India has recently introduced some crash programs[40] for the rural sector. The main programs are the following:

1. Crash scheme for rural employment: aimed at rapidly expanding employment in rural areas by hiring rural labor for labor-intensive public works.
2. Marginal farmers and agricultural labor scheme: specifically aimed at providing employment opportunities to underemployed "marginal" farmers and agricultural laborers by providing subsidized credit support for agricultural and subsidiary occupations like dairy, poultry, fishery, and horticulture operations.
3. Small Farmers Development Agency: This program was aimed at "small but potentially viable farmers" and its objectives included, making available to them farm inputs, including credit, enabling them to participate in available technology, to practice intensive agriculture, and to diversify their activities.

Despite these crash programs and other attempts to provide employment opportunities in development plans, the employment position in some of the South Asian countries—particularly India and Bangladesh—has deteriorated further. This raises the important issue of the implementation of planned policies. The development plans of the South Asian countries are replete with policy plans and ambitious targets, but the achievements, in most cases, fall severely short. This performance gap leads not only to an acute sense of national frustration, it also makes the plans appear as nothing more than so much paper and wishful thinking. Feelings about the performance gap are so strong that two members of the Committee on Unemployment recently proposed penal action against those responsible for the nonimplementation of employment programs. In the words of one committee member, "It is not enough to recognize in theory the necessity for tackling the problem of unemployment. It is also necessary to translate this theory into action."[41]

NOTES

1. For a discussion of various concepts of unemployment and the problems in measuring it, see Betty G. Fishman and Leo Fishman, *Employment, Unemployment, and Economic Growth* (New York: Crowell, 1969); Seymour L. Wolfbein, *Employment and Unemployment in the United States* (Chicago: Science Research Associates, 1964); and U.S. Government, *Economic Report of the President* (Washington, D.C., 1975).

2. U.S. Government, *Economic Report of the President,* pp. 86–102.

3. For a detailed discussion, see J. S. Uppal, *Disguised Unemployment in an Underdeveloped Economy* (New York: Asia Publishing House, 1973).

4. Amartya Sen, *Employment, Technology and Development* (Oxford: Clarendon, 1975), p. 119.

5. Gunnar Myrdal, *Asian Drama: An Inquiry into the Poverty of Nations* (New York: Pantheon, 1968), p. 2221.

6. Government of India, Planning Commission, *Report of the Committee on Unemployment Estimates* (New Delhi, 1970), p. 30.

7. Ibid., p. 31.

8. S. Selvaratram and L. S. Fernando, "Measurement of Employed and Unemployed in Ceylon," in Ronald G. Ridker and Harold Lubell, eds., *Employment and Unemployment Problems of the Near East and South Asia* (New Delhi: Vikas, 1971), p. 359.

9. Sultan S. Hashmi and Syed Mushtaq Hussain, "A Review of Projected Manpower Labour Force and Employment for Pakistan," in Ridker and Lubell, eds., *Employment and Unemployment Problems,* p. 359.

10. Ronald G. Ridker, "Employment and Unemployment in Near East and South Asian Countries," Ridker and Lubell, eds., *Employment and Unemployment Problems, p. 15.*

11. Edgar O. Edwards, ed., *Employment in Developing Nations* (New York: Columbia University Press, 1974), p.10.

12. Ibid., p. 100.

13. R. C. Bhardwaj, *Employment and Unemployment in India* (New York: Humanities Press, 1969), p. 83.

14. Computed from data in Government of India, *Report of the Committee on Unemployment* (New Delhi, 1973).

15. Iftikhar Ahmad, "Employment in Bangladesh: Problems and Prospects," in E. A. G. Robinson and Keith Griffin, eds., *The Economic Development of Bangladesh within a Socialist Framework* (New York: Wiley, 1974), p. 247.

16. H. N. S. Karunatilake, *Economic Development in Ceylon* (New York: Praeger, 1971), p. 168–169.

17. Government of India, Planning Commission, *Towards an Approach to the Fifth Plan* (New Delhi, 1972), pp. 5–6.

18. Government of India, Planning Commission, *The Fourth Plan: A Mid-Term Appraisal* (New Delhi, 1972), p. 47.

19. C. B. Mamoria, *Agricultural Problems of India* (Allahabad: Kitab Mahal, 1966), p. 727.

20. Quoted in *ibid.,* p. 728.

21. Tarlok Singh, *Poverty and Social Change* (Bombay: Oxford University Press, 1945), p. 136.

22. Shakuntala Mehra, "Surplus Labour in Indian Agriculture," *Indian Economic Review,* April 1966, p. 112.

23. J. S. Uppal, "Measurement of Disguised Unemployment in Punjab Agriculture," *Canadian Journal of Economics,* vol. 33, no. 4 (November, 1967), 590–596.

24. Government of Bangladesh, Planning Commission, *The First Five Year Plan, 1973-78,* (Dacca, 1973), p. 17.

25. Government of Pakistan, Planning Commission, *The Third Five Year Plan, 1965-70* (Karachi, 1965), p. 149.

26. Government of Ceylon, Department of Labour, *Survey of Employment, Unemployment and Underemployment of Labour* (Colombo, 1959–60).

27. H. H. S. Karunatilake, *Economic Development in Ceylon,* p. 168, 361.

28. Government of India, Ministry of Food and Agriculture, *Indian Agriculture in Brief* (New Delhi, 1975), p. 120.

29. Ahmad, "Employment in Bangladesh," p. 251.

30. Government of Bangladesh, Planning Commission, *The First Five Year Plan, 1973-78.* (Dacca, 1973), p. 441.

31. Ibid., p. 442.

32. India, *Fourth Plan: Mid-Term Appraisal,* pp. 44-45.

33. W. Arthur Lewis, *The Theory of Economic Growth* (London: Allen and Unwin, 1955), p. 356.

34. Myrdal, *Asian Drama;* vol. 3, p. 1647.

35. Ibid., p. 1649.

36. India, *Fourth Plan: Mid-term Appraisal,* pp. 44-45.

37. Ibid., pp. 45-46.

38. Government of Pakistan, Planning Commission, *Preliminary Evaluation of the Third Five Year Plan* (Islamabad, 1970), p. 169.

39. Government of India, Planning Commission, *Fourth Five Year Plan: A Draft Outline* (New Delhi, 1968), p. 111.

40. For details, see Sen, *Employment Technology and Development,* pp. 135-145.

41. Quoted in Ruddar Datt and K. P. M. Sundharam, *Indian Economy* (New Delhi: Chand, 1975), p. 511.

6
Religious and Social Values

The people of South Asia are deeply religious, and all facets of their lives including their endeavors for material advancement are affected by their religious beliefs and values. The ways and extent to which noneconomic factors, especially religious beliefs, influence economic behavior in a society is a matter of considerable controversy among economists.[1] The theorists question the validity of applying noneconomic criteria to economic phenomena that presuppose specialization and division of labor. They contend that noneconomic factors lack objectivity for want of rigorous analysis and quantification. Also, cultural factors change but slowly; thus, in the analysis of short-run processes of change, these noneconomic factors do not have much relevance.

Karl Marx contended that the social and cultural aspects of human evolution are the consequence rather than the cause of economic factors. However, this atomistic conception of the social process is criticized by social scientists like Schumpeter, who maintain that "economic man" is a myth and that the unity of social life and the inseparability of its various elements preclude any dissection of man and society into political, social, cultural, ethical, and economic parts.[2] According to J. R. Hicks, since policy is a reconciliation of political, social, cultural, sociological, and economic considerations, any attempt to formulate policy without due consideration of noneconomic factors "will be greatly misleading."[3] The case against the theorist viewpoint has been well summed up by Boulding:

I have been gradually coming under the conviction, disturbing for a professional theorist, that there is no such thing as economics—there is only social science applied to economic problems.[4]

The Indian Planning Commission is cognizant of the interrelation between noneconomic factors and economic development.

The existing social and economic institutions have . . . to be appraised from time to time in relation to their role in the nation's development. To the extent they do not adequately fulfill the social purpose or fail to secure the economic aims of planned development, they have to be replaced or transformed.[5]

The term "noneconomic factors" is, however, vague and can encompass a wide variety of factors. Social scientists have varying opinions on the identification and effectiveness of noneconomic factors in the process of economic development. Parsons stresses the "relation of the individual to society" in the process of economic transformation.[6] Kuznets lists "secularism, egalitarianism, and nationalism" as preconditions of industrial revolution.[7] Hagen stresses the "relationship between personality, society, and economic growth."[8] McCleland has attempted to identify variables which produce innovative and creative personalities.[9] In McCleland's formulation, the number of people with "n" achievements is one of the most important determinants of economic development. Max Weber and R. H. Tawney[10] stressed religion as an important element in economic growth. Denison finds education to be the single most important factor in development, accounting for as much as 23 percent of growth of the American economy during the period 1909–1929.[11]

Having noted some views on the relevance of noneconomic factors in the development process, we need to identify the relevant factors in a given economy, assign them relative weights, and calculate their precise relationship to economic growth and to noneconomic factors. Economists like Denison have developed statistical techniques to estimate the contribution of various factors to economic growth.

Noneconomic factors frequently discussed in the literature on South Asian economic development include religion and religious values (such as attitude toward present life and life after death), social institutions (such as caste and the extended, or joint, family system), social customs (such as the dowry system), social classes, political factors and political institutions (such as national integration and administrative structure), regionalism and provincialism, and education. Religion, the caste system, and the extended family system have been the subject of most debate, and we shall discuss the impact of these three factors on the economic development of South Asia.

RELIGION AND ECONOMIC DEVELOPMENT

How does religion impinge on the process of economic development? Economic development is the result of society's efforts for material advancement. Individuals in a society make efforts to satisfy their desires, and these efforts result in the production of goods and services which are consumed or are accumulated and reinvested for further production. Basically, therefore, desire, effort, consumption, savings, and reinvestment are the crucial elements affecting the development process. The impact of religious values on these basic elements would thus determine whether a particular religion was conducive or inimical to economic development. Some religious codes are more compatible with economic development than others. According to Lewis:

> It is possible for a nation to stifle its economic growth by adopting passionately and intolerantly religious doctrines of a kind which are incompatible with growth. Or it is possible alternatively for conversion to a new faith to be the spark, which sets off economic growth. . . . If a religion lays stress upon material values, upon work, upon thrift and productive investment, upon honesty in commercial relations, upon experimentation and risk bearing and upon equality of opportunity, it will be helpful to growth, whereas in so far as it is hostile to these things, it tends to inhibit growth.[12]

We do not wish to go so far as to compile a list of favorable and unfavorable religions, but it is interesting to note comments on certain major religions as they affect economic development. Boeke distinguishes between Eastern and Western cultures in his general remarks:

> The oriental is, unfortunately, totally lacking in organizing power where modern Western enterprises are concerned. Where industry is dominated by common sense reasons, Eastern society is molded by fatalism and resignation . . . Eastern culture, in this way, comes to a standstill and stagnation means decline.[13]

There appears to be a general consensus on the favorable impact of the Protestant Reformation on economic development. Max Weber and R. H. Tawney emphasize the connection between the Protestant Reformation and economic growth through the puritanical injunction to work and achieve spiritual satisfaction through work. Kapp summarizes the impact of the Protestant Reformation as follows:

Protestant ethics not only provided the religious sanction for sustained activities but it channelled human energies into an inner drive towards work. Indeed, what took place under the combined impact of economic and intellectual development was nothing less than the emergence of a new personality structure which was well suited for the production of wealth.[14]

In Catholicism, on the other hand, according to Donald Smith,

the praise of poverty, as a condition more conducive to the realization of spiritual values in this life and the bliss of heaven throughout eternity, has been a major theme until very recently and was repeated in Pope Paul's address to Colombian peasants in 1968.[15]

These religious attitudes have certainly stood in the way of economic advancement. However, as Smith points out, the emphasis in Catholicism is now shifting from "paternalistic charity" to "economic growth" and more equitable distribution as a matter of justice.[16]

Muslim scholars contend that Islam, the dominant religion in Pakistan and Bangladesh,[17] does not stand in the way of development efforts. It is claimed in fact, that:

Money, according to Islamic jurisprudence is good and a Muslim should acquire it by work and through legitimate means . . . technological and economic development are man's major task on earth, assigned to him by God. Active participation in developmental efforts, not other worldly preoccupations, characterize the life lived in obedience to the divine will.[18]

According to Jean Herbert:

Generally speaking, Islam is optimistic and transcendentalist, it does not favor either asceticism or extremes of ecstacy, but it does admit the concepts of gainful work, family ownership, earthly happiness and comfort.[19]

Endorsing the generally favorable view of Islam, the Pakistan Planning Commission exhorts "The cultural and religious heritage of the country should be preserved and not allowed to be destroyed by the ruthless pursuit of economic development."[20]

The major religions which have generally been regarded as inconsistent with economic advancement are Buddhism and Hinduism. Buddhism, the dominant religion in Sri Lanka, is said to emphasize asceticism, abstinence, cultivation of the spirit, and promoting the monastic way of life. In Buddha's Noble Truths (suffering is universal, the cause of suffering is desire, the removal of desire is the cure for suffering) the elimination of desire is the crucial goal. Nirvana—the ultimate goal of all according to the Buddhist faith—is the state of "desirelessness". Emphasis on the monastic life and elimination of desire goes against the very essence of economic development—rooted in the pursuit of material and economic goals. In examining Hinduism, the dominant religion in India and Nepal, we see considerable controversy on the question of whether its basic tenets are conducive or inimical to economic growth. The negative and commonly held view is that the basic values of Hinduism (ascetism, fatalism, the cyclical view of time, the caste system, etc.) are enormous obstacles to economic development.[21] According to Dalt and Sundharam:

> In India the Hindu religion has been emphasizing renunciation of worldly things and has always urged its followers to discount the material things of the world. The Hindu accepts his status in life, his occupation, his caste and his wealth as well as his possessions as a result of his "Karma." . . . Hence, in a real sense Hindu religion has been acting as a disincentive to economic growth because of its faith in a preordained order of life.[22]

On the other hand, some scholars believe that the "gospel of the Hindus distinctly prefers a life of action to that of renunciation"[23] and that the Hindu philosophy contains and sanctions all the characteristics of the Protestant ethic, such as

> a belief in an orderly universe subject to deterministic laws, the ability to anticipate a course of events and behave accordingly, with the possibility of control, based on knowledge; a strong sense of responsibility for one's actions and their consequences, and a capacity to organize one's life under a systematic methodical discipline which will maximize the goals one has set oneself.[24]

Some writers quote historical evidence against the contention that Hindu spirituality has fostered a pessimistic attitude and a universal indifference to material attainments. According to V. G. Kale:

> If the Indian mind had been exclusively taken up by thoughts of the other world, as has been frequently asserted, the Indian people would not have figured in history as great empire builders, conquerors, and daring colonizers.[25]

The pessimism, fatalism, and belief in predestiny responsible for stagnation of the Indian economy cannot, according to Jathar and Beri, be attributed to Hinduism; these are products of the political anarchy and social upheaval which prevailed in India during the sixteenth and seventeenth centuries.

When governments were more robbers than protectors of the people . . . when people stood to lose in a moment the fruits of years of industry by the rapacity of a chance invader or oppressive ruler, the incentive to the production and accumulation of wealth was bound to be very weak. It is natural that hope and ambition faded from the outlook of the people under these conditions, and fatalism took possession of their minds.[26]

Let us now examine the basic beliefs of Hinduism and their impact on the economic development of South Asia in general and India in particular.

THE ESSENTIAL FEATURES OF HINDUISM

We shall, in this section, mention only those major aspects of Hinduism that have a direct bearing on economic activity. At the outset, it may be noted that Hinduism is not a unified religion, there is no single sacred book that explains all of its teachings. Hinduism attempts to be all things to all men. For scholars and thinkers it offers a highly abstract philosophy or metaphysics explaining the nature of the universe, the dynamics of life, the cycle of birth and rebirth. For the layman, it provides a wealth of rituals and a multiplicity of gods. It draws its doctrines from a large number of writings and scriptures, including the Vedas and the Upanishads and the epics, *Ramayana* and *Mahabharata*. Hinduism has countless "gods, a multiplicity of "sects," "cults," and "philosophies." This bewildering diversity, sometimes gives the impression that Hinduism is not a religion but only a way of life. Authors like Tilak and Radhakrishnan have, however, attempted to reveal the basic unity of Hindu thought and belief.

The Philosophical Tenets of Hinduism[27]

One Ultimate Reality: The Universe and Humans. The one ultimate reality, despite the seemingly thousands of gods of different shapes and forms worshipped by Hindus, is the infinite universe, which is ultimately permanent and unchanging and which transcends the form, name, and personality. The *purusha* or *atman*—the real self and spiritual component of all things—is, as are all things in the universe, the manifestation of the ultimate reality. According to the Upanishads,

> The essential self or the vital essence in man is the same as that in an ant, the same as that in a gnat, the same as that in an elephant, the same as that in these three worlds, indeed the same as that in the whole universe.[28]

The essential self in humans, the *atman,* being part of the eternal, infinite universe is also eternal. As Krishna says in the *Bhagavad Gita,* "He who thinks that this slays and he who thinks that this is slain; both of them fail to perceive the truth; this one neither slays nor is slain. . . . He [the self] is said to be unmanifest, unthinkable and unchanging.[29]

But, unfortunately, the human is ignorant about the true self and assumes there is a single, complex, changing individual—the empirical, or *guna,* self—among many, living in a world of many changing objects (therefore an illusory, impermanent world). In this way, the essential self—the *atman*—is imprisoned in the finite body. It is limited to the world of the senses and possesses an ignorant and misguided mind. It fails to realize its own reality and is egotistical in understanding because it thinks of itself as a particular individual reveling in its uniqueness. The gulf between the *atman*—the infinite, real self—and the finite *guna*—the empirical self—is the major problem facing humankind. According to the Hindu view of life, closing this gap is the ultimate aim of human endeavor.

Hinduism classifies the different tendencies and characteristics observed in *guna,* or the empirical self, into three basic categories: *sattva,* which inclines one to intellectual activity; *rajas,* leading to vigorous action; and *tamas,* which inclines one to devotional activity. The combination of these tendencies is what determines the overall personality type among different persons. Each person is bound to a particular *guna,* or activity. It is through concentration on one's particular *guna* that an individual can achieve *atman.* Corresponding to each *guna* category there are three different paths: the path of discipline in knowledge, the path of discipline in work, and the path of discipline in devotion, which guide an individual toward the realization of infinite *atman.* According to the *Gita,* one should actively engage in one's duty according to one's own *guna* but should at the same time dissociate the self from the activity. This is the essence of nonattachment: an important precept in the *Gita.*

The above explanation of the relationship between the universe and humankind leads to the following inferences:

1. The empirical, finite self is separated from the real, infinite *atman* because of its nonrealization of the ultimate reality and its attachment to the illusory world and *gunas.* This gap between the *atman,* and the *guna* self stands in the way of achieving the spiritual and ultimate goal—*moksha.* One could infer from this view that renunciation of *gunas* (activities) would be an effective way to bridge the gap.
2. In order to free oneself from the *guna* self, it is necessary to undertake seriously and cooperate fully in work activity appropriate to that *guna* self, progressively transcending it. This implies that salvation from work is through work itself.

These two interpretations run parallel to one another and represent a dualism in Hindu philosophy.

The Transmigration Principle. The principle of rebirth, or the transmigration of the soul, is fundamental to the Hindu philosophy and has a great impact on the mode of thinking and way of life of the people of the Hindu faith. The self, separated from the "ultimate reality" wanders from one form to the other in search of *moksha* (salvation). Since the self is part of the "ultimate infinite universe," it is not restricted to any particular form or shape. Like a liquid, the self may fit itself to any type of container; until separated from *atman,* it may crawl as a snake, wander as an elephant, bloom as a flower, or meditate as a seer, "far from the madding crowd." As Welty puts it:

> The entire universe is a collection of temporary living quarters for selves struggling toward liberation and final release from their wanderings. Life is like a journey over a bridge, across which man must travel to reach his destination but upon which he does not build permanently. It is a lower stage of experience necessary before passing into the higher level of identification with the Supreme Reality.[30]

The fundamental question, then, is how to achieve identification with the Supreme Reality and escape from this cycle of birth and rebirth to achieve *moksha* (salvation)?

The Law of Karma. The short answer to the above question is that the misguided and mistaken empirical, or *guna,* self must be disciplined to tread the right path, to realize the true spiritual self or *atman.* This path is defined in practical terms as *dharma.*

Karma literally means 'actions' or 'deeds'; the law of karma operates like a law of causation, whereby the life of the individual self is determined by its actions—the present life is the result of actions in the past life, and actions in the present life will determine the pattern for future life. No action is lost, and, as Attreya describes

> No one can escape or evade the good or evil consequences of his deeds. . . . If he does not meet the consequences in this life here and now he must do so in some other life. . . . Life here must presuppose a previous life to account for the inequalities of circumstances and life. Death must lead to another life to make the dying person undergo retribution for what he has done in life. . . . Rebirth or reincarnation is, thus, not only a fact known directly to seers but also a logical necessity.[31]

Hindus justify the pleasures and sufferings of life in the material world of human existence through *karma,* which operates like an "iron law of inescapable retribution." According to Max Weber, Hinduism is indeed a perfect example of a religion providing a rationalistic explanation for existing incongruities of suffering, fortune, and merit.[32]

The role of "actions" raises some important questions relating to the realization of the "real self," or *atman*. (a) Should we cease to perform actions? In other words, does renunciation of all worldly activity provide the solution? (b) Is there any ordering of good actions versus bad actions? (c) Can an individual be guided to perform good actions? The answer to the first question is found in the sacred book, the *Bhagavad Gita*. It is maintained that action is necessary, "for no one can remain even for a moment without doing work; every one is made to act helplessly by the impulses born of nature." The crucial thing is to engage in worldly activity without becoming attached to it. As the *Gita* teaches:

> To action alone hast thou a right and never at all to its fruits; let not the fruits of action be thy motive; neither let there be any attachment to inaction. . . . Therefore, without attachment, perform always the work that has to be done, for man attains to be the highest by doing work without attachment.[33]

To distinguish among various actions, there seems to exist some ordering (or spiritual progression) for an individual to achieve liberation from the endless torment involved in the cycle of birth and rebirth. As Welty describes it,

> A man is closer to the ultimate Reality than an animal, an animal is closer than a plant and a plant is closer than a lifeless object . . . justice and mercy are valued more highly than injustice and cruelty. Spiritual values such as beauty, love and righteousness are of more importance than intellectual values such as logic, keenness, clarity and other skills. Below the spiritual and intellectual skills come biological values such as health and vitality and finally material values such as wealth and the like.[34]

In this ordering, actions involving spiritual values come first and material pursuits last. It is the saint and not the practical man who occupies the place of honor. It is austerity, detachment from material things, and sacrifice—not the accumulation of wealth or political or social power—which gain respect and admiration in traditional Hindu society. There is a popular saying in India: "It is the renunciation rather than the accumulation of wealth that matters."

This emphasis on the law of *karma*, and the implied spiritual progression, has a great effect on an individual's behavior in seeking personal *moksha* (salvation) and also in his interpersonal relations with the society as a whole. Hinduism provides a set of aims and objectives to be achieved by an individual in his effort to realize the *atman*. These rules, contained in the *purusharthas* (the four aims of man), apply to the various stages of his life (*ashrams*) in this illusory world of matter and the senses. The four *purusharthas* as presented in the *Mahabharata* are (1) *dharma,* or morality, (2) *artha,* or means of life, (3) *kama,* or enjoyment of the means of life, and (4) *moksha,* or final liberation through realization of the *atman.* These objectives are to be achieved in four stages of life: (1) *brahmacharya ashrama,* or student stage, (2) *grihastha ashrama,* or stage of the householder, (3) *vanaprastha ashram,* stage of withdrawal from the social world, and (4) *samnyasa ashrama,* stage of contemplation and meditation.

Dharma is the set of moral guidelines to be followed by the individual in his everyday life. Some important virtues stressed are truth, nonviolence, sacrifice, purity, and renunciation or detachment. Nonviolence stems from the belief that essentially all forms of life are related to the Supreme Reality and should, therefore, be respected. Great emphasis is placed on detachment from all associations with the material world. *Artha* is the set of guidelines to be followed in the acquisition and use of the material means for sustaining life.

The following statements from the Hindu classics suggest some of the attitudes toward the material things of life. In the *Mahabharata* it is said:

> What is here regarded as *dharma* depends entirely upon wealth (*artha*). One who robs another of wealth robs him of his *dharma* as well. Poverty is a state of sinfulness. All kinds of meritorious acts flow from the possession of great wealth, as from wealth spring all religious acts, all pleasures, and heaven itself. . . . He that has no wealth has neither this world nor the next.[35]

The famous treatise, the *Panchatantra,* contains the following observation:

> The smell of wealth is quite enough to make a creature's sterner stuff. And wealth's enjoyment even more. Wealth gives constant vigour, confidence, and power. Poverty is a curse worse than death. Virtue without wealth is of no consequence. The lack of money is the root of all evil.[36]

These statements suggest a strong preference for the acquisition and accumulation of material wealth. But material wealth is to be sought in ways consistent with the requirements of detachment or renunciation required by *dharma* as explained above.

Kama prescribes enjoyment of the material means of life and of the senses. It is explained as follows:

Kama is the enjoyment of the appropriate objects of the five senses of hearing, feeling, seeing, tasting, and smelling, assisted by the mind together with the soul. The ingredient in this is a peculiar contact between the organ of sense and its object, and the consciousness of pleasure that results from the contact is called *Kama*.[37]

Kama is recommended as one of the basic goals of life to enable the individual to fulfill the common desires of the body: food, drink, and sex. The nonsatisfaction of these common desires would create frustrations, which would stand in the way of the mind's striving for the ultimate objective—*moksha.*

Moksha, as mentioned earlier, is the ultimate human goal. The *guna* (or empirical self), engaged in worldly activities and following the requirements of *dharma, artha* and *kama,* should realize that it is a part of the Ultimate Reality. When this realization is attained, the *guna* self achieves *moksha,* or liberation. The real self, the *atman,* completely free of the bondages of the material world—including the cycle of birth and death—lives in the world but nonattached. The material world, with all its worldly things, seems "illusion."

Welty sums up the essence of this philosophy:

Hinduism synthesizes the spiritual and material ways of life by advising man to renounce the passion and attachment which accompany action, but not action itself. It believes that the renunciation of all earthly matters, along with an exclusive preoccupation with the contemplation of spiritual matters, can be reconciled with the individual's responsibility to participate in the affairs of his community and society.[38]

An evaluation of the essential elements in the Hindu philosophy reveals a great deal of dualism. There are certain elements in the philosophy which are "other worldly" and nonmaterialistic, e.g., the material is an illusion; human desires and attachment to worldly matters lead to unhappiness and misery; the individual has no control over either present or future lives since these are the product of *karma;* and preference is for renunciation over acquisition and accumulation. However, there are other elements which seem to sanction materialistic values. The *purushartha* of *artha* lauds wealth and its accumulation. The *Panchatantrata* attributes most of the evils of the world to a lack of money. The law of dharma exhorts the individual to perform his duty diligently, since the path of *moksha* lies in the performance of one's duty. The impact that these elements of Hindu philosophy have on economic development will be examined later in this chapter.

Hindu Social Organization   The social organization of the South Asian countries has been marked by two important institutions: the joint family and the caste system, each of which exerts a profound influence on the processes of economic and political development in those countries.

The Extended Family. While a typical family in Western developed countries is nuclear, or individual, consisting of wife, husband, and minor children, family life in the South Asian countries—and also in most other underdeveloped countries in the world—is organized on an "extended" or joint basis. In South Asian society, the joint family is usually patriarchal—a multigenerational, joint-kinship organization—consisting of parents, married sons with their wives and children, all unmarried children, and sometimes such other dependents as grandparents, uncles, cousins, and nephews and even more distant relatives in need of support. The family members jointly own property and share the work and income of the family. The size of the family may vary from four to as many as thirty, some of the members may be living in different places; but the main distinguishing feature of the joint family is its moral responsibility to share work and income with all of its members. Other features of the joint family system that specifically affect economic development are given below:

1. Generally the oldest male member is head of the family. Important decisions concerning the disposition of family property, the marriage of family members, and so on are taken by the head of family, who may be guided by other members. The roles of all members of the family are clearly defined and are based on their position in the family hierarchy.

2. The immovable property of the family is owned jointly and the head of the family is bound by customary laws—deemed sacred—to use the property prudently in the common interests of the family. In the event of the death of the family head or serious quarrels among members, the immovable property may be divided according to customary law. The joint family would then break up into smaller families, which, in the course of time, would again become large joint family units. Movable property, such as jewelry and clothing is exclusively owned by individual family members.

3. The incomes of all family members are joined in a common pool, which is drawn upon by family members according to their needs. If a relative, however distant, becomes impoverished, the joint family has the moral responsibility to support him.

4. The work of the family—farm operations in the case of an agricultural family—is shared by all family members. In such a situation, it is natural for all members of the family to feel that they are employed, even if some of them may be contributing virtually nothing to the total family output.

5. The marriage of a family member is a family responsibility. The

choice of marriage partner is arranged by the family, after consideration of several factors, including caste and family status, and the marriage is financed from family funds. Children of married sons are primarily members of the family and only secondarily offspring of a specific couple. Through male children the family extends and progresses. Many children thus symbolize a happy and lucky family. In the faces of its children the family sees a long line of future generations.

The origin and continuation of the joint family system may be traced to various socioeconomic and religious factors. For artisan and agricultural families, the joint family provided a type of cooperative structure. Some scholars trace the origin of the system to the emergence of societies from a pastoral stage to agricultural and industrial stages. According to Seligman:

> Where the hunting and root-grubbing stage was supplemented by developed agriculture, the labour of man in tilling the soil, constructing the house and maintaining the patrimony became of signal importance. The male is now the chief factor in the economic process, and we accordingly find the patriarchal family.[39]

Economic causation was reinforced by such religious precepts as *dharma* (moral and spiritual duties) and the *ashrams* (stages of life). Reverence for and even worship of life as well as departed elders—taking the form of obedience to them; placing one's earnings and labor at their disposal, and living as part of the joint family—is an important element of *dharma.* Further, according to the doctrine of *ashrama,* to marry and secure the continuity of the family line is a religious duty leading ultimately to spiritual progression. In the words of Manu, the Hindu seer:

> A man conquers the world by the birth of a son, he enjoys eternity by that of a grandson; and the great-grandfathers enjoy eternal happiness by the birth of a grandson's son.[40]

Some students of social organization in India claim that for various reasons, such as the waning influence of religion—especially among Western-educated youth—lack of employment opportunities, and the mounting economic hardship of large-size families, the joint family is losing its importance. On the other hand, recent statistical studies have shown that this is still the predominant family system in India. A United Nations survey in Bangladesh found that 78 percent of the workers belonged to extended families and had dependents other than their wives and children.

The Caste System.   Another social institution which has played a crucial role in shaping the socioeconomic life of the people of South Asia is the caste system. There are four major castes and a multitude of subcastes. Theoretically, the caste system applies only to Hindu society, but, in practice, the system has, in varying degrees, also affected other religious communities in the region, including Islam,[41] which, philosophically, is essentially an egalitarian religion. Caste not only determines the social status of different groups but also molds the behavior of the group and its members. Caste also regulates communication and interpersonal relations with members of other groups. The word caste[42] is used to refer to division of Indian society on a functional, racial, and sectarian basis.

On a functional basis, Indian society is divided into four *varnas,* or classes:

1. Brahmans, the priestly class, consisting of priests and teachers; their chief task is the preservation and dissemination of knowledge and the performance of religious ceremonies
2. Khashatriya, the military and administrative class; they are responsible for the protection and administration of the society. The sacred book, the *Bhagavad Gita* lists their attributes as "heroism, vigour, steadiness, resourcefulness, not fleeing even in battle, generosity, and leadership"[43]
3. Vaishyas, the class of producers and merchants; their chief functions are agricultural and pastoral operations, the distribution of goods, and the lending of money
4. Shudras, the class of laborers and servants; of them the *Bhagavad Gita* commands: "the *dharma* of Shudra . . . is action consisting of service."

Then there are the racial castes, such as the Rajbansi and the Chandals in Bengal; the Ghar and the Chero in Uttar Pradesh and Bihar; and the Jats, the Gujar, and the Meo in Rajasthan and Punjab. Finally, there are the sectarian castes, which originated from religious sects, such as the Kabir pathis, followers of Saint Kabir; and the Lingayat caste in Bombay, founded by a religious leader who denied the supremacy of the Brahmans. Most of these racial and sectarian castes are, however, also linked to the four *varnas* as explained above.

These four *varnas* seem to have originated as a grand scheme of social classification of individuals according to their *gunas,* or attributes for maintaining social order and economic prosperity. It seems that this functional division of society (or division of labor—which economists like Adam Smith have praised for its contribution to specialization and economic growth) was given religious sanction at some later date. The performance of one's duty in accordance with one's *varna* constituted one's *dharma* and led the way to the achievement of the real self, or *atman*. According to the *Gita,* "the duties of *Brahmanas, Khashatriyas, Vaishyas* and *Shudras* have been assigned according to the *gunas* born native."[44] The laws of Manu link caste, actions, and rebirth: "A Shudra who is pure, the servant of his better, gentle in his speech, and free from pride . . . attains in his next life a higher caste."[45]

It is also contended by several writers that the caste system had its origin in maintaining distinctions between the fair-skinned Aryans, who invaded India from the north many centuries ago, and the dark-skinned peoples whom they conquered. Once the Aryans had imposed their superiority, religious sanction was given to the divisions according to castes.

Whatever might have been the factors responsible for the origin of caste, there is no denying that the system created serious divisions in Indian society with far-reaching socioeconomic ramifications. Ghurye mentions the following salient features of the caste system in India:

1. The segmentation of society
2. Hierarchy
3. Food taboos and restrictions on social intercourse
4. Civil and religious disabilities—privileges of different groups
5. Restrictions on choice of occupation
6. Marriage restrictions[46]

Indian society is divided into several hundreds of castes and subcastes, each of which, according to Srinivas, "is a homogeneous group with a common culture, with a common occupation or occupations, practicing endogamy and commensality."[47] The individual caste member has greater loyalty toward his caste than toward the society at large. Thus, the existence of castes has obstructed the national integration of Indian society. The castes have a hierarchial structure, with certain castes considered higher than others. Marriage within the caste is an important social requirement. Marriage outside one's caste, though increasingly practiced by educated urban classes, is generally shunned and brings disrepute to the family.

The four major castes (*varnas*) in order of their social and religious importance are Brahmans, Khashatriyas, Vaishyas, and Shudras. Each of these main castes are further divided into subcastes, each with its place on the social ladder. The castes and subcastes exhibit some degree of craft-occupation exclusiveness. For most Indians, caste circumscribes occupation. For instance, most Hindus engaged in priestly duties are likely to be Brahmans; sweepers, clothes washers, and scavengers are most likely to be Shudras. It is true that with increasing population, industrialization, and the ambition of the lower castes to rise in the caste hierarchy, many Indians are deserting their caste-dictated occupations; but it is still very unlikely that a Brahman would be doing a sweeper's job or a Shudra would become a priest in a Hindu temple.

In the hierarchical caste structure, the Shudras have suffered a great deal of religious and hence social and economic disability. The Shudras or Untouchables (also called the backward classes or the *harijans*), numbering about one-third of India's population, or 150 million in 1951, have been relegated to the lowest position in the society. Such menial jobs as the removal of night soil (in a country largely without modern sanitary facilities) or the disposal of dead animals, including the tanning of hides, have been and still are the main Shudra occupations. Educationally, they have remained the least-educated segment of Indian society. The higher castes have kept the Shudras in an inferior position by practicing ritualistic notions of purity and pollution, reinforced by the religious doctrine of *karma,* whereby caste is the outcome of deeds in a previous existence.

There have been several attempts by religious reformers like Guru Nanak and Kabir and by social reformers like Gandhi to improve the lot of the Shudras. Since independence the government of India has passed legislation aimed at improving the social and economic conditions of "the backward classes." The constitution of India forbids discrimination on the basis of caste. Much progress has been achieved in this respect. The level of education among the *harijans* and their economic well-being have improved. Above all, these classes are losing their social and religious stigma; but they still have a long way to go to achieve social integration within society. More will be said in the final section of this chapter about efforts to weaken the hold of the caste system.

THE IMPACT OF HINDUISM ON ECONOMIC DEVELOPMENT

Our examination of the essential features of the philosophy and social organization of the Hindu religion has revealed a certain amount of dualism. There are some elements in Hindu thought that might stand in the way of economic activity, on the other hand, there are elements that could be seen as conducive to economic effort—or at least as not impinging on economic activity. In this section we will discuss the overall impact of various Hindu philosophical and social elements as they affect economic development in South Asia in general and India in particular.

Elements in Hindu Philosophy That Retard Economic Activity   The view that Hinduism is inimical to economic development is supported by those elements that seem to favor fatalism, resignation, other worldliness, and asceticism.

The law of *karma* tends to relate cause (actions) and effect (rebirth in the next life) over a time exceeding the life span of an individual. The elements of cyclical time and cosmic causation involved in the theory of *karma* are of such vast dimension in time and space that the individual feels helpless and insignificant. Acceptance, obedience, and a belief in fatalism are fostered—rather than confidence in his own powers. According to Kapp, "Such commitments will lead either to the use of magic or to resignation and acceptance of the status quo, or whatever may befall the individual."[48] To the extent that the process of economic development depends upon the conviction that man is the maker of his destiny and that economic progress emerges from deliberate effort to change the existing situation, belief in and resigned acceptance of preordination would be a hindrance to economic development.

The belief that the present life is the result of actions in a previous life and, further, that present actions will determine the next life renders the present life transitory and secondary. It promotes the view that the pains and pleasures of this life are *maya* (illusion) and that involvement in them blocks the realization of the ultimate goal. All of this fosters endurance, contentment, submission, withdrawal—attributes that are inimical to economic effort and development.

Some elements of Hindu philosophy can be interpreted as antimaterialistic. The acceptance of one's *dharma,* nonattachment to worldly things; the teachings of the *Gita* that man should perform his work without attachment to the fruits of his action—are some such elements. These views may well deprive an individual of the motivation necessary to pursue economic activity and improve his material condition. Also, "in a transitory world of appearances desireless action without attachment to its fruits runs the risk of degenerating into ritualistic performance of one's duties"[49]—an attitude to work that is unlikely to generate much ambition or the energy and enterprise that are its necessary accompaniment.

Elements in Hindu Philosophy That Promote Economic Activity.   The view that Hindu philosophy does not hinder economic activity and in some ways might actually encourage it is supported by some of the teachings of the Hindu scriptures (and/or interpretations of them), by historical evidence, and by practical aspects of the Hindu religion.

The *Gita* emphasizes the virtue of seriously performing one's duty while not expecting any reward. This emphasis on the life of action without attachment seems to effect a reconciliation between the spiritual and material aspects of life. The doctrine of *karma,* which as discussed earlier, is said to be the root cause of pessimism, asceticism, and renunciation, can be interpreted quite differently. *Karma,* rather than being a deterrent to action, can serve as a powerful incentive to action, because it makes man himself the shaper of his fortune and destiny. Moreover, the exhortation to disinterested action (that is, disinterest in the fruits of action) could create an ethic of modest living and effort for the common betterment. These traits could serve development efforts by providing incentive and ethical justification for hard work, resulting in greater productivity, and an abstinence from conspicuous and unproductive consumption—promoting, in the long run, capital formation.

One of the *purusharthas* (human aims) is *artha,* which guides the acquisition and use of material means for sustaining life. The statement in the *Panchatantra* that "wealth gives constant vigour, confidence and power. . . poverty is a curse worse than death" is a strong spur to the individual acquisition of wealth, although such wealth is required to be used with detachment. *Kama,* another of the *purusharthas,* urges the fulfillment of the physical needs and desires of the body (for food, drink, and sex) through the means achieved by *artha*—which would certainly seem to encourage pursuit of the material means of life and a high level of consumption—two of the cornerstones of economic activity.

Thus, the contradictory teachings and interpretations of Hindu philosophy and their impact on economic activity present an unresolved dualism. Different authors have drawn different conclusions from these contradictory statements. Kapp, for example, maintains that the values of the Hindu religion are a major barrier to the process of economic growth and that the lasting solution of the problem of economic development can be found only in introducing gradual and systematic changes in these values.[50] Gunnar Myrdal also seems to believe that the

> religiously sanctioned beliefs and valuations, not only act as obstacles among the people to getting the plan accepted and effectuated but also as inhibitions in the planners themselves insofar as they share them or are afraid to counteract them.[51]

On the other hand, some writers feel that the negative role of Hinduism is exaggerated and that, in fact, the Hindu religion can make positive contribution to economic effort. Singer, for example, claims that Hindu philosophy contains and sanctions all of the characteristics of the Protestant ethic, which is believed to have contributed so much to economic growth in the Western world.[52] Some scholars (e.g., V. G. Kale) quote historical evidence against the contention that the Hindu religion has fostered pessimistic attitudes and an indifference toward material attainment. Reference is made to the achievements of the ancient Hindus in the fields of mathematics, philosophy, and astronomy. The question is, in the face of these achievements, how can the Hindu mind be characterized as obsessed with other worldliness, pessimism, and ascetism? It is quite possible that the attributes of pessimism, fatalism, and belief in predestination might not be an inherent part of the Hindu religion but a result of the conditions of political anarchy and social upheaval which prevailed in India during the sixteenth and seventeenth centuries.

Some scholars have pointed out that Hinduism is not alone in stressing "other worldly" themes. M. N. Srinivas comments,

> As I understand it, Christianity too is other worldly, and it glorifies poverty and humility. Yet it is in the Christian countries that the Industrial Revolution was born and developed.[53]

And, according to Jathar and Beri,

> The modern Christian world no longer takes in a literal sense the Biblical view that a rich man by reason of his riches is in a parlous state so far as his spiritual destiny is concerned. Christian divines of the present day, for instance, would be ready to allow that a business man . . . has as good a chance of securing a place in heaven as any one else.[54]

If the "other worldly" emphasis in Christianity has not hindered economic development of the Christian, Western world, why then are similar beliefs in Hinduism held responsible for India's economic stagnation? We tend to agree with Jathar and Beri:

> No religion, however unworldly its character, is able to overcome permanently the natural impulse of man to improve his economic condition. . . . It is only when general economic outlook is hopeless . . . that the average man seeks the consolation of a religion preaching quietism and fatalistic resignation and uses it as a kind of anodyne to steep his senses into forgetfulness of the evils by which he is surrounded and which he must endure because he is unable to cure them. When opportunities for ameliorating his earthly condition by positive effort present themselves, adherence to a philosophy and to a religion which would turn people away from purposeful material activity tends to become purely formal.[55]

Viewing religious belief in this way it would seem that the interpretation and emphasis of religious precepts is a function of economic conditions.[56] Thus, any emphasis on other worldliness, asceticism, and so on in Hinduism may be seen as the effect, rather than the cause, of India's economic difficulties. The effective antidote would be building a framework in which rewards and efforts are strongly correlated. In the Indian context this would necessitate a change in the production relations on land, better irrigation facilities to save peasants from the vagaries of nature.[57]

Dube observes an "unfortunate tendency on the part of some writers to equate the conceptuality of Hindu society in classical texts with contemporary society."[58] But what is the actual behavior of Indian workers when faced with making decisions on the allocation of their scarce resources and the combination of inputs in their economic enterprises? If the workers adhere to religious principles of another worldly nature, one would expect their behavior patterns to be irrational. One supporter of the irrationality premise is Kusum Nair, who, on the basis of her interviews with peasants, cites examples to show that the Indian farmer has a low ceiling of aspirations and that he has no motivation to work once he has earned sufficient to satisfy his basic needs.[59] She cites the behavior of a worker who does not return to work after lunch when he has earned enough money to buy meals for the day, even though he suffers from poverty. Another farmer does not care to use irrigation facilities since his need for the year, consisting of two bags of rice, are met with the existing facilities. In the language of economics, Nair is subscribing to the backward-bending supply curve of labor. We cannot comment on these instances in the absence of more information. The phenomenon of the backward-sloping supply curve of labor is, however, observed all over the world—in developed as well as underdeveloped countries. The difference, among cultures and among individuals, lies in the precise point on the supply of labor curve where this behavior actually occurs. It would mostly depend upon the relative preference for leisure over work, which in turn is determined by a number of variables which might include religious beliefs and cultural patterns.

Opponents of the "irrationality" thesis, on the other hand, cite various studies to argue that the Indian farmer is quite rational in achieving optimal levels of output from given inputs and technology. W. David Hopper's study shows that the Indian farmer uses his resources rationally, as each resource is employed to the point where it receives income equal to its marginal product.[60] Raj Krishna illustrates, through the examination of input-output relationships in agricultural operations that Punjab farmers switched to new varieties of cotton when they were convinced that longer staple cotton fetched higher returns than the old varieties.[61] As regards the institutional framework, Hanumantha Rao argues that the choice of tenure arrangements are mostly based on economic considerations. The peasant resorts to crop sharing only if returns are certain, otherwise he elects a fixed contractual payment system when returns are uncertain.[62] Raj Krishna goes so far as to suggest that, notwithstanding the sacredness of the cow in the Hindu religion and culture, Hindus sometimes slaughter cows if ecological and price considerations make it economically advantageous to do so.[63] These and similar studies led Schultz to remark,

> It will come as a surprise to find that farmers in poor countries are in general not inefficient in using (allocating) the agricultural factors of production that they have at their disposal. These farmers are as a rule subject to particular economic restraints that are typical of traditional agriculture. . . . Thus the popular assumption that a different (better?) allocation of the existing poor collection of agricultural factors in these communities would substantially increase agricultural production is inconsistent both with economic logic as applied to the behavior of farmers in such an equilibrium and with the available empirical evidence.[64]

Srinivas endorses Schultz's point of view when he claims that the tragic poverty of the Indian farmer and the ever-present threat of starvation forces him to be nothing but practical.

> He (the peasant) is naturally deeply interested in agriculture and everything related to it—land, water, manure, cattle, labor, pests, etc.—one often comes across pretty strict bookkeeping even between the members of an elementary family. Money from the sale of surplus crops belongs to the man, while the money obtained by the sale of milk, butter, buttermilk, eggs, and fowl belongs to the wife. The better off peasant teaches his son the value of money and thrift early in life.[65]

Commenting on the attitude of Indian people toward the material aspects of life, Max Weber remarks, "The acquisitiveness of Indians of all strata left little to be desired and nowhere is to be found so little antichrematism and such high evaluation of wealth."[66]

In general, we believe that most of the elements in the Hindu religion do not adversely affect the pursuit of material advancement by its adherents. Any seeming attitude of helplessness, resignation, or fatalism among Hindus does not, in Singer's words, "create the human condition—it explains and justifies it."[67] As the process of economic development provides better living standards to the millions of the Indian subcontinent, pessimism will be replaced by optimism and, in place of fatalism, the masses will come to have self-confidence and a belief in their own efforts.

The Economic Impact of the Joint Family System   There is also considerable controversy on the impact of the institution of the joint, or extended, family system on the economies of South Asia. Some writers have extolled this institution as being conducive to cooperative effort and the psychological and social well-being of the Asian people, while others have characterized it as a cause of inertia, idleness, and aversion to risk taking. The most important argument in favor of the joint family system is that it provides security to minors and to the sick, the old, and the disabled in poor societies that cannot afford the social security systems and other welfare schemes developed in economically advanced societies. As Jathar and Beri point out, through the joint family system,

> To every one is guaranteed at least a bare subsistence. . . . Children who may happen to be orphans are cared for and not turned adrift into the world before they are in a position to face its troubles. Similarly, the joint family system affords a safe and respectable asylum to unfortunate widows, for whom an escape by remarriage from their helpless condition is not ordinarily available. . . . The infirm, in spite of their disability, are made to fit into the household economy, being assigned work suited to their strength and capacity.[68]

Thus, the joint family serves two vital purposes: first, it bears some of the social costs for which the economy as a whole does not provide; second, by providing a psychological cushion against the frustrations and miseries of chronic poverty, it is able to protect society from the potential disruptiveness of neglected and alienated indigents.

The joint family system acts as a form of cooperative structure in which the acutely scarce resources of a poor country (e.g., land) are pooled for joint ventures. In the South Asian economies, with increasing population pressure on small-size landholdings, this aspect of pooled resources has special significance. In India, for instance, 71 percent of family holdings are below 5 acres in size. Imagine the consequences of subdividing these already minimal family holdings in the event of a breakdown of the joint family system. Most of the resulting subdivisions would be too small to cultivate. Savings are also encouraged by avoiding wasteful duplication of household equipment; thus a small income can go a long way to maintain a comparatively large family. In other words, joint families secure "economies of scale" in the use of scarce resources and equipment. Above all, the joint family system fosters the virtues of self-discipline, sacrifice, and reverence. These are human qualities which promote human happiness and create an environment in which people, even in abject poverty, can survive with dignity and peace of mind.

The arguments against the joint family system center around (1) its impact on the personality of individual members and (2) its effect on employment, labor supply, and capital formation. Most Western writers stress the effect of the system on personality. It is claimed that in the extended family the individual is submerged in the group, that he has no chance to assert himself and gain life experience and self-confidence through trial and error; that this produces a meek personality trained in the virtues of resignation and obedience to elders—personality traits that do not produce entrepreneurship, the mainspring of economic progress.

The joint family system is also criticized for fostering idleness or voluntary unemployment in that there is no necessity for "surplus" family workers to seek work elsewhere, since the family has the moral responsibility to share work and income with all members. As explained in chapter 3, this creates a type of unemployment situation known in the literature on economic development as "disguised unemployment." A person is disguisedly unemployed when he feels he is working but, in fact, he does not contribute significantly to the income of the family enterprise, that is, his marginal product is zero or close to zero. Thus, the moral obligations implicit in the system hide and support a considerable amount of unemployed manpower. In this respect the joint family system definitely stands in the way of a fuller utilization of the labor force in the South Asian economies.

The joint family system can also stand in the way of family planning. In the first instance, the system encourages reproduction in several ways, for example, by placing a high value on male children. The usual constraint on having more children—the cost of rearing them—does not operate, since the burden is borne by the entire joint family.

The moral responsibility of the joint family to share its income with all family members according to their needs rather than according to their contribution to the family's income could adversely affect savings in several ways. Conspicuous consumption is a feature of the joint family in the celebration of weddings and other family occasions, and on other displays of wealth that enhance the family's prestige. Moreover, if in any season a joint family enjoys a good harvest or a good income from business, distant relatives may come and ask for monetary help by presenting their misfortunes. Much of the economic surplus can thus be consumed by disguisedly unemployed family members and distant relatives, who, under a nuclear family system, would have to be more self-reliant. Displays of wealth, moral responsibilities, and social traditions all have the effect of reducing potential savings and diverting potential surpluses from productive to nonproductive uses.

On balance, it would seem that the adverse effects of the joint family on individual personality are greatly exaggerated and more than outweighed by the psychic and moral support the family provides to its individual members—especially to the old, the very young and the sick. The families in South Asia most famed for their prowess in business and industry, such as the Birlas, Dalmias, Jains, and Tatas in India, and the famed twenty-two leading families (such as Adamji, Adam, Bawany, Bashir, Dada, Dadabhoy, Dawood, Habib, Karim, Maulabaksh, Shahnawza) of Pakistan,[69] are in fact organized on a joint family basis.

However, there is no denying that the system does foster disguised unemployment and adversely affects capital formation, especially within rural households.

Fortunately or unfortunately, depending on one's point of view, the joint family system is losing its grip for a variety of reasons that include urbanization and its resulting mobility, the spread of Western education and a growing stress on individualism. Increasing population pressure on land in the rural areas is also adding to the economic and psychological strains and leading to family quarrels and mutual jealousies in joint families. The victims of this declining family system are the aged, the disabled and sick, and the orphans and widows, who, in the absence of social welfare programs, are thrown on the mercy of the liberated, individualistic, and often indifferent members of nuclear families.

The Economic Impact of the Caste System   The institution of the caste system has received severe condemnation in the literature and it is generally believed to be inimical to economic development. In an earlier section, we explained the origin and structure of the caste system, and we shall now summarize the main arguments advanced against and in favor of the system.

The fact that caste prescribes, or at least circumscribes occupation prevents occupational mobility—which is crucial for economic development. Changes in occupation deemed important for economic efficiency are rendered difficult by the fact that these may endanger one's social and caste status. Persons of higher castes find it difficult to enter occupations or adopt practices normally expected of lower castes. This feature of the caste system prevents correspondence between aptitude and function. According to Ketkar:

> The moment you divide your men into watertight compartments on the mere accident of birth irrespective of their temperaments and qualifications and at the same time refuse them their birthright to develop their natural capacities and faculties to the highest possible limit, you deny your nation all the advantages that otherwise would have added to the store of national wealth and well-being.[70]

Caste may also prevent the introduction of certain improved techniques, such as the use of certain types of fertilizer (e.g., bones, night soil, or fish) and the maintenance of compost piles. In many scientific laboratories, research is hampered because high castes show a reluctance to handle dead animals or to clean equipment and must wait for low-caste servants to do so. The adherence to caste-prescribed occupations interferes with the adjustment of supply and demand forces in the labor market. One often observes unemployment among high castes, not because of the lack of work opportunities but, because there are considerable restrictions and prejudices against the available types of work. Consequently, many jobs deemed unfit for upper castes remain unfilled resulting in unemployment and loss of potential output to the country. The hampering effect of caste, preventing a fair and rational relationship between individual aptitude, performance, and earning, frustrates the creative powers and lowers the aspirations—especially of lower-caste workers—thereby causing a serious waste of individual capacities and labor resources. Various aspects of the caste system make it difficult to combine technical and professional skills, manual labor, and entrepreneurship in large-scale enterprises; these elements are often isolated from one another, belonging to separate castes. Also, in a caste-dominated society roles tend to be assigned or chosen on the basis of caste rather than merit. This fosters nepotism and results in waste of ability and loss of productivity.

Some writers claim that the link between caste and occupation is not as rigid as is generally assumed. Nijhawan cites the examples of agriculture and the Indian army. Agriculture, which absorbs 70 percent of the South Asian population, is not a prerogative of any one caste; similarly in the Indian army, people belonging to different castes rub shoulders with one another.[71] Srinivas[72] and Gore[73] in their studies have shown that people would seize more favorable opportunities in "inappropriate" occupations if given the opportunity, notwithstanding their caste status. Also, in several cities, some people have deliberately given up their traditional occupations, thereby changing their status. In general, we do not agree with Nijhawan's examples of agriculture and the army. Even in agriculture, different castes undertake different specific occupations. For instance, it would be uncommon to find high castes working as share croppers or in such occupations as carpenters and blacksmiths in rural areas. Even in the Indian army it is not uncommon to see different roles traditionally assigned on the basis of caste.

The most damaging aspect of the caste system has been the polarization of society resulting from discrimination and segregation on the basis of caste. As Karve describes an Indian village,

> The habitation area . . . of the untouchables is always separate. If a village is situated on a bank of a river or stream, the untouchables must use the water only from the lower reaches while the place of bathing, fetching water . . . of the touchables was always on the upper reaches. In some villages the village street is divided into two parts, one higher and the other lower and only the latter can be used by the untouchables.[74]

In spite of the fact that discrimination on the basis of castes is illegal, it is not uncommon to find the Untouchables (or *harijans*) being denied access to common village wells and entry to temples and other public places. The degree of discrimination, however, differs among different regions and caste groups. The actual position of the Untouchables is determined not so much by their legal rights as by their social and economic dependency. Since most of the peoples of lower caste belong to the lower economic strata, it will take a long time before they achieve their legal right to social and economic equality as guaranteed under the constitution of India. The government has adopted several social and economic measures to ameliorate their condition, but such centuries-old distinctions die hard.

Casteism, by fostering a false and distorted sense of superiority among the high castes and an inferiority complex among the lower castes, has been responsible for a loss of confidence and self-respect among millions of lower-caste people. It has also created a sense of moral aloofness, indifference, and detachment among castes. An important effect of this is an erosion of sympathy and compassion for other castes, especially the lower ones. As Shils explains:

> [Caste] inhibits the growth of those sensibilities which are required for the perception of the moral quality of other human beings. It is the caste system which cuts human beings off from each other by denying to them the possibilities of connubial and commensal intimacy and their more basic affinity as moral entities. It is the caste system which deadens the imagination of the state of mind of other human beings. It is the caste system, perhaps even more than the other factors like poverty and the crushing ubiquity of other human beings which makes the upper caste Hindus, from whose circles most Indian intellectuals are recruited, fundamentally and humanly insensate to the mass of the population who belong to the lower strata.[75]

Swami Vivekananda has in strong words castigated this moral aloofness:

> In India there is a howling cry that we are very poor, but how many charitable associations are there for the well-being of the poor? . . . Are we men? What are we doing for their livelihood, for their improvement? We do not touch them, we avoid their company. Are we men?[76]

Thus the South Asian nations are confronted by moral contradictions or double standards. On the one hand, Hinduism stresses the oneness of all life and teaches compassion for all living things, on the other, Hindus show an inhuman aloofness and detachment toward millions of lower caste members.

The aloofness, detachment, discrimination, and segregation create antagonisms and ill will which mark all intergroup relations in this caste-ridden society. Group loyalties are solidified at the expense of larger and higher loyalities. The development of a spirit of national unification, national solidarity, and mass participation is also hindered—without which neither national economic development nor political democracy can be achieved. These pernicious class divisions based on caste and social status give rise to a general climate of suspicion and distrust, which renders social and community action difficult. Development efforts, such as the community development project[77] and national extension service, have failed to achieve the desired results because of the lack of cooperation and collective effort.

The caste system has been defended on certain grounds. The most frequently mentioned argument in favor of caste is that it provides for division of labor, which in turn promotes economic strength and efficiency. It is claimed that the ancient Hindus instituted the caste system to achieve the advantages of division of labor—later, it was greatly extolled by Adam Smith. The system also helped the transmittal of skills from one generation to the next. This feature was especially important when there was no organized system of public instruction or technical training. In this way, the caste system may have been beneficial in preserving the skill of the artisan in the face of fierce foreign competition. The caste group has been compared with the medieval guilds in Europe, which served as mutual benefit societies or cooperative organizations for the economic and social benefit of their members. In Low's words, "the caste organization is to the Hindu his club, his trade union, his benefit society and his philanthropic society."[78] Viewed from this angle, caste has provided a positive meaning, direction, and thus, contentment to the Indian people. Career and occupation being predetermined by caste, the system relieved the individual of the burden of choice in selecting a profession. It also enabled Hindu society to survive the shock of foreign invasions without itself suffering disintegration during its long and checkered history.

It may, however, be noted that all the merits claimed for the system pertain to earlier periods and to its division of labor aspects. But the evils resulting from the social segregation and polarization of the society render the system, in the words of Jathar and Beri,

> one of the greatest drags on progress devised by the perverted ingenuity of man. It operates, at present as a vast engine of oppression and intolerance and is a malignant force making for social and political disunity and weakness. . . . It is probably the greatest political handicap under which the Indian people are labouring at present and it has been a source of political weakness in the past.[79]

It is for these evils that casteism has been subjected to strong condemnation by various reform movements in India. The Buddha was the first to condemn the system, in the sixth century B.C., asserting that a person's worth should be determined by right conduct and right knowledge, not by caste position. The next major challenge to the caste system came from Muslim saints, who preached that people of high or low social status had equal dignity in the eyes of God. Attempting to synthesize Hinduism and Islam, medieval religious leaders such as Ramanand, Ramanujan, Kabir, and Guru Nanak (the founder of the Sikh religion) attacked casteism explicitly and vigorously. In more recent times, Gandhi and the Indian National Congress attacked the caste system and specifically made the removal of untouchability a cornerstone of the struggle for India's independence. The constitution of India, promulgated on January 26, 1950, provides for the abolition of untouchability and forbids its practice in any form. The Untouchability (Offences) Act 1955 provides penalties for practicing any form of social and/or religious discrimination. It also contains provisions against discrimination in occupational, professional, and trade situations. To redress the centuries-old neglect of and discrimination against the Untouchables, the Indian constitution requires that positions in the civil service be reserved for them and special representation be provided for them in Parliament and in the state legislatures. These legal provisions as well as various economic and social benefits have gone a long way in improving the social and economic conditions of the Untouchables. In addition, such factors as the spread of mass education, the increasing mobility of labor through industrialization and urbanization, the introduction of universal adult suffrage, and the improved transportation system have also helped weaken caste rigidities. In urban areas, the hold of the caste system has weakened considerably from persons of different castes working together in modern factories and workshops; their children attend the same schools and colleges; they sit together in movie houses, buses, and trains. It is in village India that the caste system still has its hold. As Kingsley Davis remarks, "As long as the village predominates, caste will be hard to eradicate, especially since it is now deeply rooted in the religion and morals of the Hindus."[80]

What, then, may we conclude about the degree of direct relationship between the religious values of a population and their level of economic achievement? As pointed out earlier, religion, though important, is only one of several factors which affect attitudes toward material attainment. The importance of religion lies in its all-pervasive impact within a society, while other factors may have only a limited effect. Theoretically it is possible for a group espousing a religion with materialistic values to fail to achieve material growth if other environmental factors are not conducive to economic development. For example, though it is commonly held that Protestant ethics contributed to the growth of Western capitalistic societies, yet, in Oriental and

African communities that have adopted Protestantism, religion has not served as a catalyst for economic transformation. Thus, although religion as a system of values has a certain significance in economic development, its effect may be negated by other socioeconomic and political factors. In fact, Protestantism grew along with industrialization in Europe where these and other factors became integrated parts of an indigenous, developing society. Such can never be the case in countries where either or both factors are recently superimposed on societies that have their own equally old and integrated traditions.

Let us now examine the relative impact of Hinduism vis-à-vis, say, Islam on economic development. Hinduism, as explained in this chapter, has various spiritual and social components. Hinduism contains both pro- and antimaterialistic elements, while Islam is, by and large, mostly promaterialistic. We may reiterate here that the antimaterialistic elements of Hinduism tend to yield to the promaterialistic as Hindu societies progress to higher stages of economic development. The caste system, with its regressive and negative effects, is a part of the Hindu social system—one that other religions do not explicitly sanction. Thus, we can assert that, in planning for the economic development of India with its predominantly Hindu population, the influence of Hinduism with its antimaterialistic elements and caste system constitutes a greater hindrance than does the influence of Islam on Islamic developing economies. It should be further emphasized that even when India attains economic growth sufficient to mitigate the antimaterialistic elements in Hinduism, it will have to fight consistently against the regressive and negative aspects of the caste system, which otherwise could prove a formidable hindrance to progress.

NOTES

1. For an excellent discussion on this aspect, see Inder P. Nijhawan, "Socio-Political Institutions, Cultural Values, and Attitudes: The Impact on Indian Economic Development," in J. S. Uppal, ed., *India's Economic Problems: An Analytical Approach* (New Delhi: Tata McGraw-Hill, 1975), pp. 23–42.

2. Joseph Schumpeter, *History of Economic Analysis* (London: Oxford University Press, 1954), ch. 3.

3. John R. Hicks, *Essays in World Economics* (Oxford: Clarendon Press, 1965), p. 24.

4. Kenneth Boulding, *A Reconstruction of Economics* (New York: Wiley, 1950), p. vii.

5. Government of India, Planning Commission, *Third Five Year Plan, 1960–65* (New Delhi, 1961), p. 8.

6. Talcott Parsons, *Toward a General Theory of Action* (Cambridge, Mass: Harvard University Press, 1951).

7. Simon Kuznets, *Modern Economic Growth* (New Haven, Conn.: Yale University Press, 1966), ch. 1.

8. E. Hagen, *On the Theory of Social Change* (Homewood, Ill.: Dorsey, 1962).

9. David McCleland, *The Achieving Society* (Princeton, N.J.: Van Nostrand, 1961).

10. Max Weber, *Protestant Ethic and the Spirit of Capitalism* (New York: Scribner, 1956); R. H. Tawney, *Religion and the Rise of Capitalism* (New York: Harcourt & Brace, 1952).

11. E. F. Denison, *The Sources of Economic Growth in the United States and The Alternative Before Us* (New York: Committee for Economic Development, 1962).

12. W. Arthur Lewis, *The Theory of Economic Growth* (London: Unwin, 1963), pp. 105, 107.

13. J. H. Boeke, *Economics and Economic Policy of Dual Societies* (New York: Institute of Pacific Relations, 1953), pp. 39, 101–102, 106.

14. K. William Kapp, *Hindu Culture, Economic Development, and Economic Planning in India* (Bombay: Asia Publishing House, 1963), p. 6.

15. Donald E. Smith, ed., *Religion, Politics, & Social Change in the Third World* (New York: Free Press, 1971), p. 198.

16. Ibid., p. 199.

17. The religious composition of the South Asian countries is as follows:

	Hindus	*Muslims*	*Christians*	*Buddhists*	*Others*
India	80.70%	11.10%	2.60%	0.60%	5.00%
Pakistan	1.33	97.10	1.11	0.00	0.46
Bangladesh	14.52	83.56	0.38	0.60	0.94
Sri Lanka	18.65	5.97	8.58	65.67	1.13
Nepal	89.60	1.86	1.80	3.40	3.34

SOURCE: Derived from Clarence Maloney, *Peoples of South Asia* (New York; Holt, Rinehart & Winston 1974), pp. 156, 157.

18. Ibid., pp. 204, 212.

19. Jean Herbert, *An Introduction to Asia* (New York: Oxford University Press, 1965).

20. Government of Pakistan, Planning Commission, *The Third Five Year Plan, 1965–70* (Karachi, 1965), p. v.

21. See Milton Singer "Religion and Social Change in India: The Max Weber Thesis Phase Three," *Economic Development and Cultural Change*, vol. 14, (July 1966) 1–3; M. N. Srinivas, "A Note on Mr. Gaheen's Note," *Economic Development and Cultural Change*, vol. 7, October 1958, pp. 36; and D. G. Karve, "Comments," *Economic Development and Cultural Change*, vol. 7, October 1958, pp. 79.

22. Ruddar Datt and K. P. M. Sundharam, *Indian Economy* (New Delhi: Chand, 1975), p. 117.

23. G. B. Jathar and S. G. Beri, *Indian Economics* (Bombay: Oxford University Press, 1949), p. 96.

24. Singer, "Religion and Social Change" p. 501.

25. V. G. Kale, quoted in Jathar and Beri, *Indian Economics,* p. 93.

26. Jathar and Beri, *Indian Economics,* p. 95.

27. For an excellent discussion on the philosophical aspects of Hinduism, see John Koller, *Oriental Philosophies* (New York: Scribner, 1970).

28. Quoted in Paul Thomas Welty, *The Asians: Their Heritage and Their Destiny* (Philadelphia: Lippincott, 1973), p. 62.

29. Quoted in Koller, *Oriental Philosophies,* p. 35.

30. Welty, *The Asians,* p. 63.

31. Quoted in Kapp, *Hindu Culture,* p. 14.

32. Quoted in ibid., p. 15.

33. Radhakrishnan, ed., *The Bhagavad Gita* (London: Allen & Unwin, 1948), pp. 119, 138.

34. Welty, *The Asians*, p. 64–65.
35. Quoted in Koller, *Oriental Philosophies*, pp. 42–43.
36. Ibid., pp. 42–43.
37. Ibid., p. 43.
38. Welty, *The Asians*, p. 68.
39. E. R. A. Seligman, quoted in Jathar and Beri, *Indian Economies*, p. 87.
40. Kapp, *Hindu Culture*, p. 29.
41. Ibid., p. 23; and Jathar and Beri, *Indian Economics*, p. 86.
42. The word *caste* is taken from *casta*, the word the Portuguese applied to the practice of classification according to birth on their arrival in India in the late fifteenth century.
43. Quoted in Koller, *Oriental Philosophies*, p. 38.
44. Ibid., p. 39.
45. Kapp, *Hindu Culture*, p. 27.
46. Quoted in Jathar and Beri, *Indian Economics*, p. 79.
47. M. N. Srinivas, "Village Studies and Their Significance," *Eastern Anthropologist*, vol. 8, no. 3–4 (March–August 1955), 224.
48. Kapp, *Hindu Culture*, p. 42.
49. Ibid, p. 44.
50. Ibid, pp. 64–65.
51. Gunnar Myrdal, *An Approach to the Asian Drama: Methodological and Theoretical* (New York: Vintage, 1970), p. 104.
52. Singer, "Religion and Social Change," p. 501.
53. Srinivas, "A Note on Mr. Gaheen's Note," p. 6.
54. Jathar and Beri, *Indian Economics*, pp. 94–95.
55. Ibid., p. 94.
56. For an excellent discussion on the historical development of Hindu thought and its impact on economic development during different periods of Indian history, see Vikas Mishra, *Hinduism and Economic Growth* (New York: Oxford University Press, 1962).
57. Nijhawan, "Socio-Political Institutions," p. 39.
58. S. C. Dube, "Cultural Problems in the Economic Development of India," in R. N. Bellah, ed., *Religion and Progress in Modern Asia* (New York: Free Press, 1965), p. 51.
59. Kusum Nair, *Blossoms in the Dust* (New York: Praeger, 1962).
60. W. David Hopper, "Allocation Efficiency in a Traditional Indian Agriculture," *Journal of Farm Economics*, vol. 47, August 1965.
61. Raj Krishna, "Farm Supply Response in India-Pakistan—A Case Study of Punjab Agriculture," in Tara Shukla, ed., *Economics of Underdeveloped Agriculture* (Bombay: Vora, 1969), pp. 193–209.
62. C. H. Hanumantha Rao, "Entrepreneurship, Management, and Farm Tenure System," February 1967, mimeographed.
63. Quoted in Jagdish Bhagwati and S. Chakravarty, "Contributions to Indian Economic Analysis," *American Economic Review*, vol. 59, no. 4, part 2 (September 1969).
64. T. W. Schultz, "Economic Growth from Traditional Agriculture," in Tara Shukla, ed., *Economics of Underdeveloped Agriculture* (Bombay: Vora, 1969), p. 3.
65. Srinivas, "A Note on Mr. Gaheen's Note," p. 4.
66. Max Weber, *Religion in India* (New York: Free Press), 1958, p. 4.
67. Singer, "Religion and Social Change."
68. Jathar and Beri, *Indian Economics*, p. 88.
69. For details on the role of these families, see Lawrence J. White, *Industrial Concentration and Economic Power in Pakistan* (Princeton, N.J.: Princeton University Press, 1974).
70. Quoted in Jathar and Beri, *Indian Economics*, p. 83.
71. Nijhawan, "Socio-Political Institutions," p. 35.
72. M. N. Srinivas, *Religion and Society among the Coorgs of South India* (London: Oxford University Press).
73. M. S. Gore, "India," in Richard D. Lambert and Bert F. Hoselitz, *The Role of Savings and Wealth in Southern Asia and the West* (Paris: UNESCO, 1963), p. 181.
74. Quoted in Kapp, *Hindu Culture*, pp. 48–49.
75. Ibid., p. 52.

76. Ibid., p. 54.

77. For details, see Government of India, Planning Commission, *Fourth Evaluation Report On the Working of Community Projects and National Extension Service Blocks* vols. 1 and 2, (New Delhi, 1957).

78. S. Low, cited in Jathar and Beri, *Indian Economics,* p. 81.

79. Ibid., pp. 82, 83.

80. Kingsley Davis, *The Population of India and Pakistan* (Princeton, N.J.: Princeton University Press, 1951), p. 175.

7

Economic Planning
in South Asia

So far, we have discussed the nature of underdevelopment in the South Asian countries and the major problems hindering the attainment of self-sustaining economic growth. In chapter 1, the major economic and social indicators of underdevelopment were identified, such as low productivity in various sectors of the South Asian economies; low levels of consumption, savings, and investment; and imbalance in the input mix—shortage of land and capital inputs relative to the abundance of labor. The persistence of these indicators of underdevelopment has kept per capita income at static low levels since these estimates became available at the turn of the century. In chapter 1 we attempted to explain the static nature of the South Asian economies in terms of Leibenstein's hypothesis. We found that the process of economic planning had given rise to certain countervailing forces which tend to retard the further growth of these economies. Some of these retarding factors were identified as the population explosion, rising expectations, under- and unemployment, and the low rate of capital formation. In chapters 2 through 5, these retarding factors were discussed in detail, as were the attempts being made to overcome them and achieve further economic development. In chapter 6 we outlined the main social institutions and religious beliefs that provide the context within which attempts at economic development have to take place. In this chapter, we will explain the main features of such attempts.

ECONOMIC PLANNING: THE HISTORICAL BACKGROUND

A brief historical survey may be helpful to an understanding of current economic plans and policies in the South Asian nations.

From the mid-eighteenth century when most of South Asia came under foreign domination—first under the British East India Company and later under the British government—until independence in the mid-twentieth century, economic stagnation existed, as indicated by the low levels of aggregate output shown in Table 1-4. Before independence the growth of agricultural output did not keep pace with even the modest increase in population. In India, from 1900 to 1945, as against a population increase of 37.9 percent (less than 1 percent average annual increase), total agricultural output increased by only 13 percent, thus further impoverishing the economy.

It is commonly held by such nationalist Indian writers as Dadabhai Naoroji, R. C. Dutt, and D. R. Gadgil that India, before the arrival of the British government, was, comparatively, industrially advanced and materially prosperous.[1] They refer to the handicrafts and small-scale industries chiefly organized under a guild system, in textiles, stone work, jewelry, ship building, and so on, which were relatively advanced when compared with the prevailing technologies in the rest of the world. The following statement by the Industrial Commission (1918), appointed by the British government, refers to the historical excellence of the Indian handicraft industries:

> At a time when the West of Europe, the birthplace of the modern industrial system, was inhabited by uncivilized tribes, India was famous for the wealth of her rulers and the high artistic skill of her craftsmen.[2]

In the same spirit, discussing the relative position of Indian industries, Vera Anstey, an astute writer on Indian economic history, remarks:

> Up to the 18th century, the economic condition of India was relatively advanced, and Indian methods of production and of industrial and commercial organization could stand comparison with those in vogue in any other part of the world.[3]

Indian goods enjoyed a good reputation in foreign markets, which attracted European traders to India and led to the establishment of trading companies by British, French, and Portuguese merchants. Indian export markets, according to Knowles, ranged from Japan and China to Persia, Arabia, West Africa, and Europe.[4] India enjoyed a highly favorable balance of trade from the net inflow of gold and other precious metals from abroad.

With the imposition of foreign rule, competition from less expensive machine-made goods from abroad—especially after the Industrial Revolution in Western Europe—and the unsympathetic policies of the British East India Company and the British government, the decline of handicrafts set in toward the end of the eighteenth century and became very marked during the mid-nineteenth century. Surprisingly, the Indian economy underwent a rapid transformation from net exporter of industrial goods to net exporter of raw materials, from a country known for its wealth and the high artistic skill of its craftsman to a land noted for its tragic poverty and backward economy. As a nationalist Indian writer remarked in 1898:

> India, fifty years ago, clothed herself with her own manufactures, and now she is clothed by her distant masters. The same is the case with wool, silk, and other textiles, with oils and hides . . . this is our condition and when the whole situation is thus taken in at one view, we feel that we are standing on the edge of a precipice, and the slightest push down will drive us into the abyss below of unmixed and absolute helplessness.[5]

As Karl Marx observed: "India, the great workshop of cotton manufacture for the world since immemorial times became now inundated with English twists and cotton stuff."[6]

The destruction of Indian handicrafts created a serious imbalance between the agricultural and industrial sectors and the loss of a very important source of national income. Millions of workers were deprived of their traditional occupations, forcing them to fall back more and more on agriculture, the only available source of subsistence. Ironically, the result was a ruralization of the economy and a growing dependence of the people upon "the single and precarious resource of agriculture" just when the opposite process of urbanization and industrialization was taking place in Western Europe and North America. In India, this led to an overcrowding in agriculture, which in turn gave rise to such problems as the fragmentation of landholdings, disguised unemployment in the countryside, diminished savings, and the paucity of capital formation. Increasing competition among cultivators for the use of available land resulted in utterly uneconomic and exorbitant rents and also led agricultural laborers to undercut one another's wages. The overall effect of this loss of traditional industries has been summed up by Ranade:

> The country's economic life came more and more under foreign economic domination and India came to be looked upon by its rulers as a 'plantation, growing raw produce to be shipped by British Agents in British ships, to be worked into fabrics by British skill and capital, and to

be re-exported to the dependency by British merchants to their corresponding British firms in India and elsewhere.[7]

But how and why did this rapid decay come about? Many scholars have answered this question by referring to the rulers' interest in promoting British industries at the cost of Indian industry. In the words of H. H. Wilson, "The foreign manufacturer employed the arm of political injustice to keep down and ultimately strangle a competitor with whom he could not have contended on equal terms."[8] The British government adopted harsh measures to discourage Indian manufacturers. Indian artisans were prohibited from manufacturing except in the East India Company's factories, and prohibitive tariffs were levied to exclude Indian goods from English markets. A British writer, C. J. Hamilton, discusses the effect of these prohibitive tariffs:

> Had not such heavy duties and the prohibitory decrees existed, the mills of Paisley and Manchester would have been stopped in their outset and would have scarcely been set in motion, even by the power of steam. They were created by the sacrifice of Indian manufacturers.[9]

Some British writers have tried to explain the destruction of Indian handicrafts through the natural economic process of competition between expensive handmade goods and cheaper machine-made goods.[10] They also refer to the various benefits bestowed on India by the British in the form of extensive economic and social infrastructures—railways, roads, postal and telegraph systems, irrigation and power projects, and the introduction of Western education and administration. According to Sir John Marriott, an English economic historian,

> British brain, British enterprise and British capital have, in a material sense, transformed the face of India. . . . Thanks to improved sanitation, to a higher standard of living, to irrigation, to canalization, to the development of transport, and to carefully thought-out schemes for relief work . . . for these achievements India is wholly indebted to British administration.[11]

While Indian writers concede the benefits accruing from these improvements by the British government, they ascribe these acts to ulterior motives: the consolidation of British rule in India; the penetration of British goods into remoter parts of the country; the education of Indians to enable them to serve as clerks and petty administrators.

Another important factor cited in the impoverishment of the Indian economy is the huge sums remitted from India to England. British economists have justified these remittances as the salaries and pensions of British civil and military personnel and "home charges" — expenditures incurred in England by the British secretary of state on behalf of the Indian government, including part of the British government's expenditure on wars in Europe and India for "the security and defense of India." These remittances have been referred to as a "plunder,"[12] "loot," or "drain" of wealth, for which India received no economic or material returns. There are various estimates on the magnitude of this drain, ranging from between $15 and $20 million per year (Karl Marx), to £34 million per year (Dadabhai Naoroji), to £50 million per year (Prithwis Chandra Ray) from 1838 to 1888.[13] R. C. Dutt estimated the drain at nearly one-half of India's net annual revenue.

What was the effect of this huge drain of wealth from India to England? For India, many claim it meant impoverishment, the expropriation of scarce capital that should have been invested for India's economic development. For England, these remittances were a great boon and a rich source of investment. The eminent American writer and social philosopher Brooks Adams goes so far as to suggest that the Industrial Revolution in England was financed by this plunder from India.[14]

During the British occupation of India, the government adopted and promoted a laissez-faire economic policy according to the tenets of classical economics preached in the Western industrial economies. The public sector covered only postal and telegraph services, some ordnance factories, the railways, and all-India radio. (The latter two were originally started by private enterprise with handsome government subsidies, but still ran into bankruptcy and were taken over by the government.)[15] The British government in India showed complete indifference toward agriculture and industry. A department of agriculture was started in 1905 after a series of famines in the late nineteenth century, but its functions did not go beyond such steps as barring the fragmentation of holdings, constructing minor irrigation projects, running some model farms to supply good seed to cotton cultivators, and helping tea and coffee plantations — owned mainly by British interests. In the field of industrial development, while the policies adopted by the East India Company until 1858 were marked by the ruthless suppression of Indian handicrafts, the period from 1858 saw the adoption of laissez-faire policies, or what Indian writers have called "policies of neglect and indifference." From 1858 to 1914, however, British capital flowed into India and established plantations and mining industries, a jute (burlap) industry, and some consumer good industries like soap, paper, and sugar. Indian capital ventured mainly into cotton textiles. The basic and key industries were conspicuous by their absence — the only exception being the inauguration of the Tata Iron and Steel Company in 1912, which suffered heavily, initially, from foreign imports. The British government had to modify its policy of laissez-faire during World War I, when, due to enemy blockade of the sea routes imports of essential supplies, including military supplies, from Europe ceased. In the words of the Montagu-Chelmsford Report:

> Now-a-days, the products of an industrially developed community coincide so nearly in kind . . . with the catalogue of munitions of war that the development of India's natural resources becomes almost a matter of necessity for the defence of the British Empire in the East.[16]

In 1922, the British government in India began a limited policy of protecting Indian industries, and "departments of industries" were started at the provincial level to provide some assistance, such as technical and industrial training and marketing information. This protection, characterized by Indian writers as "nothing better than a perfunctory assistance, indifferently and grudgingly rendered,"[17] enabled several industries at least to survive in the face of severe foreign competition. Indian industry received a further impetus from the large local demand created by World War II. As a result, some large-scale industries developed, including iron and steel, jute (burlap), cotton, leather and tanning, woolen, chemicals, sugar, paper, and cement. Small- and medium-scale industries including glass, rubber goods, and minor chemicals also benefited. Though Indian industries gained a great deal from 1915 to 1945, their development, in the words of the Indian Fiscal Commission, "has not been commensurate with the size of the country, its population and its natural resources."[18] Most large industries depended upon imports for their supplies of accessories and machinery. Moreover, industrial development was very lopsided, with some major producer goods and key industries, such as metallurgical and chemical, not represented. The iron and steel and the engineering industries existed on a negligible scale. The consumer goods industries, however, had developed sufficiently to meet domestic demand — at existing low levels of income.

This brief presentation of some aspects of the economic history of the region helps to explain certain factors that have greatly affected the general attitude of the South Asian countries toward formulating economic policies and plans for development.

It is generally believed that, in the eighteenth century, India was industrially more advanced and materially more prosperous than Europe. The ruthless policies of the East India Company, with approval of the British government, resulted in the destruction of Indian industries and consequent "ruralization," unemployment, and impoverishment of the Indian people. The British policies in India from the middle of the nineteenth century, then prevented Indian industrialization, despite the country's rich resources of industrial raw materials. The blame for "underdevelopment" and poverty was thus laid squarely on the shoulders of the British government. Independence from alien rule was seen as the solution to the poverty problem, and this was the main slogan and rallying point of nationalism on the Indian subcontinent.

There were strong sentiments against laissez-faire policies and capitalism, which were believed to have brought about the ruin of the Indian economy and to have arrested economic growth. Study of the political and economic thinking of the Indian leadership during the preindependence period shows a strong commitment to (1) democratic socialism,[19] (2) active state participation in various aspects of the economy to achieve "social" as opposed to private gain, and (3) comprehensive economic planning covering all facets of national life. A. Vasudevan sums up the economic thinking of Nehru—the great Indian nationalist who is regarded as one of the main architects of modern India's economic and political philosophy—as follows:

> Socialism to Nehru was a cardinal doctrine, for it was supposed to end poverty and unemployment of the Indian people. . . . And also the problems of peasantry were conceived to be better solved under a planned system. He maintained that capitalism promoted monopolies and vested interests. . . . Planning meant adoption of socialist programmes in an air of political freedom.[20]

Similar sentiments on the impact of British rule on the economy and the need for state participation in economic planning for the island prevailed in Sri Lanka. Under the laws on "wastelands" enacted during the nineteenth century, the British government took title to uncultivated hill lands in Sri Lanka and sold them to British planters for the development of tea and coffee plantations.[21] Under the traditional laws, these wastelands belonged to villagers for grazing purposes; the nationalist writers viewed the British government's action as "legalized robbery." Ceylonese leaders were also resentful of the trading practices of the British-owned and managed plantations, which sold their output through British-owned export houses and shipping lines and bought their supplies from British merchants. To many Ceylonese, this was a continuing act of spoliation, as one group of foreigners shipped profits out of the country while another took jobs away from the island's inhabitants. The alien government was also condemned for its laissez-faire policy in the matter of industrial development and for failing to improve the lot of the Ceylonese people. In 1935, the Lanka Sama Sumaja party adopted as its fundamental objective the "establishment of a socialistic society" and nationalization of the means of production, distribution, and exchange.[22] The active participation of the government was sought in an all-out effort for the economic development of the island.

The major political parties in India, representing various nationalist elements, started preparing plans for economic development as an integral part of their struggle for political independence. A National Planning Committee was appointed by the Indian National Congress in 1938 under the chairmanship of Jawaharlal Nehru, who later became the first prime minister of independent India.

This committee prepared detailed studies on various aspects of the Indian economy and recommended comprehensive planning for the country. The National Planning Committee was composed of such eminent Indian economists as M. Visvesvaraya, K. T. Shah, and representatives from the major sectors: industry labor, and business. In 1944, various plans emerged from the committee: the industrialists came up with a plan popularly known as "the Bombay Plan"; Shriman Narayan, a well-known Gandhian economist, presented "the Gandhian Plan"; and the Indian Federation of Labor formulated "the People's Plan."[23] Although these various plans differed on such questions as the relative emphasis on agriculture versus industry and large-scale versus small-scale industries, they showed a general concensus on some major principles: the urgent need for planning and the need for active participation of the state in the national economy to achieve the objectives of economic growth, full employment, redistribution of income, and social justice. The recommendations of the National Planning Committee assigned a dominant role to government for the regulation and control of the economy:

> All businesses were to be licensed by public authority, banking was to be both licensed and regulated, insurance was to be supervised by a National Insurance Board, strict state control was to be exercised over the coal industry, and the sizes of manufacturing units were to be decided "in each industry by qualified authority."[24]

This important recommendation, suggesting the virtual end of laissez-faire policies, had great influence on the economic policies adopted by the South Asian countries after their independence.

These various economic plans created a strong public opinion in favor of planning and also provided the leadership with experience in the drawing up of future economic plans. The individual nations of South Asia were thus able to formulate plans for their economic development very soon after they had won independence.

ECONOMIC PLANNING: THE POST-INDEPENDENCE PERIOD

The independence of India in August 1947, accompanied by the partition of the country into India and Pakistan (which later was further divided into Pakistan and Bangladesh), led to the uprooting of about 10 million, mainly Hindu and Sikh refugees, fleeing Pakistan and Muslim refugees fleeing India. Further, the areas growing such raw materials as jute (burlap) and cotton were now in Pakistan while the industries using these raw materials were in India. The partition of India accentuated many of the problems of poverty, unemployment, food shortage, and so on, which the new nations of India and Pakistan had inherited from the British government.

Within about three years of achieving independence, the South Asian countries appointed planning commissions to draw up plans for their economic development. The Indian Planning Commission was established in March 1950 and was instructed to

1. Make an assessment of the material, capital and human resources of the country, including technical personnel and . . . formulate a plan for the most effective and balanced utilization of the country's resources;
2. On a determination of priorities, define the stages in which the Plan should be carried out and propose the allocation of resources for the due completion of each stage;
3. Indicate the factors which are tending to retard economic development, and determine the conditions which, in view of the current social and political situation, should be established for the successful execution of the Plan.[25]

From 1950 until 1975 India had completed the following five-year plans:

First five-year plan	1950–1951 to 1955–1956
Second five-year plan	1955–1956 to 1960–1961
Third five-year plan	1960–1961 to 1965–1966
Annual plan	1966–1967 to 1968–1969
Fourth five-year plan	1969–1970 to 1974–1975

The texts of these plan documents provide detailed explanations on the problems and prospects of the Indian economy. Each plan is built on the experience of the earlier one and contains discussion on patterns of investment, including the planning strategies proposed to accomplish production targets in the different sectors of the economy. The Planning Commission publishes periodic reports on the progress of each plan, recommending changes necessitated by rapid social, economic, and political change in the country. The plan documents are written in a lucid and scholarly style and display a high level of understanding of the nature and problems of the Indian economy. In fact, the Indian plans are recognized as one of the finest contributions to the literature on development economics and are widely read and used by planners and economists throughout the world.

Economic planning in Pakistan started in early 1948 with the establishment of a Development Board, later named the Planning Commission. Pakistan has completed the following plans:

First five-year plan	1955–1960
Second five-year plan	1960–1965
Third five-year plan	1965–1970
Annual development plan	1972–1973

The history of planned economic development in Nepal is short. Before 1951, some development activities were undertaken, but their scope was limited. In October 1955, the king of Nepal announced the formation of the National Planning Commission—an advisory body for all matters relating to macroeconomic planning. Its specific functions are as follows:

1. Make assessments of human resources and various other resources concerning economic development.
2. Offer suggestions for formulating all economic policies concerning economic development and development activities.[26]

Nepal has had the following plans:[27]

First five-year plan	1956–1961
Second three-year plan	1962–1965
Third five-year plan	1965–1970

In 1951, a World Bank team visited Sri Lanka and carried out a comprehensive survey of the country's development prospects, and it also drew up a development plan (1953–1959).[28] The suggested plan was not followed for lack of funds and the political debate that took place over the question of national priorities, but it did provide valuable background for future plans for the island. In 1954 the National Planning Council was created for "the preparation and coordination of development proposals and the determination of priorities." It drew up a comprehensive six-year Program of Investment (1954–1955 to 1959–1960), but because of a change of administration, this investment program was given up in 1956, and the new government presented the ten-year plan (1959–1968). In 1962, the ten-year plan encountered financial difficulties; a short-term Implementation Program (1962–1963) was adopted to complete some of the projects started earlier. In December 1971, the government of Sri Lanka announced a five-year plan (1972–1976).

Following the bitter civil war between East and West Pakistan, the new nation of Bangladesh (formerly East Pakistan) was formed in 1972. One of the first steps taken by the new government was the establishment of the Planning Commission of the People's Republic of Bangladesh. In November 1973 the first five-year plan (1973–1978) was adopted for reconstruction and development of "war-torn" Bangladesh.[29]

General Features of the Plans   The economic plans adopted by the South Asian countries have a striking similarity in objectives, methodology, and planning techniques. The differences involve economic questions dealing with the role of the public versus the private sector, the regulation and control of private enterprise, and land reform. Rather than discuss the plans of individual nations, we will summarize the main measures common to the South Asian economic plans. We will point out the differences in emphasis, however, as necessary.

The development plans are comprehensive in the sense that they cover many aspects of their societies, from increasing the gross national product to the development of art and music, from the welfare of the lower castes and uneducated segments of the population to improvement of transportation and communications. We have already discussed some of this in chapter 1. Some writers have criticized this approach as spreading scarce resources too thinly instead of concentrating on areas with high growth potential.[30] But the attitude of the South Asian countries is well explained by the Pakistan Planning Commission:

> Man does not live by bread alone and the national plan has to take into account not only the production and distribution of goods, but also social services and civilizing activities . . . though the social objectives of Pakistan have not been defined it is certain that they are higher than a mere provision of a standard of living very near the minimum requirements of human life.[31]

It is obvious that the planning technique which considers all "social objectives higher than mere material gains" would produce a lower growth rate.

The main objectives of development plans in South Asia[32] are:

1. To secure an increase in national income
2. To achieve a planned rate of investment to bring the actual investment income ratios to a higher planned level
3. To provide additional employment

4. To adopt measures to alleviate critical bottlenecks in the process of economic development, viz:
   a. Population growth
   b. Agricultural production
   c. Manufacturing capacity of producer goods' industries
   d. Economic and social infrastructure
5. To reduce the inequalities in the distribution of income and wealth and to reduce the concentration of economic power and resources

Increase in National Income The growth objective of the development plans was quantified in terms of the increase in annual net national product and per capita income. Table 7-1 gives the targets and realized rates of growth in national income for India and Pakistan.

Table 7-1 Annual Growth Rates of National Income in India and Pakistan

Country and plan	Growth of net national product (target)	Growth of net national product (realized)	Growth of per capita net national product
India			
First Plan	2.5%	3.5%	1.6%
Second Plan	5.0	4.0	1.8
Third Plan	5.0	2.9	0.4
Fourth Plan	5.5	3.7	1.6
Annual Plans		3.9	1.6
Pakistan[a]			
First Plan	3.0	2.4	0.0
Second Plan	5.2	5.3	2.7
Third Plan	7.5	3.0	0.7
Annual Plan	6.6	6.5	3.6

[a]Figures of the First, Second, and Third plans include statistics of Bangladesh (formerly East Pakistan).

SOURCE: Government of India, Planning Commission, the various *Five Year Plan* documents.
Government of Pakistan, *Pakistan Economic Survey,* 1972-1973 (Islamabad, 1973).

Table 7-1, along with figures on the rates of economic growth in Bangladesh, Nepal, and Sri Lanka given in Table 1-5 show that (1) the realized rates of growth are, in most plan periods, short of the target rates, and (2) the growth rates in per capita income are grossly inadequate (and even negative for Bangladesh and Sri Lanka in some periods). Overall, the rates of growth in per capita income show signs of stagnation for India and Nepal, with declining trends in the cases of Bangladesh and Sri Lanka. In Pakistan, however, we observe an improvement made during the annual plan (1972–1973) over the earlier plan periods. The main reasons for the stagnation of these economies are the existence of some retarding factors already discussed in chapter 1.

Increase in Rates of Investment   Planning commissions in the South Asian countries realize that it will be essential to increase the rates of saving and investment to achieve higher planned rates of growth. In chapter 3, we discussed the problems and processes of capital formation in South Asia. Estimate figures of various components of capital formation in Table 3–1 indicate the following trends.

The South Asian countries, except Sri Lanka, started their economic plans with very low rates of saving and investment. During the 1950s total gross investment in proportion to national income was around 6 percent in India and Pakistan (which then included the present Bangladesh). With a capital-output ratio of 3:1 (as discussed in chapter 3) the 6 percent investment rate would yield 2 percent growth in national income with zero increase in per capita income, assuming an annual population increase of 2 percent. This explains why, as shown in Table 7–1, the growth of per capita net national product during the first five-year plan was only 1.6 percent in India and zero in Pakistan.

Investment rates have increased during the plan periods; in Pakistan the rate of investment rose from 7.5 percent in 1954–1955 to 13.4 percent in 1969–1970. In the case of Sri Lanka, the rate of investment remained around 14 percent during the decade 1960–1970. The 13.0 percent gross investment rate in Pakistan during 1969–1970 included foreign capital amounting to 2.7 percent of the national income, while in the case of India, foreign capital was quite low, only 1.5 percent.

The South Asian countries would have to increase their investment rates to about 17 percent to achieve the planned growth rate of 6 percent in national income. For these countries, this would mean an increase in investment of about 4 percent, assuming minimal dependence on foreign capital, a realistic assumption considering the present international situation. As discussed in chapter 3, the projected increase in capital required would have to come either from household savings or government savings through excess revenues over general expenditures. But, poverty, the revolution of rising expectations, and the inability of democratic governments to restrain private consumption are some obstacles to increasing household savings.

Providing Additional Employment   Unemployment plagues the South Asian countries and constitutes a serious threat to their economic and political stability. In chapter 5, we have discussed in detail the nature, causes, and magnitude of the problem. Unemployment has been classified as urban (open unemployment) and rural (hidden, or disguised, unemployment and underemployment). The magnitude of each category of unemployment was discussed along with the efforts to alleviate it. We observed that although the planning commissions in the South Asian countries were quite aware of the seriousness of the problem, nevertheless they have failed to utilize their labor resources—and this failure is responsible for continuing mass poverty. There is an urgent need on the part of these countries to reevaluate their policies for providing jobs for the unemployed millions. Failure to deal with this serious problem threatens the political and social stability that is a basic requirement for what is called "democratic planning" in South Asia.

Checking Population Growth   Chapter 2 discusses the problem of population explosion in South Asia. The impact of population increase on income and employment levels was examined and we found that increasing population is a critical factor for economic development. Many of the economic problems facing the South Asian countries include unemployment, food shortages, small fragmented landholdings, low rates of capital formation, housing shortages, inadequate transportation, schools, and hospitals. Increasing population neutralizes many of the gains won from development efforts. As the figures in Table 1–2 show, the annual growth rates in the national income of the South Asian economies, ranging from 4 to 5 percent from 1950 to 1970, have been reduced to the extremely low figures of 0.5 to 2.5 percent in per capita income, when population increase is taken into account. The South Asian governments are keenly aware of the seriousness of the population problem and have adopted measures for reducing the birth rate in hopes of checking the increasing population pressures. The efforts at population control are being thwarted, however, by the falling death rate. Examining the demographic statistics presented in Table 2–7 would show a declining trend in birth rates, but death rates have declined even more. It will take several years for birth rates to decline sufficiently to balance the sharply declining death rates. Only then can the population size be expected to benefit economic development. According to some projections it might be around 1985 when this desirable demographic situation could emerge. Unfortunately, by that time, in the words of the Indian Planning Commission: "Population growth on this scale can be a crippling handicap."[33] Unless some miracle occurs (and the South Asian people do believe in miracles) or the governments of South Asia adopt some drastic measures to decrease births, future economic prospects may well be darkened by the demographic tragedy. Maybe with deteriorating economic conditions, the governments would simply be compelled to take drastic measures. The Bangladesh Planning Commission considers "no civilized measure too drastic to keep the population within control."[34]

   The Development of Agriculture and Industry There are conflicting views on the relative priority of agriculture and industry in underdeveloped countries. The case for according priority to agriculture rests on the following arguments.

   The economic history of modern industrialized nations is cited to support the importance of agriculture in economic expansion. In England, the remarkable progress of agriculture during the first quarter of the eighteenth century laid the ground for industrial expansion. In Germany, the periods of agricultural expansion synchronised with rapid industrial development from 1850 to 1900. The recent experiences of the Soviet Union and the People's Republic of China show a similar relationship between the expansion of the agricultural and industrial sectors. Agricultural improvements foster industrial development in several ways. First, increasing agricultural incomes provide saving and investment funds for the industrial sector. (This is true, for example, in the case of Japan). Second, improved agricultural output frees farm workers to move into nonagricultural sectors of the economy. Expansion in the primary sector helps overall economic development by meeting the demands of the country for food, providing raw materials for industry, and increasing foreign exchange earnings through exports of raw materials. All these arguments that favor the priority of agricultural over industrial development apply to South Asian.

   It is contended, however, that expansion of the industrial sector is a prerequisite for economic growth. It may be noted that the classical theory of comparative costs in international trade is sometimes cited to suggest that the factor endowment position of South Asia, characterized by abundant labor, is conducive to specialization in raw material production. Trade may then be established for industrial goods. In doing so, it is contended that both the underdeveloped and the developed nations would gain. This theory is, however, not taken seriously these days, as it basically assumes static factor endowment ignoring the fact that it changes with the changes in economic development. Emphasis on industrial development for economic growth is suggested on the grounds that the gap in per capita income between the developed and underdeveloped countries is largely reflected in the disparity of their economic structures. In general, countries with higher per capita income have larger proportions of their gross national product originating from the industrial sector.[35] Also, due to the introduction of synthetic substitutes for raw materials (e.g., plastics in place of jute, synthetic materials for cotton, wool, and rubber), the growth of import demand for raw materials in the advanced countries has diminished and currently it lags behind the growth in their domestic incomes. The volume of exports from the underdeveloped countries expanded at the rate of 3.6 percent annually from 1950 to 1970, while exports from the developed countries increased at the rate of 6.2 percent. This export lag has resulted in deterioration in their terms of trade. Thus, in view of unfavorable trends in the world trade of primary goods, the industrialization of underdeveloped countries is looked upon as the only effective answer. Some South Asian countries—India, Bangladesh, and Sri Lanka—have already faced this deterioration in their export earnings from the declining demand for their raw materials, specifically jute (burlap) and tea. Against the declining foreign exchange earnings of the South Asian countries, their demand for the import of capital goods, including heavy machinery essential for economic planning, has increased creating deficits in their balance of payments. One way to cover this deficit, in the long run, is to adopt import substitution policies, requiring the development of industries that produce previously imported manufactured goods. India and Pakistan are following the import substitution policies in their industrial development plans. Industrial development is also supported to achieve a higher rate of economic growth, since the net value of output per person is higher in industry than in agriculture. Industrialization provides scope for internal and external economies—economies of scale and interindustrial linkages (or complementarities) greater than in agriculture. Thus, industrial expansion creates employment opportunities for surplus agricultural labor, and it also provides income and the resultant savings for further investment. Industrial development is also of direct benefit to agriculture since it provides crucial inputs such as fertilizers, machinery, power, and technical knowledge. Finally, to the extent that the agricultural sector is a deficit sector incapable of generating sufficient savings for improvement, industry draws financial resources from outside. This agricultural and industrial interdependence would suggest a balanced development of both to ensure stable overall economic growth.

Any imbalance in the development of the two sectors, where one developed faster than the other, might create problems—industry might be short essential materials or services, and agriculture might not find a market for products. Thus, if the industrial sector developed while the agricultural remained stagnant, inflationary pressures might result with good industrial incomes increasing demands for scarce agricultural products. This is exactly what hapened in India near the end of the second five-year plan (1960-1961) when a priority for industrial development caused shortages of agricultural products. If, however, increased agricultural production is not accompanied by corresponding industrial expansion, demand for agricultural products will fall short of supply creating depressed agricultural prices with an accompanying fall in income and hampered growth.

The South Asian countries have generally followed a policy of balanced development for the different sectors of the economy. In India, highest priority was given to agriculture in the allocation of planned investment funds during the first five-year plan. The Indian Planning Commission recognized the fact that

> without a substantial increase in the production of food and raw materials needed for industry, it would be impossible to sustain a higher tempo of industrial development.[36]

Investment priority was shifted to industrial development in India's second five-year plan when emphasis was placed on capital goods and heavy industries. The third five-year plan gave priority, again, to the agricultural sector. In this way India has been trying to achieve balanced development by shifting investment priorities from one sector to the other, gaining experience from the successive plans. The investment strategy followed by India has been described by the Indian Planning Commission as follows:

> The basic objective is to provide sound foundations for sustained economic growth . . . In the schemes of development, the first priority necessarily belongs to agriculture . . . The growth of agriculture and the development of human resources alike hinge upon the advance made by industry . . . Agriculture and industry must be regarded as integral parts of the same process of development.[37]

The Pakistan Planning Commission emphasizes both sectors—their objectives are to accelerate the transformation in agriculture and "to develop basic industries for the manufacturing of producers' goods."[38] In Bangladesh's first five-year plan, however, "the main thrust of the plan is on the agricultural sector," but the Planning Commission recognizes that "the requirements of a high rate of growth in agriculture have been neglected in terms of interrelated investment in the rest of the economy."[39] Accordingly, the Bangladesh Planning Commission provides for a balanced pattern of investment between the agricultural and industrial sectors, 24.0 and 19.7 percent of the total investment, respectively. The Nepal and Sri Lanka Planning Commissions also stress this balanced technique of investment.

Program for Agricultural Development A review of the plan documents of the South Asian countries would show the following common objectives and programs of agricultural development, as stated in Pakistan's third five-year plan:

(i)   to increase the real income of farmers at least at the same rate as the per capita increase in the non-agricultural sector,

(ii) to move towards self-sufficiency in food requirements to the extent compatible with the other needs of the economy including foreign trade, aiming, at the same time, at improved nutritional standards in food consumption, and

(iii) to promote agricultural development on a sound, self-propelling basis by further improvements in agricultural organizations, and by intensified programs such as for the developments of marketing, cooperatives, storage, credit, educational, and other institutional and infra-structural facilities.[40]

To the above objectives, the Bangladesh Planning Commission adds, "creating employment opportunities for the rural unemployed and underemployed so as to enable them to attain a basic minimum level of consumption."[41] Sri Lanka's Planning Commission calls for the establishment of "new income-generating activities in agriculture. The emphasis is on subsidiary food crops, horticulture, cotton, mulberry, animal husbandry and fisheries."[42] The increase in food production is planned to be achieved through:

(i)   Reclamation of new land or the process of extensive cultivation,

(ii) Provision of agricultural inputs; water from major and minor irrigation projects, fertilizers, improved seeds at reasonable prices,

(iii) The extension of the high-yielding varities of seeds, multiple cropping programmes and the spread of technical know-how for improved agriculture.[43]

To provide the improved seeds, fertilizers, and better implements, the National Planning Council of Nepal established the Agricultural Supply Corporation;[44] Pakistan, India, and Sri Lanka distribute these items through cooperative societies. India utilizes the institution of community development projects for the task of rural uplift.[45] These projects are organized on the "self-help basis"; the efforts of the people are united with those of the government agencies to improve the economic, social, and cultural conditions of communities enabling them to contribute fully to national life and progress.

What has been the progress of agriculture under the various development plans? The agricultural sector has had varied success. In some areas the successes have been notable, for example, in the provision of irrigation facilities, in the introduction and acceptance of new varieties of seeds (wheat, *jowar, bajra,* and corn), and in the improvement in terms of trade for agriculture. The progress of agriculture in India from 1950 to 1970, summed up by V. V. Bhatt, applies to most South Asian countries.

> A right foundation has been laid, a foundation that has linked research with education, extension work and actual agricultural operations. At the same time, an institutional framework has been created for the adequate and timely supply of inputs like fertilizers, pesticides, and water and provision of credit and marketing facilities. Further remunerative prices have been assured so as to make agriculture a commercially viable and attractive proposition.[46]

In quantitative terms, in India the annual average rate of growth in agricultural output from 1950–1951 to 1970–1971 was 3.3 percent (food grain output was 3.5 percent and nonfood grain 2.9 percent).[47] Food grain output per hectare of cultivated land increased by 1.9 percent annually in that period as well. During the first and second plans in Pakistan, the annual growth rate in agriculture was over 3.5 percent, which the Pakistan Planning Commission hails as "one of the most heartening aspects of the entire development effort . . . and was one of the highest rates found in any developing country."[48] In Sri Lanka, the annual rate of growth in agricultural output was 2.3 percent from 1957 to 1968.[49] A growth rate of about 3.5 percent per annum may be impressive in an absolute sense as the Pakistan Planning Commission claims, but viewed against the increase in population and the increased demand of agricultural products from planned investments under development plans, the realized growth in agriculture is inadequate. It is certainly so in terms of ushering in a "self-generating economy," capable of fast and "self-sustained growth," the objectives stated in South Asian plan documents.

Another failure in rural economic development may be pointed out. In spite of huge investments in agriculture, the South Asian economies are still dependent on the capriciousness of the monsoons. Recurring monsoon-related floods and droughts in India, Pakistan, and Bangladesh easily wipe out all gains from rural economic development. These economies, thus, still continue to "gamble in monsoons." Ultimately, the only solution would be extensive development of flood control and irrigation facilities.

Programs for Industrial Development   Industries are classified into the following categories in the development plans:

1. large scale and heavy industries:
   a. producer goods industries
   b. consumer goods indusries
2. Small-scale industries
3. Cottage and handicrafts

The development plans of India, Pakistan, and Sri Lanka emphasize large-scale industry whereas Bangladesh and Nepal have placed priority on small-scale and cottage industries. The objectives of their industrial development are stated as follows:

1. large-scale and heavy industries—producer goods:
   a. according to the Indian Planning Commission, "to make the economy self-sustaining in such as steel, machine building and the manufacturer of producer goods and reduce as rapidly as possible, the need for external assistance to purchase these goods and also permit a broadening of the export base."[50] For the Pakistan Planning Commission, emphasis on the capital goods industries stem from the statements, "to maintain the contribution of the industrial sector to the saving effort and to extend the import substitution programme over a much wider front."[51]
2. to produce agricultural items such as agricultural machinery and fertilizers
3. to produce machines for manufacturing consumer goods

Most of the basic industries started under economic development plans are to be managed under the "public sector" according to the industrial policy statements issued in India and Pakistan.

1. Consumer goods—large-scale industries such as sugar, textiles, paper, bicycles (a) to meet the demand for consumer goods arising from the increased tempo of investment under development plans and (b) to increase levels of aggregate employment and output
2. Cottage and small-scale industries—utilizing the indigenous raw materials and manpower. According to the National Planning Council emphasis in Nepal is placed on cottage industries (a) to provide off-season employment opportunities and (b) to meet many local consumer needs.[52]

The Pakistan Planning Commission adds the following to the above objectives:[53]

(i) to adapt small industries to meet changing technological, economic and social conditions,
(ii) to stimulate production of implements and equipment required for agriculture,

(iii) to bring about a closer relationship between the small and larger industries, through the production of spare parts and accessories or components for large scale industries.[53]

To achieve the above objectives, the development plans provide for the establishment of several new undertakings while encouraging those already existing.

As already mentioned, most of the heavy producer goods industries have been established in the public sector for which a great amount of financial resources have been allocated. In India and Pakistan, progress in the field of capital goods industries has been impressive. According to the Indian Planning Commission:

> Increases in capacity have been most notable in production of steel and aluminum, a wide range of machine tools, industrial machinery, electrical and transport equipment, fertilizers, drugs and pharmaceuticals, petroleum products, cement, minerals and a variety of consumer goods. There has also been a large increase in the manufacturing capacity for power generators. All this has contributed to the strengthening of the industrial structure and a valuable potential for sustained industrial progress in the future has been created.[54]

These gains in the capital goods industries have brought about a change in the structure of Indian industries in favor of the machinery and capital goods sector.[55] From 1950–1951 to 1965–1966 the manufacturing sector increased its machinery output from 8 percent to 22 percent. During the same period consumer goods industries declined from 67.9 percent to 34.0 percent. In India, although the gains in output were not consistent, consumer goods showed an average annual growth rate of 6.6 percent from 1950 to 1970. Indian plans for the development of cottage and small-scale industries contained several provisions: allocation of raw materials, imported components, and equipment; the provision of credit at favorable interest rates and easy terms through the nationalized banks; specially established institutions—the Industrial Finance Corporation at the central and state levels; cooperative societies—for technical assistance through the establishment of service institutes and extension centers throughout the country and marketing assistance in the national and foreign markets. The small-scale and cottage industries have shown considerble progress (average annual growth rate was 5.1 percent from 1950 to 1970) and, according to the Indian fourth five-year plan,

> Apart from quantitative growth, there has been significant improvement in the quantity and quality of the products of many small scale industries . . . Products of some of these industries are exported. Production of a number of new items, parts and components requiring

high technology and precision has been successfully undertaken in the small scale sector.[56]

In spite of these impressive results, however, the industrial growth achieved during the plan periods has not even made a dent on the problem of unemployment. From 1951 to 1967, the total labor force increased by 4.7 million, but factory employment absorbed only 2 percent of this increase.[57] Proportionally, workers in industry, mining, and construction have remained at approximately 11 percent of the total work force during this period. Furthermore, the industrial share of national income has increased only from 17.0 percent in 1948–1949 to 20.0 percent in 1972–1973.[58]

According to the Pakistan Planning Commission "the growth and diversification of . . . industry has been remarkably rapid."[59] Pakistan began with virtually no industry in 1947; the contribution of the manufacturing sector to the gross national product was only 7.0 percent in 1949–1950, and this mainly from small-scale industries. From 1960 to 1970 large-scale industries in Pakistan grew at an average rate of almost 15 percent per year; the contribution of their large-scale industries to the manufacturing sector increased from 1.5 percent to 7.4 percent in that period. The measures adopted by Pakistan to achieve this remarkable growth rate were a liberalized import policy for industrial machinery, a tax holiday for new industries ranging from four to eight years, a relaxation of price and distribution controls, credit facilities, and facilities for profit and capital remittances to foreign firms.

Removal of Inequalities in the Distribution of Income The governments of the South Asian countries recognize the growing inequalities in the distribution of wealth and income; and reducing these inequalities is one of the major objectives of their development plans. Various plan documents clearly express this objective and explain measures to achieve it. The following quote from India's fourth five-year plan explains their position on the nature, the causes, and the measures suggested to alleviate inequalities.

The process of development might lead, in the absence of purposive intervention by the state, to greater concentration of wealth and income . . . Therefore, the attainment of objectives of equality and social justice requires more comprehensive planning and greater command over resources than has been attempted so far. Preventing increase in concentration of economic power is a part of this problem. Actions under the Monopolies Act, Government's powers of licensing and allocation judiciously used, and purposeful policies of public financial institutions and the nationalized banks are expected to play a significant role in this regard. A dilemma has to be faced. The largest corporate groups are the most advantageously placed to seek and obtain foreign collaboration and to expand or to initiate a number of large and new activities. Therefore, acting through them may appear the easiest and quickest way of development. In the process there is inevitably an increase in concentration of economic power . . . While large corporate enterprises would have scope for taking up new ventures in technologically challenging fields, deliberate encouragement will be given to wide entrepreneurship.[60]

The major provisions for the achievement of a more equitable distribution of income and opportunities in other South Asian countries are already covered in chapter 4.

An analysis of this quote indicates the following important aspects on inequality in income distribution:

1. income inequality is the result of economic planning in a capitalistic economy,
2. large corporate groups promote economic development which leads inevitably to a concentration of economic power,
3. income equality can be achieved through measures such as antimonopoly legislation and the judicious allocation of material and financial resources, including encouragement of wider entre-preneurship.

Besides the steps listed above, other measures included in the South Asian economic plans are:

4. land reform measures including a ceiling on land ownership, fixation of fair rent, and protection of the rights of tenants and landless labor,
5. nationalization of industrial and financial institutions,
6. encouragement of cottage and small-scale industries in the rural sector,
7. expansion of employment opportunities in both the rural and urban areas, and
8. increase in the degree of progressiveness in the tax rates on income and wealth.

What has been the result of all these egalitarian measures? In India, the planned, equitable, distribution of income has not been realized. We may repeat the findings of the Committee on Distribution of Income (1964) appointed by the Indian Planning Commission.

Even after 10 years of planning and despite fairly heavy schemes of taxation on the upper incomes, there is a considerable measure of concentration in urban incomes. This would also hold for rural incomes, as in their cases, even the burden of taxation is not heavy on the higher ranges of income.[61]

The statistics on income distribution in India collected in an all-India household survey (1960 to 1968) show that the share of the upper 20 percent households had increased from 48.1 percent to 53.3 percent of disposable income while that of the bottom 20 percent decreased from 5.9 to 4.8 percent.[72] In terms of the Lorenz ratio it registered a decline from 0.41 in 1962 to 0.46 in 1968. As mentioned in chapter 1, various estimates on the proportion of the Indian population living below the "poverty line" suggest that the figure has increased or remained substantially the same from 1960 to 1970.[63]

The income redistribution policies in other South Asian countries have also been largely ineffective. Sri Lanka's Socio-Economic Survey of 1969–1970 shows sharp disparities in incomes and living standards.[64] In Pakistan, according to the Planning Commission, wide disparities in income distribution between the lowest and highest income groups exist, particularly in the urban areas.[65]

There are several causes for the continuation and even the increase in inequalities of income redistribution. An important cause of income inequality, according to Minhas, was the failure to change property relations.

> Aside from a programme of land reform and ceiling legislation which was in various stages of implementation, no basic alteration in poverty relations was envisaged. In other words, the objectives of "reduction of disparities in income and wealth" and "prevention of concentration of economic power" were sought to be achieved not through redistribution of property and wealth, but through other means.[66]

Minhas also finds fault with the distribution of benefits from government agencies among different income classes. He stresses a basic fact,

> Whether it was the operation of public sector enterprises or the construction of infra-structure facilities in the field of irrigation, flood control, power, transport, etc., or the operation of a licensing system for control of investments and imports, or the distribution of food and fertilizers, etc., the basic fact of the distribution of public largesse to the not-so-poor was ever present.[67]

Minhas is also critical of generous subsidies granted to higher income classes in various forms.

> We built temples of modern industry which were over capitalized. Elaborate townships were provided and included in capital charges and economic rents were not charged . . . Huge dams, flood controls, irrigation and power facilities were built with public funds, but the

collection of development levies and the charging of proper irrigation rates and tariffs were forgotten.[68]

To Minhas one solution to the problem of inequality in income distribution lies in adopting a policy of realistic radicalism. "To win back the credibility among the masses," he says, "the planners must translate political slogans into realistic radicalism."[69]

The Socialistic Policies In the earlier chapter on historical background opposition against laissez-faire and capitalism was noted along with a strong preference in favor of state participation[70] (used synonymously with socialism) as a technique for economic planning in South Asia. It is, however, interesting to note that rather than adopting the traditional form, the South Asian governments mention several variants of socialism in their respective development plans.

Pakistan's third five-year plan mentions "Islamic Socialism" as the ultimate aim of all efforts in economic and social spheres. Islamic Socialism, according to the Pakistan Planning Commission, "is almost interchangeable with" the welfare state. In addition to the welfare goals, Islamic Socialism implies that the cultural and religious heritage of the country should be preserved and kept from destruction by a "ruthless pursuit of economic development."[71] A review of Pakistan's development plans shows that Islamic Socialism is more a "religious goal" than an economic policy. The Pakistan Planning Commission elaborates on the concept further:

> Our approach to economic planning has been pragmatic all along . . . The government has limited its own role to providing a suitable framework for the private sector and to the creation of those facilities which the private sector had neither the ability nor the willingness to develop. There has been no undue intervention in the private sector. In fact, the government has gradually removed most of the administrative and bureaucratic controls which hampered progress of the private sector.[72]

In Pakistan, the role of government is limited to providing "economic and social overheads," some fiscal measures to achieve a more equitable distribution of income, including land reform. Although the proportion of public investment to total investment in Pakistan increased from 4.8 percent in 1950 to 20.1 percent in 1970, most of the public investment (90.2 percent of total public investment) was in the economic and social infrastructure, notably water and power, transportation and communication, housing and education.[73] The government of Pakistan left the development of other industries to private enterprise.

The Bangladesh Planning Commission, similarly, mentions the attainment of socialism as one of the objectives of economic development. It, however, calls for gradualism in the transition from capitalism to socialism "dictated by the needs of expedience and orderly functioning of the economy since too abrupt a dislocation at one time may seriously disturb the production system."[74] Socialism is defined there as extending "by stages the sphere of state participation consistent with the ability of the state to organize efficiently."[75]

The five-year plan of Sri Lanka (1972–1976) refers to the socialist aspirations of the people which would be fulfilled through

> removal of the privileged position of groups in key sectors of the economy by land reforms, ceiling on ownership of house property and measures for the social ownership or the social control of industry and commerce.[76]

At present, twenty-two state-owned industrial corporations in several areas such as paper, oil and fats, leather goods, sugar, cement, salt, textiles, steel, lumber, and petroleum are functioning in Sri Lanka. Most of these state-owned industrial enterprises are, however, small in scale. Their five-year plan provides for starting large-scale industries either under complete or partial government ownership. The Sri Lanka Planning Commission does not demarcate any areas for private or public sectors as does India. Sri Lanka's private sector is provided with several financial and tax incentives which should allow it to play a significant role in the national plan for development.

India's objective is to build a society with a socialistic pattern, which, according to the Indian Planning Commission

> means that the basic criteria for determining lines of advance is not private profit but social gain, and that the pattern of development and the socio-economic relations should be so planned that they result not only in appreciable increases in national income and employment but also in greater equality in income and wealth.[77]

The objective of the socialistic society is based on the following provisions in India's constitution:

> The state shall, in particular, direct its policy towards securing—
> a. that the citizens, men and women, equally, have the right to an adequate means of livelihood;
> b. that the ownership and control of the material resources of the community are so distributed as best to subserve the common good;
> c. that the operation of the economic system does not result in the concentration of wealth and means of production to the common detriment (Article 39).

More specifically, their objectives for a socialist society have been (1) major decisions to be made by agencies informed by social purpose;

(2) benefits to accrue gradually to the relatively less privileged classes of society; (3) a progressive reduction to be made of the concentration of incomes, wealth, and economic power; (4) greater opportunities to be provided for vertical mobility in labor; and (5) the public sector of the economy to undergo rapid expansion. The main instruments to achieve these objectives have been economic planning, growth of the public sector with regulation of the private sector, and land reforms and other methods for a more equitable distribution of income and wealth. As noted earlier, since 1950 India has had four five-year plans and two annual plans. They provided huge investments in all sectors of the economy for achieving "rapid and self-generating economic growth." We have already noted the results of India's planning in the growth of national income and employment.

India's plans provided for a rapid growth of the public sector especially in heavy capital goods industries and financial institutions. According to the Indian Planning Commission:

> The adoption of the Socialistic Pattern of Society as the national objective, as well as the need for planned and rapid development, require that all industries of basic and strategic importance or in the nature of public utility services should be in the public sector.[78]

In India, from 1951 to 1972, the number of commercial and industrial undertakings in the public sector increased from 5 ($37 million invested) to 113 ($8 billion invested).[79] The proportion of the public sector in gross capital formation increased from 41.0 percent in 1951 to 50.1 percent during 1972.[80] The role of the public sector in India is defined in various industrial policy statements which divide the sphere of industries into the following three sectors:

1. Core industries—of basic, critical, and strategic national importance (heavy and capital goods industries); these are divided into (a) industries reserved for the public sector, and (b) industries in the public sector where large private industrial houses will be eligible to participate (also called the joint sector).
2. Other industries—including consumer goods industries, of both large- and small-scale, in which private enterprise will be allowed to function within the overall industrial plan.

Industries in the private sector are subject to strict regulation and control by the government in terms of their production, distribution, and pricing policies.

Commercial banks and life insurance companies were nationalized with a view toward directing financial resources according to the planned targets, especially in agriculture and small-scale industries. The wholesale trade in food grains was taken over by the government in April 1973, but after a year, the nationalization was rescinded due to the confusion and chaos following the takeover.

In order to achieve a more equitable distribution of income and wealth, land reform legislation was introduced involving

1. abolition of absentee landlords
2. fixing of ceilings on land ownership
3. provision for security of tenure to tenants
4. regulation of rent

Absentee landlords (also known as *zimidars* or intermediaries) owning very large estates, up to several thousand acres, were required to surrender their ownership rights when fair compensation was paid by the cultivating tenants in whom the ownership then was vested. The process was completed by 1955 involving 6.2 million acres of land and conferment of ownership rights to about 3 million tenants and share croppers.[81] This was a significant achievement indeed. A ceiling of about 30 standard acres[82] was imposed throughout India. The fixing of ceilings on land ownership was not really successful because of the large number of illegal land transfers made to evade the spirit of the law. According to the Indian Planning Commission, "on the whole it would be correct to say that in recent years, transfers of land have tended to defeat the aims of the legislation for ceilings and to reduce its impact on the rural economy."[83] Rent was regulated and maximum rent payments were fixed from one-fifth to one-third of the gross produce in different parts of the country. Laws were also enacted to provide tenants with security from eviction at the whim of the landowners. Provisions were also made to allow them to become owners of the land they cultivated. These laws have, however, been observed more in name than in fact because as the Indian Planning Commission admits,

> when there is pressure on land and the social and economic position of tenants in the village is weak, it becomes difficult for them to seek the protection of law. Moreover, resort to legal process is costly and generally beyond the means of tenants. Thus, in many ways, despite the legislation, the scales are weighed in favor of the continuance of existing terms and conditions.[84]

Aside from the program of land reforms and ceiling legislation, no basic alteration in property regulation was envisaged in India. It was assumed that poverty and the inequality in income distribution would be solved by the huge investments made during the five-year plans.

What has been the outcome of India's socialistic society? Some critics call it nothing more than a mixed economy in which the public sector has taken over those functions for which private enterprise has no sufficient resources.[85] In this sense, India's socialist society is grounded more or less in pragmatism. Minhas has, however, strong opinions against India's practice of socialism.

> Let us, however, try to see what Indian socialism has turned out to mean in practice. The socialistic intentions of independent India were pitted against the outmoded attitudes of a strongly feudal and caste status-conscious society, which has been unwilling to accept the rigorous code of private as well as public behavior implied in the concept of socialism.[86]

The Indian public sector has been criticized for inefficiencies and its inability to generate expected surpluses for investment and growth. According to Padma Desai and Jagdish Bhagwati:

> The public sector has not generated the expected surpluses of investment and growth. And their management has suffered from the constraints imposed by their bureaucratic structure and the absence of any ultimate penalty for inefficiency.[87]

As already mentioned, the inequalities in income distribution continue to persist or may even have increased despite the socialist slogans. Although national income and per capita income have increased, the poorer segments of society have not benefited.[88]

The development of the Indian and the other South Asian economies presents a paradox. On the one hand, India has built up a well diversified industrial structure; capital goods manufacturing capacity for various industries has been developed, along with the technical capacity to erect irrigation dams, power mills, and factories. All these skills and knowledge are, in fact, being exported to various countries in Africa, the Middle East, and South America. On the other hand, the peoples of India and the rest of South Asia are among the poorest in the world. The poverty, according to Pramit Chaudhuri,

> is all too real and one hardly needs any statistics to show that after twenty years of planning, the Indian poor have little to be thankful about. Indeed, in some ways his lot is worse, because with the growth in population his access to agricultural land, housing, water and transport has in many cases deteriorated.[89]

We can now summarize the major achievements and failures of planning in South Asia.[90] There have been impressive gains in national income, but because of the failure to check population increase these gains have been reduced to insignificance. The small gains in per capita income hardly made a dent in poverty and the standard of living. The South Asian countries have learned the art of planning; some, notably

India, have developed advanced and sophisticated technology, and great strides have been made in the fields of education and public health. India and Pakistan have built a well-diversified industrial structure. India has made it possible to expand production capacity in vital sectors such as iron and steel, mining, and power generation. In the field of rail and road transportation and communications, virtual self-sufficiency has been realized for the price of equipment and rolling stock. Some success has also been achieved in educating farmers for using new items—fertilizers, small-scale machinery, and financial institutions. Banks and cooperative societies have been expanded to provide farmers with credit at easy terms and to educate those persons interested in starting small-scale industries.

Although the South Asian nations have succeeded in expanding their productive means, they have failed miserably in their redistributive efforts. The inequalities in income and wealth continue to persist, or have even increased, causing frustration among the unfulfilled who believed the promises made in the development plans. The result has been a revolution of rising expectations. There has also been great disappointment in the inability to provide employment opportunities, as needed, to an increasing labor force.

The future economic well-being and political stability of these countries may depend on their ability to utilize their vast labor resources and to distribute their gains more equally than has been the case in the past. Industrial expansion in the public sector would seem to provide the greatest opportunities toward this end.

INDIA AND CHINA: DEVELOPMENT CONTRASTS

While evaluating the development of South Asia, the question of their performance (especially India's) relative to that of China's is often raised. The question is natural because at the start of economic planning in India and China during the 1950s, both nations had several quite similar characteristics. They had similar factor endowment situations with abundant labor and little capital, industrial underdevelopment, extreme poverty, disease, and ignorance, and rapidly increasing populations affected, for centuries, by Western colonialism. These two countries embarked upon economic planning during the early 1950s with differing political philosophies. India functioned under a democratic form of government while China functioned under a communistic system. Both declared their development objectives as plans for the economic betterment of their peoples. To some extent, their relative successes were expected to be interpreted as the efficacy of democratic versus communistic governments for solving the problems of underdevelopment in general. Their experiences could conceivably be extended to the situations faced by other developing nations.

How do we actually contrast the development experiences of India and China during the last twenty-five years? There are a host of difficulties of both a conceptual and an operational nature involved in such a comparison.[91] The major difficulty is a scarcity of reliable data for China. For India, massive quantities of data are available for almost every aspect of the economy, from government as well as nongovernment agencies. Also, there is easy access to it by scholars for scientific scrutiny and evaluation. For China, sources of information are limited and their reliability is questionable. The main data sources are "bits and pieces of information which are allowed to trickle in,"[92] the assertions of China-watchers from mainland America, and the impressions of visitors to a few factories and communes under guided tours.[93] In spite of the limitations of the data, there are several studies comparing the development of India and China during various periods.[94] The pioneering study by Malenbaum showed that for the 1950s, China's growth rate in real per capita income was two to three times higher than India's.[95] Malenbaum attributed China's higher growth rate to a faster rate of capital formation and also to a bigger investment in agriculture. Since then, there have been more studies but with different conclusions. Barry Richman finds that

> China has done considerably better with regard to both economic and social development than India has to date; and China has gone much further in creating an overall social environment conducive to sustained economic growth and development in the future.[96]

The most important factor in explaining China's superior economic development, according to Richman, is "the apparent significantly greater willingness and ability of the Chinese people to work hard and effectively on a national scale for goals which inspire them."[97] Thomas Weisskopf, on the basis of data for the period 1952 to 1970, has concluded similarly that,

> The record of economic growth has unquestionably been better in China than in India. Most estimates on the average annual rate of growth of real output in China from 1952 (after an initial period of recovery) to the early 1970's range between 4 and 6 percent. The corresponding figure for India, based on official estimates, is 3-1/2 percent. With population growing at about 2 percent per year in each country, the average annual rate of growth of per capita output has probably been twice as high in China (2–4 percent) as in India (1–1-1/2 percent).[98]

Weisskopf ascribes the rapid growth of the Chinese economy to the "exceptionally rapid growth of Chinese Industry." "Chinese agricultural growth," Weisskopf suggests, "may have been slighty less than that of India."[99] In a study, with abundant statistical data on the growth of various sectors in the two economies, Subramanian Swamy concludes that "the growth rate of the Chinese and Indian economies has been the same over the period 1952-1970."[100] For the industrial sector, Swamy finds that, "the average rate of growth of industrial production during 1952-1970 was 6.7 percent in India." As regards agricultural output, he finds that for China "the years 1952-70 form a period of significant 'ups and downs,'; the rates of growth 4.2 percent during the 1950's, 1.6 percent during 1958-63, 5 percent during 1963-65, zero percent during 1965-70." For India, he finds, however, that "the trend rate is steadily upward from 2.3 percent in the 1950's to 2.6 percent during 1958-63, to 3.3 percent during 1963-70."[101]

While studies do not concur on the relative growth rates of India and China, there is general concensus in the literature on some issues. For example, China has been very successful in her egalitarian policies. A vast redistribution of wealth has been effected and occupational income differentials have been narrowed. As a result of this income redistribution, Joost Kuitenbrouwer found that China

> has overcome and eradicated the basic expressions and effects of poverty such as hunger and malnutrition. Also its whole population has the real opportunity to participate in the production process, receive a reasonable share of the social product in accordance with its work, while it can also on reasonable terms acquire the basic goods it needs and make use of the collective services for the country's and one's personal development in such fields as health and education.[102]

India, however, has not really employed income and wealth redistribution policies. The quantitative data from various Indian studies indicate that the degree of income inequality has actually increased since 1950 and the proportion of the population below the "poverty line" has risen. Although India has made great strides in public health, education, and other social and welfare measures, their benefits have not extended to all levels of the population. The common man in India finds it difficult to appreciate the relationship between national development and his personal benefits. In China, as a result of reducing income differentials between the rural and the urban sectors, and between different industries and social classes, great progress has been made toward achieving social equality. The gap between different groups—urban and rural, educated and uneducated, upper and lower classes—has been greatly reduced. India's record, however, in striving for social equality has been less than commendable. Although India has undertaken several measures to ameliorate the social and economic conditions of the lower castes and the weakest segments of the population, Indian society, especially in the rural areas, still practices class and caste distinctions with all the attendant evils, and socioeconomic consequences.

The main thrust of Chinese success is based on the utilization of massive labor resources. Through carefully worked out labor-utilization programs Chinese planners are able to achieve balanced distributions of employment opportunities in both urban and rural sectors. The educated personnel that cannot be absorbed in urban enterprise are moved by political persuasion, or even by force, and "sent down" to rural communes where they are organized into production teams to develop the local economy. In many instances, "Chinese factories are overstaffed and no workers are dismissed even when higher productivity would make it possible to use fewer men."[103] Labor which cannot be absorbed in rural communes is enrolled in "production and construction units" to "people the desert regions, develop their agriculture and to provide military reserves."[104] High labor-intensive techniques of production are employed in the rural sector, in handicrafts and in factories to utilize as much labor as possible. Even primitive technologies, with very low levels of specialization, are employed to manufacture goods and provide services that otherwise would require capital-intensive techniques of production. Producing steel in backyard furnaces illustrates the extent of labor-intensive technology used in China. It is quite evident that China has achieved nearly "full employment," although there may be substantial "disguised unemployment," and the employment pattern may not conform to Western norms of economic efficiency. India, unfortunately, has failed to provide employment for her growing labor force. As pointed out earlier in chapter 4, the Indian economy suffers from serious urban unemployment including a deteriorating situation of the educated unemployed, the rural unemployed, and the underemployed. India has no plan to "send down" her urban unemployed to the rural sector as it is already overpopulated with surplus laborers.

DEVELOPMENT DIRECTION: AN OVERVIEW

The discussion above on the comparative economic development of India and China suggests some vital issues bearing on the direction of development. We now turn to a consideration of some of the most important.

Indian plans emphasize a maximization of the growth rate by using capital-intensive technology in major industrial enterprises and irrigation projects in an economy possessing abundant labor and a dearth of capital. It was more or less assumed that the other planning objectives, namely providing employment opportunities, reducing income disparities, and remedying poverty would result from industrial growth. This strategy of growth glossed over the apparent, and logical, eventualities that capital-intensive technology could neither absorb the current labor surplus nor any further increases in the labor force. The problem of inequalities in this society, characterized by a vastly unequal wealth distribution, would, in turn, be aggravated by the production of luxury goods and services instead of the basic goods needed by the majority of the population. China has instead given priority to the utilization of labor for the production of goods and services that meet essential needs, generating the workers' enthusiasm from this concerted development effort.

In India, planned policies were formulated within existing confines: a social framework based on the caste system, a property system based on private ownership of both land and industry by a small elite, and a traditional political structure inherited from local monarchies and consolidated by the colonialism of the British. Although various official Indian statements call for changes in these institutions, Gunnar Myrdal has remarked that "the combination of radicalism in principle and conservatism in practice . . . was quickly woven into the fabric of Indian politics."[105] Each of these institutional factors constitutes a barrier to the achievement of planned objectives. For example, the Indian plans persistently call for land reform measures, which in a legal sense, should enable a lower caste, powerless landless tiller to gain hold of land from a high caste, powerful landowner. Anyone with a modicum of understanding of the Indian social situation and power structure would understand the helplessness of the (moneyless) landless against the (monied) landowner. It is obvious that short of a thorough reorganization of rural social and political structure no dent can be made in the fundamental agrarian problem. Only if land is taken from the landed and given to the landless can they attain such property.

China recognized the necessity of changing the social structure in such a way as to facilitate an economic transformation. For example, the abolition of private property as a means of production allowed China to achieve a fair measure of equality in the economic and social realms of national life. Although this policy disrupted a number of individual lifestyles, the Chinese seem to be attaining better and more equitable living conditions for their general population. In the pursuit of economic development, China did not ignore the potential of using vast human labor resources along with technology no matter how primitive or crude the process. For example, the countryside medicine men became "barefoot doctors," and even folksingers and dancers were encouraged to provide entertainment for the rural population. As Padma Desai remarks, "What the Chinese seem to have accomplished is widespread distribution of food and most rudimentary types of shelter, education and medicine to its population."[106]

In India's planning, modernization seems to be the most important aspect of development. Modernization is interpreted as wholesale adoption of Western standards; especially in the area of consumer goods and services. Sizeable resources have been deployed to produce them—mainly luxury items such as automobiles, refrigerators, electrical gadgets, motor scooters, and luxury apartments. Basic necessities for the general public have been grossly neglected. In the pursuit of modernity substantial investments were made in developing modern medicines, constructing imposing public buildings, and imparting training in expensive modern techniques while paying scant attention to "crude" indigenous medicine and rural crafts which still provide some of the basic amenities of life to the vast majority of rural Indians. They are, however, discouraged by government policy and their disappearance is creating a gap unfilled, as yet, by "modern goods" produced chiefly to cater to Westernized demands. As a result, the majority of the rural Indian population is deprived of even basic necessities including pure drinking water, sanitary facilities, and adequate shelter—this, despite two decades of economic planning.

In India, the Planning Commission is an advisory body which formulates plans but leaves it to the central government, the states, and a host of local governments to implement them within the existing political and institutional framework. According to Weisskopf, in India

> first of all, the system of parliamentary democracy for all its inability to equalize the distribution of political power does permit certain interests to mount opposition to various aspects of government policy and thus to constrain the role of the central government. Second, the federal structure of government in India (in part the result of India's ethnological heterogeneity) allocates certain critical responsibilities to state governments and thereby weakens the power of the central government and the national political leadership. Third, the extensive protection of private property rights guaranteed by the Indian Constitution (reflecting the interests of powerful propertied classes) set strict limits on the authority of the State to bring about institutional changes affecting private property.[107]

Aside from these several government levels, where plan policies tend to become often radically changed, there is the bureaucracy, which by custom serves the interests of the ruling classes and is apathetic toward the needs of the underprivileged. The political structure has been attuned, traditionally, to the formation of alliances and compromises among the various interests competing for control. Instead of functioning as faithful executors of plan policies, the bureaucrats seem to have become aligned with the diverse vested interests of landowners, industrialists, and opportunist politicians; they function to provide the necessary links for alliance formation among them. Ram Manohar Lohia, a celebrated Indian socialist thinker, had cautioned against such an outcome from the very start of economic planning in India. Lohia said in 1955 that a "structure may emerge in which the political party, the managerial class and the professional class are all fixed in their superior places and the rest of the populace is divided up into a hierarchical group of a lower order."[108] Lohia's perception of the bureaucratic implementation of plan policies is equally true for the area of land reform. The following observation of the Task Force on Land Reforms, recently appointed by the Indian Planning Commission, bear this out fully:

> In no sphere of public policy in our country since independence has the hiatus between precept and practice, between policy pronouncements and actual execution, been as great as in the domain of land reforms. The attitude of the bureaucracy towards the implementation of land reforms is generally lukewarm, and often apathetic. This is, of course, inevitable because, as in the case of the men who yield political power, those in the higher echelons of the administration also are substantial landowners. The village functionaries like Patwaries are invariably petty landowners. They are also under the sway of big landowners . . . As a matter of fact there have been cases where administrators who tried to implement land reform laws honestly and efficiently were hastily transferred elsewhere.[109]

Dandekar considers this pattern of alliances to be the principal cause of India's policy failures, especially those aiming at radical reforms.[110] Commenting on the implementation of radical reforms recommended by the Indian plans, Gunnar Myrdal has arrived at the conclusion that

> equalization has been attempted through a number of palliative measures. Many supposedly egalitarian measures actually favor middle class and upper class groups and discriminate against the masses. . . Measures specifically designed to aid the lowest strata in the population have ordinarily been poorly enforced, if at all.[111]

No wonder that in India, there is a wide gap between the statements of policy objectives spelled out by the Indian Planning Commission and actual economic development. To deal with this "implementation crisis," what India needs is a committed government cadre to frustrate the alliances of vested interests for the good of the Indian nation as a whole. The implementation of any development plan policy needs appropriate implementation machinery.

CONCLUSIONS

The countries of South Asia are suffering from underdevelopment. This statement is supported by the existence of several factors, such as low productivity and low levels of consumption, savings, and investment. Most of these symptoms have been the result of a century-long policy of colonialism and neglect accompanied by outright exploitation. This persistent policy kept per capita income at static low levels, with the standard of living among the lowest in the world.

After the attainment of independence, the South Asian countries adopted ambitious and comprehensive plans for economic and social development. Their performance during the last two decades has been mixed. Their increases in gross national product represent notable acceleration over the growth rates of the first half of the twentieth century, and they compare quite favorably with the growth rates of the presently advanced nations at similar points in their earlier developmental histories. However, the growth rates achieved by the South Asian countries will be grossly inadequate to meet the increasing demands of a considerable population growth with only a small rise in absolute income. Moreover, during the last two decades, these growth rates have been generally lower than those of other regions of the underdeveloped world.

Solutions to the serious problems of both poverty and unemployment continue to elude the efforts of the South Asian governments. How does one explain this poor performance? One possible explanation may be the Leibenstein hypothesis—that the process of economic planning in an underdeveloped economy gives rise to certain countervailing forces which tend to retard further economic growth. In the context of South Asian economic planning, some of these retarding forces are population explosion, rising expectations, low rate of capital formation, and unemployment.

In this book we have discussed these retarding forces in detail and, also, the attempts being made to overcome them. The alarming increase in the populations of the South Asian countries threatens the economic well-being and political stability of the region. Nothing short of drastic measures would save some of the South Asian countries from the crippling effects of the population explosion. The rising expectations for a better material life, in contrast to the completely inadequate growth in the supply of goods and services, have created a widening gap—a gap being filled with frustrations and social and political unrest.

Unfulfilled expectations are also making development problems more difficult because of the adverse effects on capital formation and the public attitude toward planning. Lack of capital continues to be a most serious obstacle for economic development. With continuing poverty and rising expectations the domestic capital has fallen considerably short of development needs. At the same time, the prospects of foreign aid and private foreign investments are not encouraging because of the economic and political problems facing the modern world. The South Asian countries are now emphasizing a need for self-reliance to reach their capital goals for development, but this policy seems to make a virtue out of necessity. Lack of investment, an alarming increase in population, and spreading educational facilities are accentuating an already serious unemployment problem.

The South Asian countries have failed largely to utilize their vast labor resources. This failure keeps the economies poor, and so poverty is perpetuated. Although two decades of planning has resulted in some gains in national incomes, the creation of infrastructures, and the development of human capital, the bulk of these gains seems to have accrued to the upper socioeconomic classes. The pronouncements and policies aimed at the redistribution of income and wealth largely have been a failure in the South Asian countries. The political leaderships tend to place the blame for these failures on the ineffectiveness of existing political structures to deal with the problems of corruption, smuggling, disrespect of the law, and other antisocial symptoms. In some countries in the region "states of emergency" have been declared, and their constitutions are being amended to remove obstacles to economic and social development. Once again the people are eagerly looking forward to the future, hoping for a better life for themselves and their children. The success or failure of the emergency measures, and of new and bold attempts to rejuvenate the sagging economies, will largely determine the future economic and political prospects for the countries in South Asia.

NOTES

1. See Bipan Chandra, *The Rise and Growth of Economic Nationalism in India,* (Delhi: People's Publishing House, 1969), chs 2 and 3.

2. Quoted in G.B. Jathar and S. G. Beri, *Indian Economics* (Bombay: Oxford University Press, 1949), p. 109.

3. Vera Anstey, *The Economic Development of India* (London: Longman, Green, 1929), p. 5.

4. For details on India's international trade during the eighteenth and nineteenth century, see L. C. A. Knowles, *The Economic Development of the British Overseas Empire* (London: Kelley, 1928), p. 310.

5. M. G. Ranade quoted in Chandra, *Economic Nationalism p. 57.*

6. Karl Marx quoted in P. A. Wadia and K. T. Merchant, *Our Economic Problem* (Bombay: New Book Co., 1954), p. 391.

7. Ranade quoted Chandra, *Economic Nationalism,* p. 58. According to the census of 1891, the percentage of agricultural to total population in India stood at 61.0. In 1901 it rose to 65.2, in 1911 to 69.8, and in 1921 to 70.9.

8. Ibid., p. 61.

9. C. J. Hamilton quoted in Jathar and Beri, *Indian Economics,* p. 112.

10. For a defense of british policies in India, see John A. R. Marriott, *The English in India: A Problem of Politics* (London: Oxford University Press, 1932).

11. Ibid., pp. 301–302.

12. Adam Smith, *The Wealth of Nations* (New York: Modern Library, undated), book 5, ch. 1, part 3, p. 710.

13. Various estimates quoted in Chandra, *Economic Nationalism,* ch. 13.

14. Brooks Adams, *The Law of Civilization and Decay* (London: Swan, Sonnenschein, 1895), pp. 259–260.

15. For details on this point, see S. Bhattacharya, "Laissez-faire in India," *The Indian Economic and Social History Review,* vol. 2, no. 1, January 1965, 10–15.

16. Quoted in S. C. Chakrabarti, et.al., *Economic Development of India* (Calcutta: Nabhabharat Publishers, 1965), p. 166.

17. Ibid., p. 167.

18. Indian Fiscal Commission, quoted in Jathar and Beri, *Indian Economics,* p. 411.

19. The following statements by Jawaharlal Nehru illustrate his strong preference for socialism: "The only key to the solution of the world's problems and of India's problems lie in socialism (Government of India, Ministry of Education, *Jawhar lal Nehru* [New Delhi, 1966], p. 23). "Socialism is for me not merely an economic doctrine which I favour, it is a vital need which I hold with all my head and heart (cited by John Gunther, *Inside Asia* [New York: Harper, 1942], p. 429.)

20. A. Vasudevan, *The Strategy of Planning in India* (Meerut: Menakshi Prakashan, 1970), pp. 279–80.

21. For details see Henry M. Oliver, *Economic Opinion and Policy in Ceylon* (Durham, N.C.: Duke University Press, 1957), chs. 2 and 3.

22. Ibid., p. 44.

23. For details of the recommendations of the National Planning Committee, see A. H. Hanson, *The Process of Planning* (London: Oxford University Press, 1966), pp. 27–49.

24. Ibid., p. 32.

25. Ibid., p. 50.

26. Government of Nepal, National Planning Council, *The Third Plan, 1965–70,* (Khatmandu, 1965), p. 1.

27. For an excellent description of planning in Nepal, see Y. P. Pant, *Economic Development of Nepal* (Allahabad: Kitab Mahal, 1965); and A. Blenhakker, *A Kaleidoscopic Circumspection of Development Planning* (Rotterdam: Rotterdam University Press, 1963).

28. International Bank for Reconstruction and Development, *The Economic Development of Ceylon* (Colombo, Ceylon Government Press, 1952).

29. Government of Bangladesh, Planning Commission, *The First Five Year Plan, 1973–78* (Dacca, 1973).

30. See M. R. Pai, *Planning in India: A Commentary* (Bombay: Popular Prakashan, 1966), sect. 1, pp. 1–56.

31. Government of Pakistan, Ministry of Economic Affairs, *Reports of the Economic Appraisal Committee, 1962,* (Karachi, 1963), pp. 68–69, Appendix.

32. For an excellent discussion of this topic, see Pramit Chaudhuri, ed., *Aspects of Indian Economic Development* (London: Allen & Unwin, 1971); Mike Faber and Dudley Seers, *The Crisis in Planning,* vol. 2: *The Experience* (London: Chatto & Windus, 1972); and V. V. Bhatt, *Two Decades of Development: The Indian Experience* (Bombay: Vora, 1973).

33. Government of India, Planning Commission, *Fourth Five Year Plan, 1969–74* (New Delhi, 1970) pp. 31–32.

34. Bangladesh, *First Plan,* p. 538.

35. Ruddar Datt and K. P. M. Sundharam, *Indian Economy* (New Delhi: Chand, 1975), p. 449.

36. Government of India, Planning Commission, *The First Five Year Plan, 1950–55* (New Delhi, 1951), p. 44.

37. Government of India, Planning Commission, *The Third Five Year Plan, 1960–65* (New Delhi, 1961), pp. 6–7.

38. Government of Pakistan, Planning Commission, *The Third Five Year Plan, 1965-70* (Karachi, 1965), p. 39.

39. Bangladesh, *First Plan,* pp. 32-33.

40. Pakistan, *Third Plan,* p. 396.

41. Bangladesh, *First Plan,* p. 87.

42. Government of Sri Lanka, Planning Commission, *The Five Year Plan, 1972-1976* (Colombo, 1971), p. 25.

43. Datt and Sundharam, *Indian Economy,* pp. 428-434.

44. Nepal, *Third Plan,* p. 27.

45. For details, see India, *First Plan.*

46. Bhatt, *Two Decades of Development,* p. 18.

47. Ibid., p. 43.

48. Pakistan, *Third Plan,* p. 393.

49. Birger Moller, *Employment Approaches to Economic Planning in Developing Countries* (Lund: Studentlitteratur; 1972), p. 158.

50. India, *Third Plan,* p. 64.

51. Pakistan, *Third Plan,* p. 446.

52. Nepal, *Third Plan,* p. 100.

53. Pakistan, *Third Plan,* pp. 455-456.

54. India, *Fourth Plan,* pp. 10-11.

55. "Survey of Indian Industries," *Commerce,* Annual Number, 1968 (Bombay), p. 281.

56. India, *Fourth Plan,* p. 284.

57. Datt and Sundharam, *Indian Economy,* p. 459.

58. Calculated from data in Reserve Bank of India, *Report on Currency and Finance, 1973-74* (Bombay, 1975), pp. S14-17.

59. Pakistan, *Third Plan,* p. 446.

60. India, *Fourth Plan,* pp. 14-15.

61. Government of India, Planning Commission, *Report of the Committee on Distribution of Income and Levels of Living—Part I* (New Delhi, 1964), p. 28.

62. National Council of Applied Economic Research, *All-India Household Survey of Income, Savings and Consumer Expenditure* (New Delhi, 1972), p. 26.

63. For various estimates, see A. J. Fonseca, *Challenge of Poverty in India* (Delhi: Vikas, 1972), pp. 34-35.

64. Sri Lanka, *Five Year Plan,* p. 23.

65. Pakistan, *Third Plan,* p. 30.

66. B. S. Minhas, *Planning and the Poor* (New Delhi: Chand, 1974), p. 2.

67. Ibid., p. 10.

68. Ibid., pp. 10-11.

69. Ibid., p. xvii.

70. Characterized by government ownership of the means of production, public welfare in place of private profit.

71. Pakistan, *Third Plan,* p. v.

72. Ibid., pp. iv, v.

73. M. Akhlaqur Rahman, "The Role of the Public Sector in the Economic Development of Pakistan," in E. A. G. Robinson and Michael Kidron, eds., *Economic Development in South Asia* (London: St. Martin's, 1970), pp. 70-89.

74. Bangladesh, *First Plan,* p. 2.

75. Ibid., p. 10.

76. Sri Lanka, *Five Year Plan,* p. 8.

77. India, *Second Plan,* p. 22.

78. Ibid., p. 22.

79. Datt and Sundharam, *Indian Economy,* p. 148.

80. Ibid., p. 149.

81. Ibid., p. 335.

82. Ibid., p. 340.

83. India, *Third Plan,* p. 229.

84. Ibid., p. 223.

85. Hanson, *Process of Planning,* ch. 12.

86. Minhas, *Planning and the Poor,* p. 10.

87. Padma Desai and Jagdish Bhagwati, "Socialism and Indian Economic Policy," Paper read at the Eighty-seventh Annual Meeting of the American Economic Association, San Francisco, California, December 1974.

88. V. M. Dandekar and N. Rath, "Poverty in India—Dimensions and Trends," *Economic and Political Weekly,* January 2 and 9, 1971.

89. Chaudhuri, *Indian Economic Development,* pp. 38–39.

90. For an excellent discussion of this, see Bhatt, *Two Decades of Development,* pp. 6–54.

91. For a detailed discussion, see Barry Richman, *Industrial Society in Communist China* (New York: Random House, 1969).

92. Padma Desai, "Discussion of Papers on China and India: Development During the Last 25 years," *American Economic Review,* 65, (May 1975), 367.

93. The dramatically changing impressions about China on the part of some American writers create doubts about the authenticity of their writings in the mind of Indian scholars. One may well question how it is that some American sinologists who used to be sharply critical of events in China just five years ago are now suddenly indulging in glorification. Is it a bandwagon effect of President Nixon's visit to China? One answer is provided by Padma Desai; "I cannot help recalling listening in early 1967 at Columbia University to a noted sinologist. . . . He was favorably comparing the Indian economy with the Chinese, using the Indian Plan document statistics, representing mainly *ex ante* aspirations, and Chinese *ex post* performance. I have a distinct impression that we have the reverse phenomenon. . . *ex ante* Chinese (and sinological) assertions being compared with *ex post* Indian realities." Ibid., p. 367.

94. See K. I. Chen and J. S. Uppal, eds., *India and China: Studies in Comparative Development* (New York: Free Press, 1971).

95. W. Malenbaum, "India and China: Contrasts in Development Performance," *American Economic Review,* 49 (June 1959), 284–309.

96. Barry Richman, "Chinese and Indian Development," *American Economic Review,* 65 (May 1975), 354.

97. Ibid.

98. Thomas Weisskopf, "China and India: Contrasting Experiences in Economic Development," *American Economic Review,* 65 (May 1975), 357.

99. Ibid., p. 357.

100. Subramanian Swamy, "Economic Growth in China and India, 1952–1970: A Comparative Appraisal," *Economic Development and Cultural Change,* vol. 21, no. 6, part 2 (July 1973), 82–83.

101. Ibid., p. 82.

102. Joost Kuitenbrouwer, *Growth and Equality in India and China* (The Hague: Institute of Social Studies, Occasional Papers, No. 38, April 1973), p. 1.

103. Jan Deleyne, *The Chinese Economy* (London: Deutsch, 1973), pp. 36–37. Also, see Audrey Donnithorn, *China's Economic System* (London: Allen & Unwin, 1967), pp. 185–186.

104. Deleyne, *Chinese Economy,* p. 60.

105. Gunnar Myrdal, *Asian Drama: An Inquiry into the Poverty of Nations* (New York: Pantheon, 1968), p. 276.

106. Desai, "China and India," p. 367.

107. Weisskopf, "China and India," p. 363.

108. Ram Manohar Lohia, *Wheel of History* (Hyderabad: Navahind Prakashan, 1955), pp. 51–52.

109. Government of India Planning Commission, *Report of the Task Force on Agrarian Relations* (New Delhi, 1973), p. 9.

110. V. M. Dandekar, "Next Step on the Socialist Path," *Economic and Political Weekly,* vol. 7, no. 31–33 (August 1972), 1553–1558.

111. Myrdal, *Asian Drama,* p. 762.

BIBLIOGRAPHY

REFERENCES CITED

Abramovitz, M. "Resources and Output Trends in the United States since 1870." *American Economic Review*. Vol. 46, May 1956.

_____. "Savings and Investment: Profits vs Prosperity." *American Economic Review*. Vol. 32, No. 2, June 1942.

Adams, Brooks. *The Law of Civilization and Decay*. London. Swan, Sonnenschein. 1885.

Agarwal, A. N. *Indian Economy*. Delhi. Vikas. 1975.

Agarwala, S. N. *India's Population Problems*. New Delhi. Tata McGraw-Hill. 1972.

Ahmad, Iftikhar. "Employment in Bangladesh: Problems and Prospects." In E. A. G. Robinson and Keith Griffin, eds., *The Economic Development of Bangladesh within a Socialist Framework*. New York. Wiley. 1974.

Akhtar, S. M. *Economic Development of Pakistan*. Lahore. Publishers United. 1969.

Anstey, Vera. *The Economic Development of India*. London. Longmans, Green. 1929.

Arumugam, M. "Aid Flows and Indian Economic Crisis." *Mankind*. Vol. 18, No. 4, 1974.

Baden-Powell, B. H. *Land Systems of British India*. Oxford. Clarendon Press. 1892.

Balasubramanyam, V. N. "Foreign Private Investments in India." In J. S. Uppal, ed., *India's Economic Problems*. New Delhi. Tata McGraw-Hill. 1975.

Beringer, Christopher, and Ahmad, Irshad. *The Use of Agricultural Surplus Commodities for Economic Development of Pakistan*. Karachi. Institute of Development Economics. 1964.

Bhagwati, Jagdish, and Chakravarty, Sen. "Contributions to Indian Economic Analysis." *American Economic Review*. Vol. 59, No. 4, September 1969.

_____., and Desai, Padma. *India: Planning for Industrialization*. New York. Oxford University Press. 1970.

Bhardwaj, R. C. *Employment and Unemployment in India*. New York. Humanities Press. 1969.

Bhatt, V. V. *Two Decades of Development: The Indian Experience*. Bombay. Vora. 1973.

Bhattacharjee, J. P., ed. *Studies in Indian Agricultural Economics*. Bombay. Indian Society of Agricultural Economics, 1958.

Bhattacharya, S. "Laissez-faire in India." *Indian Economic and Social History Review*. Vol. 2, No. 1, January 1965.

Blenhakker, A. *A Kaleidoscopic Circumspection of Development Planning.* Rotterdam. Rotterdam University Press. 1963.

Boeke, J. H. *Economics and Economic Policy of Dual Societies.* New York. Institute of Pacific Relations. 1953.

Boulding, Kenneth. *A Reconstruction of Economics.* New York. Wiley. 1950.

Chakrabarti, S. C., *et al. Economic Development of India.* Calcutta. Nabhabharat Publishers. 1965.

Chand, Gyan. *India's Teeming Millions.* London. Allen & Unwin. 1939.

Chandra, Bipan. *The Rise and Growth of Economic Nationalism in India.* New Delhi. People's Publishing House. 1966.

Chandrasekhar, S. "A Billion Indians by 2000 A.D. *"New York Times Magazine.* April 4, 1965.

_____. *Population and Planned Parenthood in India.* London. Allen & Unwin. 1955.

Chandhuri, Pramit. *Aspects of Indian Economic Development.* London. Allen & Unwin. 1971.

Chen, K. I., and Uppal, J. S., eds. *India and China: Studies in Comparative Development.* New York. Free Press. 1971.

Chenery, H. B., and Strout, A. M. "External Assistance and Economic Development." *American Economic Review.* Vol. 56, No. 4, Part I, 1966.

_____ et al. *Redistribution with Growth.* London. Oxford University Press. 1974.

Chugh, Ram. "Population Growth in India." In J. S. Uppal, ed., *India's Economic Problems.* New Delhi. Tata McGraw-Hill. 1975.

Cochrane, William W. *The World Food Problem: A Guardedly Optimistic View.* New York. Crowell. 1969.

Curle, Adam. *Planning for Education in Pakistan.* London. Tavistock. 1966.

Dandekar, K., and Bhate, Vaijayanti. *Socio-Economic Change during Three Five-Year Plans.* Poona. Gokhale Institute of Politics and Economics. 1975.

Dandekar, V. M. "Foreword." In N. Rath and V. S. Patwardhan, eds., *Impact of Assistance under P.L. 480 on Indian Economy.* Poona. Gokhale Institute of Politics and Economics. 1967.

_____. "Next Step on the Socialist Path." *Economic and Political Weekly.* Vol. 7, No. 31–33, August 1972.

_____, and Rath N. "Poverty in India—Dimensions and Trends." *Economic and Political Weekly.* January 2, 1971.

Dantwala, M. L. *Agriculture in a Developing Economy.* Poona. Gokhale Institute of Politics and Economics. 1966.

Darling, M. L. *The Punjab Peasant in Prosperity and Debt.* London. Oxford University Press. 1925.

Datt, Ruddar, and Sundharam, K. P. M. *Indian Economy.* New Delhi. Chand. 1976.

Davis, Kingsley. *The Population of India and Pakistan.* Princeton, N.J. Princeton University Press. 1951.

Deleyne, Jan. *The Chinese Economy.* London. Deutsch. 1973.

Denison, E. F. *The Sources of Economic Growth in the United States and the*

Alternative Before Us. New York. Committee for Economic Development. 1962.

Desai, Padma. "Discussion of Papers on China and India: Development During the Last 25 Years." *American Economic Review.* Vol. 65, No. 2, May 1975.

_____, and Bhagwati, Jagdish. "Socialism and Indian Economic Policy." Paper read at the Eighty-Seventh Annual Meeting of the *American Economic Association.* San Francisco, California. December, 1974.

Di Marco, Luis Eugenio. *International Economics and Development — Essays in Honor of Raul Prebisch.* New York. Academic Press. 1972.

Domar, E. O. "On the Measurement of Technical Change." *Economic Journal.* Vol. 71, December 1961.

Donnithorn, Audrey. *China's Economic System.* London. Allen & Unwin. 1967.

Dube, S. C. "Cultural Problems in the Economic Development of India." In R. N. Bellah, ed., *Religion and Progress in Modern Asia.* New York. Free Press. 1965.

Dutt, R. C. *Economic History of India.* New Delhi. Manager of Publications. 1960.

Edwards, Edgar O., ed. *Employment in Developing Nations.* New York. Columbia University Press. 1974.

Faber, Mike, and Seers, Dudley. *The Crisis in Planning: The Experience.* London, Chatto & Windus. 1972.

Fishman, Betty G., and Fishman, Leo. *Employment, Unemployment, and Economic Growth.* New York. Crowell. 1969.

Fonseca, A. J. *Challenge of Poverty in India.* Delhi. Vikas. 1972.

Gait, E. A. "Population." *Imperial Gazetteer of India.* Vol. 1, 1907.

Gandhi, Ved P. *Some Aspects of India's Tax Structure: An Economic Analysis.* Bombay. Vora. 1970.

_____, *Tax Burden on Indian Agriculture.* Cambridge, Mass. Harvard Law School. 1966.

Gore, M. S. "India." In R. Lambert and B. Hoselitz, eds., *The Role of Savings and Wealth in Southern Asia and the West.* Paris. UNESCO. 1963.

Government of Bangladesh, Planning Commission. *The First Five Year Plan 1973-78.* Dacca. 1973.

Government of Ceylon. *The Ten Year Plan.* Colombo. 1959.

_____, Department of Census and Statistics. *Ceylon Year Book.* Colombo. 1968.

Government of India. *Economic Survey, 1966-67.* New Delhi. 1967.

_____. *National Sample Survey Report,* No. 7. New Delhi. 1955.

_____. *National Sample Survey (18th Round), 1963-64.* New Delhi. 1970.

_____. *Report of the Committee on Distribution of Income and Levels of Living.* New Delhi. 1964.

_____. *Report of the Committee on Unemployment.* New Delhi. 1973.

_____. *Report of the Working Group on Education.* New Delhi. 1972.

_____, Fifth Lok Sabha Estimate Committee. *Family Planning Programme.* New Delhi. 1972.

_____, Ministry of Education. *Jawharlal Nehru.* New Delhi. 1966.

_____, Ministry of Food and Agriculture. *Agricultural Situation in India.* New Delhi. 1963.

_____. *Indian Agriculture in Brief.* New Delhi. 1975.

_____, Publications Division. *India: A Reference Manual.* New Delhi. 1974.

_____, Planning Commission. *The First Five Year Plan, 1950–55.* New Delhi. 1951.

_____. *The Second Five Year Plan, 1955–60.* New Delhi. 1956.

_____. *The Third Five Year Plan, 1960–65.* New Delhi. 1961.

_____. *The Fourth Five Year Plan: A Draft Outline.* New Delhi. 1966.

_____. *The Fourth Five Year Plan, 1969–74.* New Delhi. 1970.

_____. *The Fourth Plan: A Mid-Term Appraisal.* New Delhi. 1972.

_____. *Towards an Approach to the Fifth Plan.* New Delhi. 1972.

_____. *Draft Fifth Five Year Plan, 1974–79.* New Delhi. 1974.

_____. *Fourth Evaluation Report on the Working of Community Projects and National Extension Blocks.* New Delhi. 1957.

_____. *Report of the Committee on Distribution of Income and Levels of Living, Part I.* New Delhi. 1964.

_____, Planning Commission. *Report of the Committee on Unemployment Estimates.* New Delhi. 1970.

_____. *Report of the Task Force on Agrarian Relations.* New Delhi. 1973.

Government of Nepal, National Planning Council. *The Third Plan, 1965–70.* Khatmandu. 1965.

Government of Pakistan. *Twenty Years of Pakistan, 1947–1967.* Karachi. Pakistan Publications. 1967.

_____, Finance Division. *Pakistan Economic Survey, 1963–64, 1972–73.* Karachi. 1974.

_____, Ministry of Economic Affairs. *Reports of the Economic Appraisal Committee, 1962.* Karachi. 1963.

_____, Ministry of Finance. *Economic Survey, 1969–70.* Islmabad. 1971.

_____, Planning Commission. *The First Five Year Plan, 1955–60.* Karachi. 1957.

_____. *The Second Five Year Plan, 1960–65.* Karachi. 1960.

_____. *The Third Five Year Plan, 1965–70.* Islamabad. 1965.

_____. *Preliminary Evaluation of the Third Five Year Plan.* Islamabad. August 1970.

_____. *Evaluation of the Third Five Year Plan.* Islamabad. 1970.

_____. *The Fourth Five Year Plan 1970–75.* Islamabad. 1970.

Gunther, John. *Inside Asia.* New York. Harper. 1942.

Hagen, E. *On the Theory of Social Change.* Homewood, Ill. Dorsey. 1962.

Hanson, A. H. *The Process of Planning.* London. Oxford University Press. 1966.

Haq, Mahbub-Ul. *The Strategy of Economic Planning — A Case Study of Pakistan.* Karachi. Oxford University Press. 1963.

Hashmi, Sultan. "Constraints in Economic Development: The Problem of Population Growth in South Asia." In E. A. G. Robinson and Michael Kidron, eds., *Economic Development in South Asia.* London. St. Martin's. 1970.

_____, and Hussain, Syed Mushtaq. "A Review of Projected Manpower, Labour Force and Employment for Pakistan." In Ronald G. Ridker and Harold Lubell, eds., *Employment and Unemployment Problems of the Near East and South Asia.* New Delhi. Vikas. 1971.

Haskall, P. W. *Taxation of Agricultural Lands in Underdeveloped Countries.* Cambridge, Mass. Harvard University Press. 1959.

Hauser, Philip. "World Population." In National Academy of Science, ed., *Rapid Population Growth.* Baltimore. Johns Hopkins Press. 1971.

Herbert, Jean. *An Introduction to Asia.* New York. Oxford University Press. 1965.

Higgins, Benjamin. *Economic Development.* New York. Norton. 1959.

Hopper, David W. "Allocation Efficiency in a Traditional Indian Agriculture." *Journal of Farm Economics.* Vol. 47, August 1965.

India News. February 1960.

International Bank for Reconstruction and Development. *The Economic Development of Ceylon.* Colombo. Ceylon Government Press. 1952.

Jathar, G. B., and Beri, S. G. *Indian Economics.* Bombay. Oxford University Press. 1949.

Kapadia, K. M. *Marriage and Family in India,* 3rd rev. ed. Bombay. Oxford University Press. 1966.

Kapp, J. William. *Hindu Culture, Economic Development and Economic Planning in India.* Bombay. Asia Publishing House. 1963.

Karunatilake. H. N. S. *Economic Development in Ceylon.* New York, Praeger. 1971.

Karve, D. G. "Comments." *Economic Development and Cultural Change.* Vol. 7, October 1958.

Katz, Stanley. *External Assistance and Indian Economic Growth.* New York. Asia Publishing House. 1968.

Khan, Azizur Rahman. *The Economy of Bangladesh.* London. Macmillan. 1972.

————. "Some Problems of Choice of Techniques in a Mixed Economy: The Case of Pakistan." In E. A. G. Robinson and Michael Kidron, eds., *Economic Development in South Asia.* London. St. Martin's. 1970

————. "Some Problems of Choice of Techniques in a Mixed Economy: The Case of Pakistan." In E. A. G. Robinson and Michael Kidron, eds., *Economic Development in South Asia.* London. St. Martin's. 1970.

Knowles. L. C. A. *The Economic Development of the British Overseas Empire.* London. Kelley. 1928.

Koller, John. *Oriental Philosophies.* New York. Scribner. 1970.

Kothari, Rajni. "The Family Planning Programme: A Sociological Analysis." *Sociological Bulletin.* Vol. 15, No. 2, September 1966.

Krishna, Raj. "Farm Supply Response in India-Pakistan—A Case Study of Punjab Agriculture." In Tara Shukla, ed., *Economics of Underdeveloped Agriculture.* Bombay. Vora. 1969.

Kuitenbrouwer, Joost. *Growth and Equality in India and China.* The Hague. Institute of Social Studies. Occasional papers. No. 38. April 1973.

Kuznets, Simon. *Modern Economic Growth.* New Haven, Conn. Yale University Press. 1966.

————, ed., *Economic Growth: Brazil, India, and Japan.* Durham, N.C. Duke University Press. 1955.

Lakadawala, D. T., and Mody, R. J. *Financial Assets and Instruments for Mobilization of Savings.* Ahmedabad, Sardar Patel Institute of Economic and Social Research. 1975.

Leibenstein, Harvey. *Economic Backwardness and Economic Growth*. New York. Wiley. 1963.

Letwin, William. "Four Fallacies about Economic Development." *Daedalus*. Summer 1963.

Lewis, Stephen R., Jr. *Pakistan, Industrialization and Trade Policies*. London. Oxford University Press. 1970.

Lewis, W. Arthur. *Theory of Economic Growth*. London. Allen & Unwin. 1963.

Lohia, Ram Manohar. *Wheel of History*. Hyderabad. Navahind Prakashan. 1955.

McCleland, David. *The Achieving Society*. Princeton, N.J. Van Nostrand. 1961.

Malenbaum, W. "India and China: Contrasts in Development Performance." *American Economic Review*. Vol. 49, June 1959.

Maloney, Clarence. *Peoples of South Asia*. New York. Holt, Rinehart & Winston. 1974.

Mamoria, C. B. *Agricultural Problems of India*. Allahabad. Kitab Mahal. 1966.

Marriott, John A. R. *The English in India: A Problem of Politics*. London. Oxford University Press. 1932.

Mathew, E. T. *Agricultural Taxation and Economic Development in India*. Bombay. Asia Publishing House. 1965.

Mehra, Shakuntala. "Surplus Labour in Indian Agriculture." *Indian Economic Review*. April 1966.

Meier, G. M. *The International Economics of Development*. New York. Harper & Row. 1968.

Millikan, Max F. "Economic Development: Performance and Prospects." *Foreign Affairs*. Vol. 46, No. 3, April 1968.

Minhas, B. S. *Planning and the Poor*. New Delhi. Chand. 1974.

Mishra, Vikas. *Hinduism and Economic Growth*. New York. Oxford University Press. 1962.

Moller, Birger. *Employment Approaches to Economic Planning in Developing Countries*. Lund. Studentlitteratur. 1972.

Mukerji. S. B. "Studies on Fertility Rates in Calcutta." In A. Nevett., ed., *Population: Explosion or Control?* London. Chapman. 1964.

Myrdal, Gunnar. *An Approach to the Asian Drama: Methodological and Theoretical*. New York. Vintage. 1970.

————. *Asian Drama: An Inquiry into the Poverty of Nations*. New York. Pantheon. 1968.

Nair, Kusum. *Blossoms in the Dust*. New York. Praeger. 1962.

Naqvi, S. N. H. "The Foreign Capital Requirements and External Indebtedness of a Developing Country: A Case Study of Pakistan." In A. E. G. Robinson and Michael Kidron, eds., *Economic Development in South Asia*. London. St. Martin's. 1970.

National Council of Applied Economic Research. *All India Household Survey of Income, Savings and Consumer Expenditure*. New Delhi. 1972.

————. *Taxation and Private Investment*. New Delhi. 1961.

Nevin. R. *Capital Funds in Underdeveloped Countries*. New York. St. Martin's. 1961.

Nijhawan, Inder P. "Socio-Political Institutions, Cultural Values, and Attitudes: The Impact on Indian Economic Development." In J. S. Uppal, ed., *India's Economic Problems*. New Delhi. Tata McGraw-Hill, 1975.

Nurske, Ragnar. *Problems of Capital Formation in Underdeveloped Countries.* Oxford. Blackwell. 1953.

_____. "Reflections on India's Development PLan." *Quarterly Journal of Economics.* Vol. 71, No. 1, May 1957.

Oliver, Henry M. *Economic Opinion and Policy in Ceylon.* Durham, N.C. Duke University Press. 1957.

Organization for Economic Cooperation and Development. *Food Aid: Its Role in Economic Development.* Paris. 1963.

Owen, Wilfred. *Distance and Development.* Washington, D.C. Brookings Institution. 1968.

Paddock, William, and Paddock, Paul. *Hungry Nations.* Boston. Little, Brown. 1964.

Pai, M. R. *Planning in India: A Commentary.* Bombay. Popular Prakashan. 1966.

Pant, Y. P. *Economic Development of Nepal.* Allahabad. Kitab Mahal. 1965.

Parsons, Talcott. *Toward a General Theory of Action.* Cambridge, Mass. Harvard University Press. 1951.

Patel, Surendra J. *Essays on Economic Transition.* New York. Asia Publishing House. 1965.

Patel, Tara. "Some Reflections on the Attitude of Married Couples toward Family Planning in Ahmedabad." *Sociological Bulletin.* Vol. 12, No. 2, Sept. 1963.

Pentomy, DeVere E. *The Underdeveloped Lands: A Dilemma of the International Economy.* San Francisco. Chandler. 1960.

Philips, Van, and Paul, A. M. *Public Finance and Less Developed Economy with Special Reference to Latin America.* The Hague. Martinus Nijhoff. 1957.

Radhakrishnan, S., ed. *The Bhagavad Gita.* London. Allen & Unwin. 1948.

Rahman, M. Akhlaqur. "The Role of the Public Sector in the Economic Development of Pakistan." In E. A. G. Robinson and Michael Kidron., eds., *Economic Development in South Asia.* London. St. Martin's. 1970.

Raj, K. N. *Indian Economic Growth: Performance and Prospects.* Delhi. Vikas. 1965.

Rath N., and Patwardhan, V. S. *Impact of Assistance under P.L. 480 on Indian Economy.* Poona. Gokhale Institute of Politics and Economics. 1967.

Rele, J. R. "Some Aspects of Family and Fertility of India." *Population Studies.* Vol. 15, No. 3, March 1962.

Reserve Bank of India. "Estimates of Savings and Investment in the Indian Economy, 1950–51 to 1962–63." *Bulletin.* March 1965, and various issues.

_____. *Report on Currency and Finance 1973–74.* Bombay. 1975.

_____. Commerce Research Bureau. *Basic Statistics Relating to the Indian Economy.* Bombay. October 1975.

Richman, Barry. "Chinese and Indian Development." *American Economic Review.* Vol. 65, No. 2, May 1975.

_____. *Industrial Society in Communist China.* New York. Random House. 1969.

Rostow, W. W. *The Stages of Economic Growth.* Cambridge. The University Press. 1961.

Samuel, T. J. "The Development of India's Policy of Population Control." *The Milbank Memorial Fund Quarterly.* Vol. 44, No. 1, Part I, January 1966.

Schultz, T. Paul. "An Economic Perspective in Population Growth." In National Academy of Science, ed., *Rapid Population Growth,* Vol. 2. Baltimore. Johns Hopkins Press. 1967.

Schultz, T. W. "Economic Growth from Traditional Agriculture." In Tara Shukla, ed., *Economics of Underdeveloped Agriculture.* Bombay. Vora. 1969.

_____. *The Economic Value of Education.* New York. Columbia University Press. 1963.

Schumpeter, Joseph. *History of Economic Analysis.* London. Oxford University Press. 1954.

_____. *The Theory of Economic Development.* New York. Oxford University Press. 1961.

Selvaratram. S., and Fernando, L. S. "Measurement of Employed and Unemployed in Ceylon." In Ronald G. Ridker and Harold Lubell, eds., *Employment and Unemployment Problems of the Near East and South Asia.* New Delhi. Vikas. 1971.

Sen, Amartya. *Employment, Technology and Development.* Oxford. Clarendon. 1975.

Shetty, S. L. "Inter-Sectoral Equity in Tax Burden." *Economic and Political Weekly.* Vol. 7, No. 31–33, 1972.

Singer, M. "Religion and Social Change in India: The Max Weber Thesis Phase Three." *Economic Development and Cultural Change.* Vol. 14, No. 4, July 1966.

Singh, D. Bright. *Economics of Development.* Bombay. Asia Publishing House. 1963.

Singh, Tarlok. *Poverty and Social Change.* Bombay. Oxford University Press. 1945.

Smith, Adam. *The Wealth of Nations.* New York. Modern Library. Undated.

Smith, Donald E., ed. *Religion, Politics, and Social Change in the Third World.* New York. Free Press. 1971.

Snodgrass, Donald R. *Ceylon: An Export Economy in Transition.* Homewood, Ill. Irwin. 1966.

Solow, Robert. "Technical Change and the Aggregate Production Function." *Review of Economics and Statistics.* Vol. 39, August 1957.

Som, Rajan Kumar. "Population Trends and Problems in India." In S. N. Agarwala, ed., *India's Population — Some Problems in Perspective Planning.* Bombay. Asia Publishing House. 1960.

Srinivas, M. N. "A Note on Mr. Gaheen's Note." *Economic Development and Cultural Change.* Vol. 7, October 1958.

_____. *Religion and Society among the Coorgs of South India.* London. Oxford University Press. 1952.

_____. "Village Studies and Their Significance." *Eastern Anthropologist.* Vol. 8, No. 3–4, March–August. 1955

Stern, Joseph. "Growth, Development, and Regional Equity." In Walter Falcon and Gustav Papanek, eds., *Development Policy, II.* Cambridge, Mass. Harvard University Press. 1971.

Sukhatme, P. V. *Feeding India's Growing Millions.* Bombay. Asia Publishing House. 1965.

"Survey of Indian Industries." *Commerce.* (Bombay). Annual Number. 1968.

"A Survey of Employment, Unemployment, and Underemployment in Ceylon." *International Labour Review.* March 1963.

Swamy, Subramanian. "Economic Growth in China and India, 1952-1970." *Economic Development and Cultural Change.* Vol. 21, No. 4, July 1973.

Tauber, Irene B. "Japan's Population—Miracle Model or Case Study?" *Foreign Affairs.* July 1962.

Tawney, R. H. *Religion and the Rise of Capitalism.* New York. Harcourt & Brace. 1952.

UNESCO, Regional Office for Education in Asia. *Progress of Education in the Asian Region.* Paris. 1972.

United Nations. *Demographic Year Book, 1973.* New York. 1974.

_____. *The Determinants and Consequences of Population Trends.* New York. 1973.

_____. *Economic and Social Survey of Asia and the Pacific, 1974.* Bangkok. 1975.

_____. *Economic Bulletin for Asia and the Pacific, 1973, 1974.* Bangkok. 1974, 1975.

_____. *Economic Survey of Asia and the Far East 1960.* New York. 1961.

_____. *Economic Survey of Asia and the Far East 1970-1974.* Bangkok. 1971-1975.

_____. *Statistical Year Book, 1973, 1974.* New York. 1974, 1975.

_____. *Statistical Year Book for Asia and the Pacific, 1973.* Bangkok. 1974.

_____. *World Population Prospects.* New York. 1969.

_____. *Year Book of National Accounts Statistics, 1974.* New York. 1975.

_____, Food and Agriculture Organization. *The State of Food and Agriculture, 1967, 1968, 1974.* Rome. 1968, 1969, 1975.

_____. *Agricultural Commodity Projections,* Vol. 1. Rome. 1971.

United States Government. *Economic Report of the President.* Washington, D.C. 1975.

_____, Agency for International Development. *Gross National Product, Growth Rates, and Trend Data.* Washington, D.C. 1968.

_____, Department of Commerce. *Statistical Abstract of the United States, 1972-1974.* Washington, D.C. 1973-1975.

Uppal, J. S. "Attitudes of Farm Families towards Land Reforms in Punjab." *Journal of Developing Areas.* Vol. 4, No. 1, October 1969.

_____, *Disguised Unemployment in an Underdeveloped Economy.* New York. Asia Publishing House. 1973.

_____. "Implementation of Land Reform Legislation in Punjab." *Asian Survey.* Vol. 9, No. 5, May 1969.

_____. "Measurement of Disguised Unemployment in Punjab Agriculture." *Canadian Journal of Economics.* Vol. 33, No. 4, November 1967.

_____. "Work Habits and Disguised Unemployment in Underdeveloped Countries: A Theoretical Analysis. *Oxford Economic Papers.* Vol. 21, No. 3, November 1969.

_____, ed. *India's Economic Problems: An Analytical Approach.* New Delhi. Tata McGraw-Hill, 1975.

Vasuderan, A. *The Strategy of Planning in India.* Meerut. Menakshi Prakashan. 1970.

Verma, P. C. "Growth of Tax Revenue in Pakistan." *Economic and Political Weekly.* Vol. 4, No. 49, December 6, 1969.

Vorys, Karl Von. "Some Aspects of the Economic Development of India." *World Politics.* Vol. 13, 1960–1961.

Wadia, P. A., and Merchant, K. T. *Our Economic Problem.* Bombay. New Book Co. 1954.

Ward, Barbara. *The Rich Nations and the Poor Nations.* New York. Norton. 1962.

Wattal, P. K. *Population Problem in India.* Bombay. Bennett, Coleman. 1934.

Weber, Max. *Protestant Ethic and the Spirit of Capitalism.* New York. Scribner. 1956.

_____. *Religion in India.* New York. Free Press. 1958.

Weiner, Myron. *The Politics of Scarcity.* Chicago. University of Chicago Press. 1962.

Weisskopf, Thomas. "China and India: Contrasting Experience in Economic Development." *American Economic Review.* Vol. 65, No. 2, May 1975.

Welty, Paul Thomas. *The Asians: Their Heritage and Their Destiny.* Philadelphia. Lippincott. 1973.

White, Lawrence J. *Industrial Concentration and Economic Power in Pakistan.* Princeton, N.J. Princeton University Press. 1974.

Wolfbein, Seymour L. *Employment and Unemployment in the United States.* Chicago. Science Research Associates. 1964.

World Bank. *Annual Report.* Washington, D.C. 1975.

_____. *Atlas.* Washington, D.C. 1974.

World Bank. *Trends in Developing Countries.* Washington, D.C. 1973.

OTHER REFERENCES

Ahmad, Nafis. *A New Economic Geography of Bangladesh.* Bombay. Vikas. 1976.

Ahmad, Syed Jamil. *An Approach to Economic Problems of Pakistan.* Karachi. Kifayat Academy. 1969.

Bauer, P. T. *Indian Economic Policy and Development.* Bombay. Popular Prakashan. 1965.

Bonne, Alfred. *Studies in Economic Development in the Underdeveloped Areas of Western Asia and India.* London. Routledge & Paul. 1957.

Brown, Norman W. *The United States and India, Pakistan, Bangladesh.* Cambridge, Mass. Harvard University Press. 1972.

Coale, Ansley J. *Population Growth and Economic Development in Low Income Countries: A Case Study of India's Prospects.* Princeton, N.J. Princeton University Press. 1968.

Faaland, Just, and Parkinson, J. R. *Bangladesh: The Test Case for Development.* Boulder, Colorado. Westview Press. 1976.

Dean, Vera., *New Patterns of Democracy in India.* Cambridge, Mass. Harvard University Press. 1969.

Gadgil, D. R. *The Industrial Evolution of India in Recent Times, 1850–1939.* Bombay. Oxford University Press. 1971.

———. *Planning and Economic Policy in India.* Bombay. Asia Publishing House. 1965.

Ghosh, ALak. *Indian Economy.* Calcutta. World Press. 1975.

Griffin, Keith, ed. *Growth and Inequality in Pakistan.* London. Macmillan. 1972.

Jahan, R. *Pakistan: Failure in National Integration.* New York. Columbia University Press. 1972.

Khan, Nasir Ahmad. *Problems of Growth of an Underdeveloped Economy—India.* New York. Asia Publishing House. 1961.

Kidron, Michael. *Foreign Investments in India.* London. Oxford University Press. 1965.

Kishore, Barj, and Singh, B. P. *Indian Economy through the Plans.* Delhi. National. 1969.

Kurien, C. T. *Indian Economic Crisis.* New York. Asia Publishing House. 1969.

Lamb, Beatrice Pitney. *India: A World in Transition.* New York. Praeger. 1975.

Lewis, John P. *Quiet Crisis in India.* Bombay. Asia Publishing House. 1963.

Malenbaum, W. *Modern India's Economy: Two Decades of Planned Growth.* Columbus, Ohio. Merrill. 1971.

———. *Prospects of Indian Development.* New York. Free Press. 1972.

Mannan, M. A. *Economic Problems and Planning in Pakistan.* Karachi. Ferozsons. 1970.

Mason, Edward S. *Economic Development in India and Pakistan.* Cambridge, Mass. Center for International Affairs, Harvard University. 1966.

Mehta, Asoka. *India Today.* New Delhi. Chand. 1974.

Mellor, John W. *The New Economics of Growth: A Strategy for India and the Developing World.* Ithaca, N.Y. Cornell University Press. 1976.

Mohnot, S. R. *Concentration of Economic Power in India.* Allahbad. Chaitanya. 1962.

National Council of Applied Economic Research. *Development without Aid.* Delhi. 1966.

Nayar, Baldev Raj. *The Modernization Imperative and Indian Planning.* Delhi. Vikas. 1972.

Nevett, A. S. J. *Population: Explosion or Control: A Study with Special Reference to India.* London. Chapman. 1964.

Pant, Y. P., and Jain, S. C. *Agricultural Development in Nepal.* Bombay. Vora. 1969.

Papanek, G. F. *Pakistan's Development, Social Goals, and Private Incentives.* Cambridge, Mass. Harvard University Press. 1967.

Qureshi, Anwar Iqbal. *Economic Problems Facing Pakistan.* Karachi. Pakistan Publishers. 1971.

Singh, Tarlok. *India's Development Experience.* Delhi. Macmillan. 1974.

Index